AN UNCOMMON COLLABORATION

DAVID BOHM AND J. KRISHNAMURTI

Alpha Centauri Press
Ojai, California
alphacentauripress@gmail.com

Book design by Kirsten Hansen Pott.

Cover photograph by Mark Edwards. Copyright Krishnamurti Foundation Trust.

The author acknowledges with gratitude the assistance of the Krishnamurti Foundation of America and the Krishnamurti Foundation Trust, England, in photo research and reproduction.

Content reproduced with permission.

Numerous quotes [pp. 18-397; 5000 words] from THE ENDING OF TIME by J. KRISHNAMURTI and DR. DAVID BOHM. Copyright (c) 1985 by Krishnamurti Foundation Trust Limited. Reprinted by permission of HarperCollins Publishers.

Excerpts from pp. 516-17, 518-19, 521, 523, 525-6, 534-5 [864 words] from THE AWAKENING OF INTELLIGENCE by J. KRISHNAMURTI. Copyright (c) 1974 by Krishnamurti Foundation Trust Ltd. Reprinted by permission of HarperCollins Publishers.

Excerpts from pp. 9, 17, 32, 46, 104, 107, 115, 134, 140 [906 words] from THE FIRST AND LAST FREEDOM by J. KRISHNAMURTI. Copyright 1954 by Krishnamurti Writings, Inc., renewed (c) 1982 by J. Krishnamurti. Reprinted by permission of HarperCollins Publishers.

Permission to quote from the works of J. Krishnamurti or other works for which the copyright is held by Krishnamurti Foundation Trust Ltd has been given on the understanding that such permission does not indicate endorsement of the views expressed in this publication.

ISBN 978-0-6928-5427-3

Printed in the United States of America

Library of Congress Cataloging-in-Publication Data

Moody, David Edmund
An uncommon collaboration: David Bohm and J. Krishnamurti / David Edmund Moody
  p cm.
Includes bibliographical references and index.
ISBN 978-0-6928-5427-3
Library of Congress Control Number: 2017904340
Alpha Centauri Press, Ojai, CA

P	23	22	21	20	19	18	17	16	15	14	13	12	11	10	9	8	7	6	5	4	3	2	1
Y	36	35	34	33	32	31	30	29	28	27	26	25	24	23	22	21	20	19	18	17	16		

AN UNCOMMON COLLABORATION

DAVID BOHM AND
J. KRISHNAMURTI

DAVID EDMUND MOODY

ALPHA CENTAURI PRESS
OJAI, CALIFORNIA

For Marilyn

TABLE OF CONTENTS

INTRODUCTION

In a world consumed with problems of every possible kind and dimension—environmental, economic, political, religious, social, ethical, and personal—and deep-seated conflicts resulting in endemic violence, the question must arise whether the multiplicity of issues all arise from disparate sources, with little relationship among them; or whether these problems and conflicts have a common denominator. Our leaders evidently conceptualize and seek solutions on a piecemeal basis, with little attention given to the possibility that the only meaningful and enduring answer lies in understanding that our problems have a common source. To examine the matter in that fashion seems to be a radical approach in and of itself; and it opens the door to a new way of looking and behaving that may be characterized as revolutionary.

The psychological philosopher J. Krishnamurti (1895-1986) examined society and human affairs in precisely this manner. Although he lacked academic degrees or any form of institutional support beyond the barest minimum, he managed over the course of a lifetime to articulate an original, profound, and comprehensive understanding of consciousness as it functions in daily life, and to elucidate the structural features of it that lead to illusion, conflict, and disorder on an individual as well as a collective scale. In this endeavor, he touched the lives of millions, and he engaged in dialogues, many of them recorded, with hundreds of individuals who found his observations deeply insightful and vitally important. Of those with whom he engaged in this manner, none was more significant than the quantum theoretical physicist David Bohm.

Among the major innovators in intellectual history, collaboration is the exception, not the norm. Copernicus, da Vinci, Galileo, Newton,

Shakespeare, Mozart, Einstein—most of those whom we consider to represent the quality of genius were individuals who broke new ground without a travelling companion. A few prominent exceptions spring to mind: Watson and Crick; Russell and Whitehead; Freud and Jung (for a time); Rodgers and Hammerstein. These exceptions are notable, however, precisely for their infrequency of occurrence.

Among that small subset of collaborations among men of genius, the case of J. Krishnamurti and David Bohm may be the most extraordinary. Watson and Crick were both biologists; Russell and Whitehead both philosophers; Freud and Jung both psychiatrists. But David Bohm was an eminent scientist, a physicist, whereas Krishnamurti represented a blend of philosopher and psychologist, with a spiritual or metaphysical background. How did these two men find one another? What did they have in common? What did they talk about?

Over a period of two decades, 144 conversations were recorded between Bohm and Krishnamurti, and many of these dialogues were videotaped as well. Thirty-four were transcribed and edited for publication and appeared in a series of books including the following titles: *The Limits of Thought; Truth and Actuality; The Wholeness of Life; The Ending of Time;* and *The Future of Humanity.*

Krishnamurti's philosophy is personal and direct. It is not a matter of abstractions about arcane theories, much less New Age flights of fancy. He addressed everyday issues of fear, loneliness, love, death, sorrow, joy, and self-understanding. At the same time, his views are subtle and sometimes elusive. He paid great attention to the respective roles of thought, emotion, desire, intelligence, and insight, and to the possibility of a transformation of consciousness. He emphasized that he was not any kind of authority figure and that his philosophy had significance only to the extent that it facilitated the actual understanding of oneself.

Bohm is now acknowledged as among the foremost physicists of the twentieth century. His associations with Oppenheimer and Einstein are interesting in their own right, but of far greater significance were his contributions to the foundations of quantum theory. These were sufficiently radical as to mark him as a maverick in the field, and it has required decades for his contribution to be more fully appreciated. His life- and career-altering encounter with the House Committee on Un-American Activities adds another dimension to his intriguing personal story.

There can be little doubt that Bohm regarded Krishnamurti's philosophy as essential to his understanding of his own state of mind. This factor adds an intensely human and poignant element to the quality of their collaboration. The biographical information presented in the early chapters of this book should be understood in that context. The extraordinary sequence of events, political and professional, that dominated the first decades of Bohm's career must have prepared him to appreciate and explore Krishnamurti's work. The success or failure of his involvement with that philosophy represents the subtext of all that follows here.

From 1975 until 1992, I had the good fortune to work closely with both Krishnamurti (until his death in 1986) and with David Bohm. This involvement occurred in the context of the Oak Grove School, founded by Krishnamurti, in Ojai, California, where I worked as teacher, educational director, and as director. My relationship with the two men focused on educational and psychological issues, but there was a personal element as well. This background perhaps prepared me to appreciate the quality and the meaning of the twenty-plus-year dialogue that occurred between them, and it adds an element of richness and context that would not otherwise be available.

It may be many years before the collaboration between Krishnamurti and David Bohm can be fully unraveled and assessed. Their dialogue was so extensive and profound as to defy encapsulation in any single book. The aim of the present volume is to introduce their work to a larger audience, not to provide any final or definitive characterization of it. Each man was uncommonly interesting and unusual by himself, and the record of their interaction even more so. The story of their relationship is timeless.

Chapter One

THE PATH TO PRINCETON

The sequence of events that brought David Bohm into contact with J. Krishnamurti might appear at first glance rather circuitous; but, with the benefit of hindsight, his path may be seen less as a series of detours than as the shortest route between two very distant starting points.

Bohm's childhood circumstances were not conducive to the development of scientific genius. He was born in 1918 in Wilkes-Barre, Pennsylvania, a town whose primary source of income came from the mining of coal. Bohm's father, Samuel, was born in Hungary, and he immigrated to the United States in his late teens. He took a room in the home of a second-hand furniture dealer, who in turn set up Samuel with a furniture store of his own, complete with his daughter Frieda for a wife. Samuel, Frieda, David, and a younger brother lived upstairs over the store.

Samuel Bohm was not sympathetic to David's early interest in science and science fiction. He would have preferred for both of his sons to go into the furniture business. Nevertheless, David's passion for exotic other worlds and a fourth dimension, as well as for more practical pursuits, such as constructing radios from wires and crystals scavenged from a local junk yard, could not be denied. By the time he was in high school, Bohm's precocious intellect was becoming conspicuous. His math teacher, who taught for some 50 years, recalls him as one of a kind. The teacher once set his students a problem so challenging he was afraid no one could solve it, but Bohm came up with three solutions, one of which was so original he had to explain it to his teacher. Other early signs of Bohm's unfolding intellect included several inventions he conceived of in his early- and mid-teens and actively attempted to bring to market.

Among these was a dripless pitcher, cleverly constructed with a narrow collar at its lip, designed to break the surface tension of any liquid poured from it and so to facilitate a smooth flow. He also conceived of a new design for the piston engine as well as a modification in the structure of airplane wings.

David's mother, Frieda, was given to bouts of depression, and her relationship with Samuel was conflicted. When he came home from work, he belittled and insulted her, and the tension in the household was palpable. She doted upon David, but she may have been excessively concerned with his health, a tendency he evidently acquired and continued throughout his life. He was shy and physically awkward, not much good at games, and not inclined to mix it up with other boys in sports. However, he enjoyed long walks in the woods around Wilkes-Barre, by himself or with a few friends. On one of these walks, he encountered a stream that could be crossed only by means of a few stepping stones protruding above the water. Bohm tried to work out in advance how he would place his feet on each stone, but once he got started he found he had to keep moving and his plans were of no use. This experience precipitated an insight, one he often remarked upon in later years, regarding the nature of flowing movement in all facets of life.

In 1929, when Bohm was 11, the Great Depression hit Wilkes-Barre with particular force, and David was faced at an early age with the reality of economic privation. His own family remained financially stable, but many others in his community suffered acutely. Bohm began to read progressive periodicals and to develop a set of political views to the left of center. He often discussed politics with the father of one of his friends until late at night, and his exposure to the weaknesses of capitalism later had a profound effect upon the course of his career.

By the time he was ready for college, it must have been a relief to escape the narrow intellectual horizons of Wilkes-Barre. In spite of some early signs of genius, his childhood was notable less for any outstanding accomplishments than for his ability to survive, and even to thrive to some extent, in an environment far from ideal for cultivating a mind of his kind. It would still be some years before he found an intellectual atmosphere truly designed to stimulate and foster his capacities, but the transition from Wilkes-Barre to Pennsylvania State College represented a major step along this path. Pennsylvania State was not known for the quality of its physics department; the school tended to emphasize what it considered more practical pursuits, such as engineering and agriculture. Nevertheless, the scholastic regulations were somewhat relaxed, and Bohm was able to arrange an independent course of study that included work with a select few professors and other students. In his junior year, he and a fellow student tackled a graduate level textbook that presented all the mathematics then required for topics in theoretical physics, and they worked through every problem in the text. In one of his physics classes, Bohm detected a flaw in the logic of a widely accepted proof regarding the effects of radiation, and his professor explained Bohm's reasoning to the class, along with a more satisfactory solution he had developed.

The countryside around Pennsylvania State was also to Bohm's liking. Long walks through forested areas became a part of his daily routine. He had little interest in dating or conventional social activities, but on these walks he thought deeply about problems in physics, and the unfolding insights and flowering of creativity sustained him. By the time of his senior year, it was clear to Bohm that he wanted to pursue the study of physics at the graduate level. Unfortunately, the financial means to do so were not available unless he found some form of support. The mathematics department at Pennsylvania State offered a test, open to all students, with a substantial scholarship for whoever scored the highest. The test consisted of five problems so challenging that most students were able to complete no more than one or two of them. Bohm answered four of the problems correctly and had outlined a solution to the fifth when time expired.

The six hundred dollar reward for winning this contest enabled Bohm to attend The California Institute of Technology (Caltech) for his first year of graduate study. There he anticipated finding a community of peers, a set of colleagues as dedicated as he was to pursuing the beauty of scientific truth. The reality he discovered there was not as he had hoped, but once again—as with the stream he had crossed in his youth—Caltech turned out to be an important stepping stone on the way to firmer ground. What Bohm found at Caltech was in fact the antithesis of the kind of soil he required to nourish his particular brand of genius. He flourished in a cooperative atmosphere where he could investigate problems in science with a few friends at leisure and in depth, with a minimum of external requirements and constraints. In spite of its stellar reputation, Caltech was highly competitive, intensely oriented toward examinations, and committed to a mechanical, problem-solving approach to physics. Although he excelled there in certain respects—he was said to be the only student ever to work through every problem in a core course in electricity and magnetism—it soon became apparent to Bohm that he could not thrive in that environment. The physical setting was hot and dry, not conducive to the long daily walks that he required to sustain his intellectual fires. He found relief only in hikes up nearby Mt. Wilson, a three-thousand-foot climb from the campus of Caltech.

Midway through his second year, intellectual deliverance arrived for Bohm in the form of the premier American physicist, J. Robert Oppenheimer. He was in charge of the department of physics at the University of California at Berkeley, but he taught an occasional course at Caltech as well. A friend suggested to Bohm that he arrange to meet with Oppenheimer, and the two men evidently formed an immediate bond. Oppenheimer arranged for Bohm to transfer to Berkeley, with a research assistantship available as well. Early in 1941, Bohm moved from Pasadena to Berkeley, where he found an environment more compatible with the development of his capabilities.

The department of physics at Berkeley was home not only to Oppenheimer, but also to another world-class scientist, Ernest Lawrence. Unraveling the structure of the atom was at that time among the most compelling issues in physics, and the means to do so consisted of machines called particle accelerators that smashed one atom or proton into another. Lawrence had the crucial insight, for which he won a Nobel Prize, that an accelerator in the form of a circle could move particles at much greater speeds than a linear accelerator. He called his new device a "cyclotron," and, in his Radiation Laboratory, successive generations of cyclotrons, each one larger than the last, became the basis for a long and highly successful research program at Berkeley.

Lawrence was a mid-Westerner, blond and blue-eyed, affable and congenial. He and Oppenheimer both came to Berkeley in 1929, and the two men soon became good friends. Lawrence was the practical innovator, Oppenheimer the theoretician. Oppenheimer had studied at Harvard and Cambridge, and he received his Ph.D. at the age of 23. His intellectual gifts were not confined to physics but encompassed Italian poetry, Eastern philosophy, as well as fine wines. The parties he held at his home in Berkeley for friends and graduate students were memorable events, often brought to a close with a recording of Oppenheimer's favorite string quartet by Beethoven. He liked to serve a spicy Indonesian dish called *nasi goreng*, which Lawrence translated as "nasty gory."

Bohm found both the intellectual and physical atmosphere at Berkeley exhilarating. The cooler climate and easily accessible forested walks put him in his element, and the cultural milieu that Oppenheimer generated was scintillating. Bohm revered him almost as a father figure, although he was only fourteen years his senior. Richard Feynman, who later became a celebrated Nobel laureate, was one of Oppenheimer's graduate students whom Bohm befriended at that time. Far more than at Caltech, Bohm found in Berkeley the fertile mecca of theoretical physics.

The research program Oppenheimer assigned to Bohm revolved around the consequences of a collision between a proton and deuterium, a heavy form of hydrogen that contains an extra neutron. Bohm investigated this issue with characteristic diligence and depth of analysis. He completed his research in 1943, but before he was able to report the results, his work came to the attention of senior governmental officials who recognized its potential military applications. Since the country was on a wartime footing, and Bohm did not have the necessary security clearance, his research was confiscated by federal authorities, and he was forbidden even to compose his doctoral dissertation. Oppenheimer had to award Bohm his Ph.D. based purely on his personal recommendation.

As early as 1941, the principles involved in the development of an atomic bomb had become apparent to the world's most advanced physicists. Two of these, Leo Szilard and Edward Teller, approached Albert Einstein, then residing in the United States, and asked him to cosign a letter addressed to President Roosevelt, bringing this issue to his attention. Within a few months, the president acted upon their advice, and the highly secretive Manhattan Project was formed for the purpose of developing such a bomb. Although the Manhattan Project was formally under the control of the military, only the nation's leading scientists could actually carry out the necessary research. Oppenheimer was appointed to lead the scientific effort. As a result, he was away from Berkeley for months at a time, at Los Alamos, New Mexico, where most of the work on the Manhattan Project was carried out.

In his absence, Oppenheimer appointed his most senior graduate assistant, Joseph Weinberg, to conduct his courses in quantum physics, the field that studies the nature of events inside the structure of the atom. The assignment proved to be too challenging for Weinberg, however, and when his health began to suffer, the job was taken over by Bohm. It was a fortuitous turn of events, as it gave Bohm the opportunity to study the foundations of quantum physics at a deep level. This would later prove to be the cornerstone of his academic career. Weinberg and Bohm were good friends, and the two men often argued until late at night over the meaning of quantum physics. The principles involved were foreign to classical, Newtonian physics, and left a great deal of room for debate and alternative interpretations. Their conversations were not limited to physics, however, but encompassed a mutual fascination with political issues as well.

During the 1930's, a certain sympathy with Marxist ideology was not uncommon within some intellectual circles in the United States. The horrors of the Communist experiment in the Soviet Union had not yet become apparent. The Great Depression had brought home the weaknesses of the capitalistic system, and the socialist ideal was seen by many as a path to personal as well as economic salvation. Oppenheimer himself was representative of this current of thinking. He was active in several quasi-Communist organizations, and he had many friends and associates who were actual members of the Communist Party. Some of Oppenheimer's graduate students similarly absorbed this point of view, including Weinberg, Bohm, Rossi Lomanitz, and Bernard Peters. Lomanitz organized a union of the staff at the Radiation Laboratory, and Bohm attended a few meetings of the local Communist Party. These students were imbued with the ideal of a free and classless society, where each individual could flower to his or her fullest potential.

Oppenheimer would have liked for Bohm to work with him in Los Alamos, but his application to do so was denied by higher authorities on grounds that Bohm had relatives living in Eastern Europe. The actual grounds for the denial were probably political in nature, although neither Bohm nor Oppenheimer was aware of it at the time. As an alternative, Bohm was assigned to work at the Radiation Laboratory, conducting research into plasma, a fourth form of matter (after solids, liquids, and gases) that occurs at very high temperatures, when the nuclei of atoms are stripped of their electrons. In connection with this project, Bohm made his first enduring contribution to the foundations of theoretical physics. His examination of the behavior of plasmas revealed the tendency of the free electrons to act in a collective manner, as if they were in some kind of communication with one another. His description of this behavior is called *Bohm diffusion*, and it remains a basic feature of every textbook analysis of plasma.

Even while he was conducting this research, Bohm continued to refine and deepen his understanding of quantum physics. The quantum world deals with events in the land of the electron, where an Alice in Wonderland reality prevails, far removed from the principles of ordinary life. Among other things, conventional physics dictates that the electron, in its orbit around the nucleus of the atom, should quickly expend all its energy and break apart from the atom. Bohm found a way to reconfigure the mathematics that predicts this effect, and so to preserve the integrity of the atom. He wrote a paper describing his analysis, but it was not well received by either Oppenheimer or Wolfgang Pauli, two of the leading defenders of a more orthodox interpretation. Subsequent events, however, served to confirm the originality and the accuracy of Bohm's proposal, and the "renormalization" of the behavior of the electron is now standard procedure in quantum mechanics.

An abstract of Bohm's paper made its way to John Wheeler, who was at that time the head of the physics department at Princeton University. A former assistant to Einstein, Wheeler recognized the depth of Bohm's insight and promptly offered him a position as an assistant professor.

Princeton was associated with the Institute for Advanced Study, where many of the world's leading physicists, including Einstein, were employed. When Oppenheimer was selected, following World War II, to be in charge of the Institute, Bohm agreed to accept Wheeler's offer. In the fall of 1947, he joined the faculty of Princeton University and entered into an intellectual atmosphere even richer, in some respects, than what he had found at Berkeley.

Nothing in these early years suggested a propensity or preparation for Bohm's subsequent involvement with Krishnamurti, except his pellucid intellect and his determination to go to the end of whatever problem or issue occupied his attention. The experiences that would shake his faith, not in science, but in scientists, and therefore lead him to explore a wider field, still lay ahead.

Chapter Two

QUANTUM CONSEQUENCES

Bohm's first impressions of Princeton were somewhat mixed. The school was located in an industrial area, not conducive to his long, daily walks in nature. Some of the other professors seemed unavailable or indifferent to his work. Nevertheless, he had two or three good graduate students with whom he explored issues in quantum mechanics and superconductivity.

In his second year at Princeton, Bohm took a room in the home of Erich and Lilly Kahler, and there his social life fell into place. The Kahlers were emigrants from Germany, and they enjoyed a wide circle of gifted friends and associates, including Thomas Mann, Jacob Bronowski and Albert Einstein. In addition, Lilly's daughter, Hanna Loewy, a vivacious young woman, took a fancy to Bohm, and for a time the two were a couple. They contemplated marriage, but in the end Hanna decided they were not compatible to that extent. Einstein used to come over to the Kahlers' in the evening to relax and play his violin. Perhaps it was in that context that Bohm and Einstein cemented a close relationship. Hannah Loewy later remarked that Einstein considered Bohm to be his "intellectual son."

Bohm was now in a social and professional milieu that was compatible with his gifts and inclinations. He had every prospect of remaining at Princeton for a long and illustrious career, one that would enhance the reputation not only of Princeton, but of the American physics community at large. Then came a subpoena, on April 3, 1949, to appear before the House Committee on Un-American Activities.

The sequence of events that precipitated the subpoena had its roots several years in the past. The principal obstacle to development of the atomic bomb lay in the puzzle of how to extract an elusive form of uranium from the ordinary uranium found in nature. It was said that if even a country like Switzerland possessed a roomful of this material, it could rule the world. The foremost American physicist skilled in finding such a process was Ernest Lawrence, Oppenheimer's colleague at the University of California at Berkeley. Lawrence was one of the strong proponents of including Oppenheimer in the Manhattan Project.

Even before Pearl Harbor and the United States' entrance into World War II, the FBI had opened a file to investigate possible subversive activities on the part of Oppenheimer. The FBI had some reason for concern. Oppenheimer's brother, his former fiancée, and his wife Kitty had all been members at one time or another of the Communist Party; Kitty was on friendly terms with Steve Nelson, the representative of the party for the San Francisco Bay area; and Oppenheimer himself was known to be active in or sympathetic to a variety of progressive causes. The investigation into Oppenheimer assumed a sense of urgency when he was selected to become the lead scientist for the Manhattan Project. As a result, not only the FBI, but also the security arm of the United States Army, took an interest in the activities and associates of Oppenheimer. His phone was tapped, his mail was intercepted, and he was followed on many occasions. He was interviewed numerous times by Army and FBI intelligence officers. His security clearance was held up more than once. Ultimately, his participation in the Manhattan Project was assured only because he won the trust of Leslie Groves, the Army officer in charge of the project, who believed Oppenheimer was the only scientist capable of beating the Germans in the race to develop the bomb.

As a consequence of the security apparatus's concerns about Oppenheimer, his top graduate students also came under suspicion. Joseph Weinberg, Rossi Lomanitz, Max Freidman, and David Bohm were all placed under varying degrees of surveillance. Of particular note was a visit that Weinberg evidently made to the home of Steve Nelson, in April 1943. FBI agents had placed bugs in Nelson's apartment, and the agent in charge that evening reported that Weinberg told Nelson something about the nature of the Manhattan Project. Six years later the House

Committee on Un-American Activities decided to investigate the possibility of espionage at Berkeley in 1943, in spite of the fact that the FBI and Army intelligence had long since concluded that no actionable information had been found. The committee called to testify all the individuals who could possibly shed any light on this issue. The committee went out of its way to dramatize the hearings by referring to a mysterious "Scientist X" who was suspected of passing atomic secrets to the Soviet Union.

The Manhattan Project had occupied the attention of thousands of scientists in multiple locations before it came to its dramatic conclusion in Hiroshima and Nagasaki. In the months immediately following the war, many of these scientists had misgivings about the project they had participated in. The destructive potential of the bomb had been demonstrated conclusively, and the question now was what form the future would take. Many of the atomic scientists favored a future in which no one pretended there was any "secret" to the bomb, since all of the basic principles required for creating it were already a matter of public record. As a result, these scientists reasoned, the future of the bomb should lie in the hands of some kind of international body or organization, one dedicated to the responsible deployment of atomic knowledge and expertise.

Such a conclusion was not welcome within the halls of Congress, nor within the corridors of the military. The political and military leaders felt that the United States should maintain as much control over the bomb as possible. The tension between the scientists and the governmental establishment took the form of a debate over the newly formed Atomic Energy Commission, designed by Congress to administer and direct all applications of atomic energy within the United States. The scientists insisted that the Commission remain under civilian control. Ultimately, their view prevailed, although the military won substantial concessions in its desire to maintain an oversight role of the AEC. Nevertheless, some politicians continued to feel that the loyalty of the atomic scientists left something to be desired.

It was within this context that the House Committee on Un-American Activities took an interest in atomic espionage at the University of California at Berkeley. The committee was established immediately following the war in 1945. During the 79th session of Congress (1945-46), the committee held hearings for only twelve days and accomplished little of any consequence. During the 80th Congress (1947-48), the committee was more active, and held hearings on a total of 62 days. Its main focus during this period was purported Communist influence in Hollywood, and the witnesses included many well-known writers and directors. This preoccupation earned the committee its lasting reputation for exaggeration, intimidation, and political persecution. Not until the 81st session of Congress (1949-50), however, did the committee reach the apex of its activities and interests. During that two-year period, the committee held hearings on no less than 108 days, and the transcripts of the testimony given consumed over 3000 pages. The investigation into possible espionage at Berkeley was one of many topics that occupied the committee during that session.

In the course of the committee's proceedings, the notorious Scientist X turned out to be none other than Joseph Weinberg, but his testimony on three occasions gave the committee little to go on. He denied ever having met Steve Nelson, much less passing on secret information. Nelson himself appeared before the committee twice and refused to accept the committee's oath or to participate in any manner. Also on the committee's docket was Frank Oppenheimer, Robert's younger brother, then an associate professor at the University of Wisconsin. Frank admitted to having been a member of the Communist party for two years prior to 1940, but he refused to name other individuals whose participation he was aware of. In anticipation of the fallout from this refusal, Frank had tendered his resignation to the University of Wisconsin prior to his testimony. On the day of his testimony, his resignation was accepted.

As a result of his unionizing activities within the Radiation Lab at Berkeley, Rossi Lomanitz had lost his draft deferment in 1943, as well as a responsible position at Los Alamos. By 1949, however, he had become an assistant professor at Fisk University in Tennessee, when he was called to appear before HUAC. He testified on April 17, 1949. When he too refused to name acquaintances from six years earlier who might have been associated with the party, he lost his position at Fisk the next day.

Into this maelstrom strode David Bohm on April 23, 1949. A photograph of him on his way into the hearing room shows the visage of a lamb being led to the slaughter (see p. 287). His testimony, in April and June 1949, occupied 14 of the 3000 pages of transcripts the committee compiled during that session. Most of the questions directed at Bohm focused on whether he knew specific individuals suspected of Communist allegiance or sympathies. On the advice of counsel, Bohm refused to answer many questions. He offered three grounds for his refusal: the First Amendment guarantees of freedom of speech and assembly; the Fifth Amendment guarantee against self-incrimination; and the inherent right not to answer questions that might tend to "degrade" his personal and employment prospects. Present on the committee was Richard M. Nixon, a newly elected congressman from California, who pointed out with lawyerly precision that the Supreme Court had already ruled that the Constitution provides no protection for witnesses from questions that might merely tend to "degrade" them.

Fifteen months after his testimony, in September 1950, Bohm was one of 56 witnesses indicted on charges of contempt of Congress for refusing to answer all of the committee's questions. He was arrested in his office at Princeton by federal marshals on October 1, 1950, and his case was heard in federal court the following April. Following a recent decision by the Supreme Court (Blau v. United States), federal judge Alexander Holtzoff ruled that Bohm's constitutional right against self-incrimination protected him from all charges brought against him, and he was exonerated in the eyes of the law. Bohm's apprehension that his testimony might tend to degrade him in the eyes of an employer, however, turned out to be all too prescient. Following his arrest, he was forbidden by the president of Princeton (a devout anti-Communist) to set foot on campus until his case was resolved. The next year, in spite of Bohm's legal exoneration, the president intervened in what would normally have been a faculty decision and refused to renew Bohm's contract.

Bohm consulted with Einstein about what to do next. Einstein wanted Bohm to work with him at the Institute for Advanced Study (affiliated with but not under the control of Princeton). Oppenheimer himself, however, as director of the institute, refused to approve the appointment, evidently on grounds that to do so would embarrass him politically. However narrow and self-serving Oppenheimer's decision may seem today, in fact he had good grounds for concern about his own reputation, as subsequent events made clear. Einstein advised Bohm that the political atmosphere in the United States was so poisoned that he might have to seek employment abroad. He wrote a letter to a colleague at the University of Manchester in England, recommending Bohm not only as a physicist, but also for his courageous stand before the House Committee on Un-American Activities. This appeal met with no success. Finally, Einstein turned to the University of Sao Paulo in Brazil, where again he recommended Bohm in glowing terms. Oppenheimer also contributed a letter of recommendation, and this time the results were favorable. On a dark day in August, 1951, David Bohm departed the country of his birth and prepared to commence the life of an expatriate.

Even while he was enduring a period of political persecution, Bohm was intensely occupied with the foundations of quantum theory. While he conducted classes in this subject for graduate students at Princeton, it was his responsibility to present the standard, prevailing interpretation of events in the realm of electrons and other subatomic particles—the so-called Copenhagen interpretation, named for the city of residence of Niels Bohr, the leading proponent and articulator of that point of view. According to the Copenhagen interpretation, certain features of ordinary reality are entirely absent in the behavior of subatomic particles. Among other things, we cannot know or understand the actual physical reality of the mathematical formulas that describe the electron. The particles under observation in that realm are so extremely small that they defy the kind of factual understanding or description that we normally take for granted.

Moreover, a fundamental feature of all other forms of science is held to be impossible at the quantum level. Ordinarily, science seeks to explain phenomena with reference to the principle of causation. To know or understand what events or circumstances cause a given result is generally considered the sine qua non of scientific understanding. But according to the Copenhagen interpretation, we can never know what causes subatomic particles to move in one way or another. All that can ever be expressed are probabilities—the electron might do this, or it might do that, according to certain formulas that predict those probabilities with a very high degree of accuracy.

In 1951, the same year that his prosecution for contempt of Congress was heard in federal court, Bohm published a textbook that expressed the Copenhagen interpretation of quantum reality with an original and unusual clarity. *Quantum Theory* sought wherever possible to describe events in the land of the electron with reference to qualitative rather than merely quantitative concepts, and to keep all the formulas grounded in the experimental observations that had produced them, rather than simply presenting the mathematics as a set of received and given truths. Bohm's textbook remains a classic in the field and is still in print to this day.

At the time of its publication, Bohm sent copies of the book to the leading quantum theorists for their review. Einstein felt that Bohm had described the Copenhagen interpretation as well as could be done, but he was not satisfied with that point of view. He particularly objected to the notion that causation was in principle not possible to attribute to subatomic particles, and that only probabilities could be found in that realm. This issue is what precipitated Einstein's famous remark, "God does not play dice with the universe." As a result, he encouraged Bohm to continue to examine and to question the Copenhagen interpretation of quantum reality. Although Einstein himself had not succeeded in showing in any rigorous way that the Copenhagen interpretation might be limited or flawed, he remarked that, "If anyone can do it, it is David Bohm."

Perhaps as a result of Einstein's encouragement, Bohm did indeed continue to probe the fundamental logic of the Copenhagen interpretation. He found a way to rewrite the standard formulas for quantum mechanics in such a way as to preserve the principle of causation in that realm. He did so by introducing a new variable, somewhat analogous to the gravitational field or the electromagnetic field, but operating at a deeper level of physical reality. Such a variable, known technically as the *quantum potential*, lay hidden to our present tools of magnification, but might be revealed by subsequent advances in technology. The standard theory of quantum events held that, in principle, no such advances could *ever* occur, but that doctrine had its roots in the mathematical formulas.

By rewriting the formulas in a way that still explained all the existing evidence, Bohm was able to show that more subtle forms of measurement, unknown to present science, could in fact be developed.

Bohm's insight was profound and revolutionary. With the introduction of the variable of a quantum potential, Bohm demonstrated that what had been considered settled doctrine in quantum physics was not necessarily the case. To be sure, Bohm did not refute the whole of the Copenhagen interpretation; he merely refuted the cornerstone of the edifice that held that its principles were inviolable. This in itself was an achievement of the highest magnitude.

Bohm was not unaware of the significance of what he had accomplished. He told a friend he could hardly believe that he had been so fortunate as to discover something so fundamental embedded in the innermost fabric of physical reality. As a result, even on the eve of his departure from his native shores in 1951, Bohm had reason to believe that his life and career were on an upward trajectory, buoyed in spite of everything by his path-breaking contribution to physics. The messy world of politics might fail to meet his idealistic expectations, but surely the citadel of science stood as a bulwark against passion and prejudice and would ensure proper and appropriate recognition of his work.

His revolutionary insights were described in a pair of papers that were published consecutively in volume 85 of the 1952 edition of the premier physics journal, *Physical Review*. The papers were entitled, "A Suggested Interpretation of the Quantum Theory in Terms of Hidden Variables, I and II." While the influence of those papers continues to grow even to the present day, their reception by the leading lights of the physics community during Bohm's first years in Brazil was not in accord with what he must have anticipated.

Chapter Three

THE OBSERVER AND THE OBSERVED

The response of the physics community to Bohm's papers could be described as muted at best. One of the leading proponents of the Copenhagen interpretation, Wolfgang Pauli, admitted that Bohm's argument was logically sound, but he believed that what Bohm had offered was no more than a "check that cannot be cashed," since the actual existence of hidden variables had not been and, he maintained, could not be established. The implication contained in Pauli's metaphor that the check was somehow impure or fraudulent only added insult to injury. The cruelest blow, however, came from Oppenheimer himself. "Juvenile deviationism" was his assessment of Bohm's papers; and he is reported to have added, "If we cannot disprove Bohm, then we must agree to ignore him." According to another member of the physics establishment, "We say that we cannot refute Bohm; but we add that we don't believe him."

Such an attitude was not universally shared. The outstanding physicist J. S. Bell later said of Bohm's papers, "In 1952, I saw the impossible done"; and his view, rather than that of Pauli or Oppenheimer, is the one that has withstood the test of time. According to the philosopher Paul Feyerabend, moreover, Bohr himself was stunned at what Bohm had achieved.

A crucial indicator of the significance of any scientific paper is the frequency with which it is cited in the published work of other scientists. By that measure, the influence of Bohm's papers has increased with each passing decade since the 1950's. Was the unfavorable response to Bohm's papers when they first appeared the result of professional jealousy or territoriality, perhaps coupled with political considerations? There is no way to know for sure, but his letters at the time reveal that

Bohm strongly held that view. In any case, the implications for him, both personally and professionally, would be hard to overstate. He had to face the fact that even the most apparently rational individuals could be biased by self-interest or other considerations, and therefore that science was not an infallible instrument for the discovery of truth. In this manner, Bohm may have embarked on the path that led ultimately to the work of Krishnamurti.

Such a transition, however, did not occur overnight. An intermediate stage in the evolution of Bohm's thinking appeared in his next major publication, *Causality and Chance in Modern Physics*, a book composed for an audience wider than his peers. Without resorting to mathematical formulas or equations, Bohm lays bare the structure of assumptions on which prevailing opinion in the field of quantum physics was based. He does so by placing events in the land of the electron in a broader context—indeed, in the context of the whole enterprise of science. He displays his familiarity with developments not only in physics, but in medicine, geology, astronomy, and other areas of science. The scope and detail of his analysis reveals an intellectual curiosity far beyond the requirements for expertise in theoretical physics.

In his review of developments throughout many fields of science, Bohm demonstrates the manner in which causation and probability form a pair of interlocking principles, each one complementing and reinforcing the other. Science normally seeks to understand phenomena with reference to cause and effect wherever possible, but when that form of understanding eludes experimental results, the principle of probability comes into play. When we roll a pair of dice, the outcome is determined the moment the dice leave our hand, and could be predicted if we knew their precise position, height, and momentum at that instant. In the absence of such detailed knowledge, we resort to probabilities and express in numerical terms the chance of any possible outcome.

In *Causality and Chance in Modern Physics*, Bohm describes the alternative explanations of causation and probability throughout the disciplines of science, before turning to the unusual issues presented by events in the subatomic realm. The quantum world represents the limit of our technological ability to see into the fine structure of physical reality.

Matter at that level is so minute that a single photon of light can disturb a particle and prevent our understanding of its behavior, and so we resort to probabilities rather than causation to describe what occurs. But to conclude that what causes the action of the electron is forever unknowable, or does not even exist, represents an unwarranted assumption at odds with the findings of every other field of science. The Copenhagen insistence that causation is forever removed from that realm, according to Bohm, is in essence a philosophical assumption, not one grounded in evidence or empirical results. It is the product of a thinking process superimposed upon factual material, rather than something dictated by experimental results.

One of the most interesting ideas Bohm introduced in *Causality and Chance in Modern Physics* is that the universe is infinite not only in the quantitative sense of time and distance, but also qualitatively. Nature is composed of successive layers of matter and energy, and each layer has its own particular concepts and laws. It is mistaken to suppose that the quantum level is ultimate and final; there is no end, according to Bohm, of qualitative levels of reality. In this and other ways, he exposes in dispassionate but meticulous detail the false and limited nature of the assumptions underlying prevailing opinion in our understanding of the electron and other subatomic particles. *Causality and Chance in Modern Physics* represents a refutation, in prose accessible to any serious reader, of the reasoning that prevented immediate acceptance of Bohm's papers on hidden variables.

One notable visitor while Bohm was in Brazil was Richard Feynman, who later won the Nobel Prize in physics. Feynman came there in part to take bongo drum lessons, a favorite hobby of his, and while there he went on walks with Bohm, who described the substance of his papers on hidden variables. Feynman was at first skeptical, but later he came to accept Bohm's point of view. Bohm concluded that he and Feynman would remain friends for life, which proved to be the case.

Even within the relative safety of Brazil, Bohm's past political interests continued to haunt him. The situation became so severe that the head of his department felt obliged to write to Einstein for confirmation of his endorsement. Einstein replied as follows:

> Dr. Bohm, whom I have known personally for some years, is, in my opinion, a very gifted and original theoretical physicist. Professionally, he has added materially to our knowledge of quantum mechanics and has more recently become very interested in the fundamental philosophical implications of that theory. He is also an exceptionally able teacher who is an inspiration to his students. . . .
>
> [Bohm], having already achieved a very stimulating book on Quantum Mechanics and its application to the theory of atoms. . . . has become deeply interested in the following questions. Is it really necessary to assume that the processes in the molecular domain are governed by chance? . . .
>
> Dr. Bohm has a lovable personality, and with this opinion his former students and colleagues would agree wholeheartedly. . . . I have had in the past the greatest confidence in Dr. Bohm as a scientist and as a man, and I continue to do so.

A few weeks after his arrival in Brazil, Bohm was called in to the American embassy and asked to relinquish his passport. After he had done so, the embassy refused to return it for any purpose other than Bohm's return to the United States. The rationale, much less the legality, of this action remains unclear. The net effect, however, was to deny Bohm the opportunity to travel outside of Brazil unless he were to assume Brazilian citizenship and abandon his own. After three and a half years in Brazil, Bohm decided he had no alternative but to take that course. Neither the weather nor the intellectual atmosphere there were conducive to his temperament. When a position opened up for him at the Technion in Israel, he hesitated for several months but then decided to take it. In this manner, it is possible to say in retrospect that the House Committee on Un-American Activities set in motion a series of events that ultimately deprived Bohm of his American citizenship. In the annals of injustices not consonant with the principles of democracy, this one surely deserves an honorable mention.

Bohm remained in Israel for three years, during which two events of outstanding significance in his life occurred. One involved a graduate student, Yakir Aharonov, who predicted an unexpected phenomenon in the behavior of the electron based upon Bohm's papers on hidden variables. When Aharonov's prediction was confirmed by experimental evidence, it represented a challenge to the conventional understanding of quantum reality and an indirect confirmation of the legitimacy of Bohm's contribution. What is now known as the Aharonov-Bohm effect remains to this day a puzzle to theoretical orthodoxy in quantum physics.

The second major development in Israel was that Bohm met Sarah Woolfson, an artist originally from England, who would become his wife. They met at a dance, where Sarah picked out Bohm from the crowd at first sight. Sarah was known to family and friends as Saral, and she soon became his close companion. In 1957, David and Saral returned to the country of her birth, where he had been offered a research position at Bristol University. Four years later, he accepted the offer of a chair in Theoretical Physics at Birkbeck College, University of London. It was at Birkbeck that Bohm's odyssey from Wilkes-Barre to Caltech to Berkeley to Princeton to Sao Paulo to Israel to England finally came to an end. He remained in the position of professor of physics at the University of London for the rest of his life.

Among the most famous thought experiments in the history of science revolves around a hypothetical cat. The cover of the May 1994 issue of *Scientific American* depicts the fundamental issue involved. The artist has rendered a depiction of a cat, confined in a box, that is both alive, standing upright, and simultaneously dead, lying on the floor of the box. This thought experiment was devised by Erwin Schrödinger in 1937 to illustrate the problems inherent in the Copenhagen interpretation of events at the subatomic level. The title of the cover story was "Bohm's Alternative to Quantum Mechanics." The author was David Z. Albert, professor of philosophy at Columbia University, a former professor of physics, and author of *Quantum Mechanics and Experience* (Harvard University Press, 1994).

The blurb in the table of contents describing Albert's article reads as follows:

For almost 70 years, quantum theory has upended commonsense notions about reality. Cause and effect, time and place, and objective events are happily jettisoned. Yet for the past 40 years, a formulation of the theory has existed that explains events as well as the standard version, without threatening reason. The work of an expatriate American, it may be gaining adherents.

According to the Copenhagen description of events, the characteristics of any particle of matter smaller than an atom cannot be observed without disturbing the behavior of the particle being examined; or, more precisely, the particle under consideration cannot be regarded as being in one state or another until it is actually observed. Only at that moment is its formerly ambiguous condition resolved. With his parable of the cat, Schrödinger brought out the inherent strangeness of this point of view. He describes a box in which a cat is confined along with a container of poison and a source of radioactivity. The container is wired to release the poison only if it is struck by a particle of radioactivity. But according to the Copenhagen interpretation, whether or not the poison is released is only determined by the act of observation itself. In the meantime, according to this view, the cat must remain in some indeterminate condition, neither dead nor alive.

According to Albert,

> Notwithstanding the profound violence these ideas do to our intuitive picture of the world, to the very notion of what it is to be material, to be a particle, a compact set of rules has been cooked up that has proved extraordinarily successful at predicting all the observed behaviors of electrons under these circumstances.

Schrödinger's thought experiment illustrates the bizarre implications of quantum theory. Bohm's alternative avoids some of these strange implications and restores sanity to the land of the electron. Again, according to Albert,

> For some time, many physicists and philosophers have viewed this state of affairs as profoundly unsatisfactory. It has seemed absurd that the best existing formulation of the most fundamental laws of nature should depend on such imprecise and elusive distinctions.

Albert goes on to say,

> Bohm's theory is a great deal clearer than is the Copenhagen interpretation about what the world is made of. . . . Bohm's theory accounts for all the unfathomable-looking behaviors of electrons discussed earlier every bit as well as the standard interpretation does. Moreover, and this point is important, it is free of any of the metaphysical perplexities associated with quantum-mechanical supposition. . . .
>
> Despite the rather spectacular advantages of Bohm's theory, an almost universal reluctance even to consider it, and an almost universal allegiance to the standard formulation of quantum mechanics, has persisted in physics, astonishingly, throughout most of the past 40 years.

Bohm's seminal contributions to the foundations of quantum theory, in other words, were not more fully appreciated until decades had passed after he had published his pathbreaking papers at the age of thirty-three.

Schrödinger's thought experiment illuminates the fact that the apparatus we use to observe the electron has the effect of interacting and interfering with the events we are trying to observe. Such a result would be bizarre in any other field of study, but in quantum theory it is understood to be inescapable. It is enshrined in what is called the Heisenberg uncertainty principle and is considered to be a central pillar in the edifice of quantum physics. The essence of the principle is that under some circumstances the act of observation affects what is being observed.

Once this principle is grasped or acknowledged, a somewhat similar application of it can be discerned in other spheres of life. When we use a camera to photograph a flower or a mountain, the object photographed is not affected by the camera. But when human beings are photographed, their behavior is often modified accordingly. People tend to pose for the camera by gathering together into groups and smiling or adopting exaggerated expressions of affection. If the individual viewing such photos did not realize that the people were posing for the camera, he or she might assume that they were gathering in that manner for its own sake or for some other reason. This would represent a failure to recognize an intrinsic connection between the apparatus of observation and what is being observed.

If one had already elaborated the meaning of the principles involved, one might abbreviate this idea by asserting simply, "the observer *is* the observed." In any case, this is the manner of speech adopted by Krishnamurti when describing the internal, psychological landscape of thought and emotion. He expressed this view in many public talks as well as in one of his first published works, *The First and Last Freedom*, with a foreword by Aldous Huxley. Perhaps it was Huxley's name that attracted Saral Bohm one afternoon when she was browsing in the local library with her husband. In that book, she ran across the phrase, "the observer is the observed," and she brought it to his attention.

Bohm found the book fascinating, and he resolved to meet the man who had written it. He wrote a letter to the publisher and inquired whether it would be possible to arrange an appointment with Krishnamurti. The answer was affirmative, and the next time Krishnamurti was in London, the first meeting between the two men took place. According to Saral, after a period of silence or uncertainty, Bohm began to describe his work in physics and how he perceived its relationship to Krishnamurti's observations. The conversation proceeded from there in a friendly and collegial manner, something that Bohm said reminded him of his conversations with Einstein.

The year was 1961. Bohm was 43 years old; Krishnamurti was 66. The collaboration that developed between the two men was extraordinary in many respects, not the least of which was the disparity between their respective backgrounds—as will become more clear in the chapter that follows.

Chapter Four

THE WORLD TEACHER

By any measure or standard, Krishnamurti led an extraordinary life. The list of his recorded talks and dialogues runs more than 100 pages, with an average of some 45 entries per page. During a single decade, he addressed audiences in 22 nations encompassing 64 cities, some 600 talks in all. Selected talks and dialogues were published in more than 30 books, and an additional seven books were published of his written work. He founded eight schools on three continents. His message reached an audience of millions.

The philosophy Krishnamurti expressed from a public platform focused almost exclusively on elucidating the contours of daily life and consciousness. The catalogue of his most familiar topics includes the origin of conflict, the nature of fear, the problem of desire, the sources of creativity, and the essential meaning of love. He was particularly concerned with the fundamental nature of thought and its relationship to experience, knowledge, and memory. Interwoven among these themes were observations about the sense of self, ego, or individual identity. These and several related issues are examined in greater detail in the following chapter.

Krishnamurti expressed his views in ordinary, non-technical language, accessible to any audience, but much of what he had to say was original and radical in concept. He addressed elements of human nature common to all mankind, but he did so with a depth of insight that eluded many listeners. Paradoxically, he often seemed impeccably clear and yet at the same time difficult to follow to the end. Perhaps it was precisely this quality that enabled a man like Bohm to engage in hours of sustained dialogue with him, probing the meaning of his work.

The origins of Krishnamurti's career were both a blessing and a kind
of curse. From an early age, he was hailed as a spiritual teacher, and he
gathered a worldwide following predicated on that reputation. It was
only by an act of singular courage and clarity that he broke free from
those bonds while still a young man and proceeded to chart his own
course. Nevertheless, the notoriety of those early associations continued
to shape, to some degree, the manner in which his message was received
for many years. In any case, his life and work cannot be fully understood
without reference to the earlier phase of his career and the manner in
which he divested himself of it.

Jiddu Krishnamurti was born in 1895 in a small town not far from
Bangalore in the southern portion of the Indian subcontinent. He was
the eighth of eleven children. In his culture, the family name came first,
followed by the given name, and he was generally known as Krishna. As
a boy, he was fascinated by nature and would sit for hours under a tree
watching the world around him. He was not so adept at schoolwork,
which evidently bored him, and the canings he received as a consequence
proved to be no motivation. Although his family belonged to the Brahmin
caste, they were not well off. Krishna's mother, moreover, died when he
was ten years old, and so the family was poor in more ways than one.
Krishna's father kept the children together by moving to Adyar, just south
of Madras, on the coast of southern India, where he worked as a clerk for
the Theosophical Society on a large property adjacent to the ocean.

The Theosophical Society (TS) was founded in the United States in
1875 by Helena Blavatsky and Henry Olcott. She was a Russian émigré
and the author of many books, including *The Secret Doctrine*, a work
that describes an occult world hidden behind the veil of ordinary reality. He was a journalist by trade, a Buddhist by inclination, and a
student of the occult arts as well. The Theosophical Society was intended to investigate a common core of spiritual insights held to be
inherent in most religions. Its general intention was expressed in terms
of "Objects," of which there were three: the study of comparative religion, philosophy, and science; the investigation of unexplained laws
of nature and "powers latent in man"; and, above all, support for "the
universal brotherhood of humanity."

In 1907, the author, public speaker, and social activist Annie Besant was elected president of the TS. Besant had achieved fame in 1876, at the age of 27, when she became the first woman to defend herself before a court of law in England. At issue was the right to publish a slender volume entitled *Fruits of Philosophy*, composed by an American physician, that described for a general public the best medical knowledge available regarding birth control. When Besant and her associate, Charles Bradlaugh, president of the National Secular Society, re-published *Fruits of Philosophy*, they were charged by the authorities with the dissemination of obscenity, and their trial was the subject of intense public interest. Besant held forth before the court for three days, examining the issue of birth control from every angle—medical, legal, social, and moral. The quality of her logic, coupled with the persuasive beauty of her speaking voice, won over the public, if not necessarily the court. She and Bradlaugh won their case only on a technicality, but the result was widely regarded as a vindication of their position. In the year following their trial, *Fruits of Philosophy* sold over 100,000 copies.

For the remainder of her career, Besant advanced a progressive social agenda, including interventions on behalf of working women, education, and the independence of India from imperial England. The power of her voice, whether in writing or from a public platform, was a formidable factor in the politics of her age. When she assumed the presidency of the Theosophical Society, it obtained an endorsement of immeasurable value, as well as a fountain of energy and access to a wide network of resources. As might be expected from a woman of her drive, intellect, and imagination, Besant put her own characteristic stamp upon the overall outlook and intention of the TS. She maintained that human history demonstrates a pattern of periodic interventions by a World Teacher, and that it was the mission of the Society to identify and to cultivate the next manifestation of that individual. The World Teacher was represented by the Buddha, Jesus, and others who appeared at times of crisis and guided humanity toward a more enlightened future.

Besant resolved to direct the resources of the TS according to this vision. She spoke increasingly, to large audiences, on the coming of the next World Teacher, and the search for the boy or adolescent who was destined to fulfill this role began to assume a sense of urgency. In this mission, she was assisted by her associate, Charles Leadbeater, a priest from England, who had relocated to Adyar, where Blavatsky had established the headquarters of the Society. Leadbeater liked to walk on the beach in the afternoons with a retinue of his friends and associates, and there he observed Krishnamurti, then fourteen years old, playing with his younger brother, Nitya. Leadbeater claimed to have the extrasensory power of perceiving an aura of light surrounding an individual, with colors corresponding to personality characteristics, and he said that Krishnamurti's aura contained no element of self-interest. Leadbeater invited Krishna to his quarters on the Theosophical compound for the purpose of investigating his past lives, a subject in which he was considered unusually skilled and accomplished. His studies revealed that Krishna had an uncommon collection of previous incarnations, one that suggested his suitability for the next manifestation of the World Teacher.

In this assessment, Leadbeater was confirmed by Annie Besant upon her next visit to Adyar. Since Krishna and Nitya were inseparable, she resolved to take them both under her care and to raise and educate them with all the formidable range of resources at her disposal. She removed them to England, against their father's wishes, and housed them in the homes of members of the TS, where they were given tutorial instruction and exposed to the best that English society had to offer. George Bernard Shaw met Krishnamurti at dinner one evening and declared him to be "the most beautiful human being" he had ever seen. In order to facilitate the emergence and recognition of the new World Teacher, Besant created an international organization entitled the Order of the Star in the East (OSE). She appointed Krishnamurti as head of the organization, and at its peak it numbered 40,000 members worldwide. Krishnamurti wrote regular columns for the *Star Bulletin*, appeared at OSE events, and seemed to accept the grand expectations that had been placed upon him.

Underneath the surface, however, another reality was evidently at work. A letter Krishnamurti wrote in 1920 suggests he had already begun to chafe under the yoke of the OSE. Within another few years, he started to articulate his own, independent message, one steeped in human psychology and not shaped by any esoteric doctrine. He spoke of the human condition as a whole, with a depth of understanding that many listeners found extraordinary, but without reference to anything occult, preordained, or extra-worldly.

A salient factor in the unfolding independence of Krishnamurti's mind may have been the death of his brother, Nitya, in 1925. The two young men had moved to Ojai, California in 1922 in an effort to find a climate conducive to arresting the progression of Nitya's tuberculosis, from which he had been suffering for two years. The Ojai Valley lies about eighty miles north of Los Angeles and fifteen miles inland from the sea. Its Mediterranean climate seemed beneficial to Nitya's health, and when Krishna travelled to India for a Theosophical conference, he expected Nitya to survive for the foreseeable future. But the ship on which he travelled received a telegram late one night: the fever and other symptoms of tuberculosis had flared up unexpectedly and taken Nitya's life. The shock of this event may have accelerated and even crystallized Krishna's increasing detachment from the principles and ideology of Theosophy.

In 1929, at the age of thirty-four, Krishnamurti acted to dissolve the organization (now called Order of the Star) that had been formed to cultivate and introduce him to the world. He did so in a memorable address in which he stated, in effect, that organized religion is inherently inimical to the discovery of truth. He had no quarrel with organizations designed for practical purposes, but once it is intended to claim a monopoly upon truth and to evaluate individuals according to whether they belong, or how far they have advanced, no organization can be conducive to psychological freedom.

Perhaps the most salient of the passages from this talk was Krishnamurti's declaration that "truth is a pathless land." This statement was an unmistakable reference to a central Theosophical principle, formulated and elaborated by Leadbeater, of a precise "Path" to spiritual enlightenment, with clearly demarcated stages along the way, and progress along the Path assessed by those who claimed access to occult powers and sources of wisdom. To say that truth is a pathless land represented a definitive repudiation of that philosophy and perhaps the most succinct explanation why Krishnamurti felt compelled to dissolve the Order of the Star.

In the years that followed, Krishnamurti continued to refine and to elaborate his message. He articulated a coherent and original understanding of the nature and structure of consciousness, with an emphasis upon the problems of everyday life. His talks were transcribed, edited, and published as pamphlets under the imprint of Krishnamurti Writings, Inc., or KWINC. He and others referred to his philosophy as his "teachings," although he preferred to call them not the teachings of Krishnamurti, but rather the teachings of life.

Krishnamurti's travels were interrupted by World War II, during which he remained at his home in Ojai. At that time, Aldous Huxley, the world-renowned intellectual and author of *Brave New World*, was living with his wife in Santa Barbara, less than an hour's drive from Ojai. With his encyclopedic mind, Huxley was aware of Krishnamurti, and he initiated a meeting. During those years the two men became very close. They often went for walks together in the hills surrounding Ojai, and their conversations encompassed world events, the natural world, and psychological issues. Krishnamurti later seemed to regard his relationship with Huxley as a kind of model for an ideal friendship, one where both individuals feel able to confide whatever is on their minds or to sit together in silence by the side of a stream.

Huxley evidently felt a comparable rapport. He visited Krishnamurti regularly or invited him to his second home in Wrightwood, in the mountains east of Ojai, and it was Huxley who encouraged him to commit his thoughts to the printed page. His first efforts of this kind consisted of detailed descriptions of scenes from nature, coupled with accounts of individuals who had come to seek his counsel or advice. Huxley considered these compositions "marvelous and unique," and they were published by Harper and Row in three volumes, under the title *Commentaries on Living*. A subsequent book, *The First and Last Freedom*, was a compilation of excerpts from his public talks, and it contained a foreword by Huxley. He later said of one of Krishnamurti's talks, "It was like listening to a sermon of the Buddha."

During the decade of the 1950's, Krishnamurti continued to refine his message and to enlarge his audience. He gave public talks throughout the world without charging admission or requesting his listeners to join any organization. This was the state of affairs in 1961, at the time that David Bohm reached out and began to establish a relationship with him. Neither man could have foreseen what was about to ensue. Their compatibility and their conversation endured for over two decades. Each man evidently recognized in the other a collaborator who was profoundly interested in discovering the truth, regardless of where it might lead. On that basis, a deep bond between the two men was sealed.

Krishnamurti's philosophy, as it developed over the course of his lifetime, consisted of several interrelated elements. These had primarily to do with relationship, thought, emotion, and identity. He considered thought to be essentially the product of memory, of the past—a mechanical, conditioned process that governs most of consciousness. The various emotions of love, fear, joy, sorrow, and so on are among the products on which thought attempts to exert its influence. Superimposed upon thought and emotion is the overriding sensation of a personal identity, "me," the thinker or observer who believes he or she is in charge of the whole affair. Krishnamurti maintained that this arrangement of the landscape of consciousness is untenable. He argued that sheer observation, not only of the outer world, but especially of the inner world of thought and emotion, is the vehicle for clarity and the liberation of the mind.

According to Krishnamurti, however, such observation is not easily achieved, for the mind is quick to introduce value judgments and to justify, suppress, or otherwise distort many of the thoughts and emotions that commonly occur in daily life. He therefore advocated what he called a "choiceless awareness" of consciousness. Perhaps the foremost impediment to achieving such an awareness is the observer, the thinker, who stands apart from the data of consciousness and feels that he or she is an independent entity who monitors, controls, and decides what course of action to take. Krishnamurti considered this sense of identity to be an illusion created by thought, not an independent or objective reality. This illusion is so powerful and pervasive that it is difficult to imagine what consciousness or daily life would be like without it, much less to achieve such a state of mind. Nevertheless, to do so is imperative and requires a deep insight into the whole structure of the thinking process. The thinker, the observer, by its very nature, introduces an artificial division in consciousness, when in fact he or she is inseparable from the events under observation. Krishnamurti often expressed this insight by declaring that the thinker is the thought; the observer is the observed.

Krishnamurti's philosophy is far more comprehensive, subtle, and complex than this brief summary suggests. He strongly discouraged anyone, however, from assuming the role of his representative or interpreter; he insisted that his teachings be taken on their own terms and speak for themselves. Rather than attempt any further summary of his outlook, therefore, it seems prudent to elaborate his message with closer, more detailed reference to his actual public talks. The following chapter is devoted to this purpose.

In addition to his public talks and dialogues with individuals and small groups, Krishnamurti established several schools over the course of his lifetime. Five of these were in India, one in England, and two in the United States. Prior to the dissolution of the Order of the Star, Annie Besant had secured three properties in the Ojai Valley exclusively for Krishnamurti's work, and these remained under his control. One of these was the residential property where he and Nitya stayed beginning in 1922. A second property was located in the "Upper Ojai," just outside the valley, and in 1946 Krishnamurti, Aldous Huxley and others established there the Happy Valley School (since renamed the Besant Hill School), although he subsequently disassociated himself from it. Besant also purchased 150 acres in the heart of the Ojai Valley, where Krishnamurti gave public talks for many years, and where he established the Oak Grove School in 1975.

Krishnamurti continued to give talks, conduct individual and group dialogues, and oversee the operation of his schools for the remainder of his life. At 90 years of age, in 1986, he died in Ojai of pancreatic cancer. All of his schools continue to flourish, and the voluminous recordings of his talks and dialogues are preserved in archives on three continents. New volumes of his work continue to be published; access to his teachings is available online; and new memoirs of the man and analyses of his work continue to see the light of day. As a result, the final measure of his influence, the magnitude of his impact, is not yet possible to assess and may not be for years to come. As with many individuals whose work is original and profound, it may be centuries before his contribution comes more clearly into focus.

Chapter Five

CHOICELESS AWARENESS

Subsequent to the dissolution of the Order of the Star, Krishnamurti's message remained reasonably consistent over the course of many years. He always spoke extemporaneously, however, and he always sought new language to refine his presentation. The more mature expression of his views occurred after the period of lying fallow during World War II. His work is so voluminous that it defies any easy or straightforward summary, but the task of creating a fair description becomes more manageable by considering two volumes of his published talks. One volume appeared a few years after World War II, and the other some thirty years later; these books effectively capture the beginning and the conclusion of the latter half of his career.

The First and Last Freedom was published in 1954 by Harper and Brothers. In his foreword to this book, Aldous Huxley places Krishnamurti's philosophy in the context of humanity's use of symbols in all the domains of life:

> Man is an amphibian who lives simultaneously in two worlds—the given and the home-made, the world of matter, life and consciousness and the world of symbols. In our thinking we make use of a great variety of symbol-systems—linguistic, mathematical, pictorial, musical, ritualistic. Without such symbol-systems we should have no art, no science, no law, no philosophy, not so much as the rudiments of civilization: in other words, we should be animals.
>
> Symbols, then, are indispensable. But symbols—as the history of our own and every other age makes so abundantly clear—can also be fatal. Consider, for example, the domain of science on the one hand, the domain of politics and religion on the other. Thinking in terms of, and acting in response to, one set of symbols, we have come, in some

small measure, to understand and control the elementary forces of nature. Thinking in terms of, and acting in response to, another set of symbols, we use these forces as instruments of mass murder and collective suicide. In the first case the explanatory symbols were well chosen, carefully analysed and progressively adapted to the emergent facts of physical existence. In the second case symbols originally ill-chosen were never subjected to thorough-going analysis and never re-formulated so as to harmonize with the emergent facts of human existence. Worse still, those misleading symbols were everywhere treated with a wholly unwarranted respect, as though, in some mysterious way, they were more real than the realities to which they referred.

Huxley proceeds to elaborate upon this theme, and he uses it to introduce Krishnamurti's teachings, the essence of which he characterizes as follows:

The liberating process must begin with the choiceless awareness of what you will and of your reactions to the symbol-system which tells you that you ought, or you ought not, to will it. Through this choiceless awareness, as it penetrates the successive layers of the ego and its associated sub-conscious, will come love and understanding, but of another order than that with which we are ordinarily familiar. This choiceless awareness—at every moment and in all the circumstances of life—is the only effective meditation.

Unlike some of Krishnamurti's subsequent publications, *The First and Last Freedom* does not consist of a single series of talks, but rather of excerpts evidently compiled over a period of years (the excerpts are not dated). This construction is the work of his editor, but the subject matter is familiar to anyone acquainted with Krishnamurti's work. The book is divided into twenty-one topics, each consisting of five to seven pages, as well as replies to thirty-four questions, two or three pages each. The titles given by the editor for the topics in the first section include Self-Knowledge, Belief, Fear, Awareness, Desire, Self-Deception, and Time and Transformation. The answers to questions include On Nationalism, On Belief in God, On Love, and On the Known and the Unknown.

Among the themes that receive close attention in this volume is relationship, considered in its entirety. According to Krishnamurti, life is relationship; to be is to be related. Relationship is with people, nature, things and ideas, and to understand oneself is to discover what one is from moment to moment in relationship:

> Before we can find out what the end-purpose of life is, what it all means—wars, national antagonisms, conflicts, the whole mess—we must begin with ourselves, must we not? It sounds so simple, but it is extremely difficult. To follow oneself, to see how one's thought operates, one has to be extraordinarily alert, so that as one begins to be more and more alert to the intricacies of one's own thinking and responses and feelings, one begins to have a greater awareness not only of oneself but of another with whom one is in relationship. To know oneself is to study oneself in action, which is relationship.

In another passage, he continues with this theme:

> Relationship, surely, is the mirror in which you discover yourself. . . . Relationship is a process of self-revelation, and, without knowing oneself, the ways of one's own mind and heart, merely to establish an outward order, a system, a cunning formula, has very little meaning. What is important is to understand oneself in relationship with another. Then relationship becomes not a process of isolation but a movement in which you discover your own motives, your own thoughts, your own pursuits; and that very discovery is the beginning of liberation, the beginning of transformation.

Observations about the nature of thought are also woven into almost every topic. In considering the activity of the mind, for example, he says:

> What is the function of the mind? . . . It is all a process of thinking, is it not? Otherwise the mind is not there. So long as the mind is not thinking, consciously or unconsciously, there is no consciousness.

Only a mind that is quiet can fully understand any problem or see something new. For this purpose, thought, which is the action of knowledge, a movement in the field of the known, must go into abeyance:

> To understand anything, any human or scientific problem, what is important, what is essential? A quiet mind, is it not?—a mind that is intent on understanding. It is not a mind that is exclusive, that is trying

to concentrate—which again is an effort of resistance. If I really want to understand something, there is immediately a quiet state of mind. When you want to listen to music or look at a picture which you love, which you have a feeling for, what is the state of your mind? Immediately there is a quietness, is there not?

The network of issues addressed in this volume is oriented toward "self-knowledge," which is not of a piece with ordinary knowledge of the outer world. Perhaps in order to avoid confusion on this point, in later years he discontinued use of this term, although he still emphasized the issue in other language.

The fundamental understanding of oneself does not come through knowledge or through the accumulation of experiences, which is merely the cultivation of memory. The understanding of oneself is from moment to moment; if we merely accumulate knowledge of the self, that very knowledge prevents further understanding, because accumulated knowledge and experience becomes the center through which thought focuses and has its being.

The world is not different from us and our activities because it is what we are which creates the problems of the world; the difficulty with the majority of us is that we do not know ourselves directly, but seek a system, a method, a means of operation by which to solve the many human problems.

The exposition ultimately points to or revolves around the sense of self, the thinker or observer who feels he or she is overseeing the activities of consciousness. Krishnamurti maintains that the separation between the thinker and the thought is illusory and the source of psychological discord and conflict.

Surely the only thing which can bring about a fundamental change, a creative, psychological release, is everyday watchfulness, being aware from moment to moment of our motives, the conscious as well as the unconscious. When we realize that the disciplines, beliefs, ideals only strengthen the 'me' and are therefore utterly futile—when we are aware of that from day to day, see the truth of it, do we not come to the central point when the thinker is constantly separating himself from his thought, from his observations, from his experiences? So long as the thinker exists apart from his thought, which he is trying to dominate, there can be no fundamental transformation.

The First and Last Freedom explores a rich set of interrelated topics, of which the summary given here represents only a brief distillation. A somewhat comparable set of topics was on display twenty-five years later in Saanen, Switzerland. In this exquisite, bucolic setting, Krishnamurti gave an annual series of talks for the last two decades of his life. He typically spoke on alternate days for two or three weeks to an audience of a thousand or more, gathered from all parts of Europe and beyond. This extended series of talks allowed the opportunity for a more complete and coherent exposition of his philosophy. The last series of talks at Saanen occurred in July, 1985, and it represents a final statement of Krishnamurti's overall outlook.

In the first talk on Sunday, July 7, Krishnamurti began as follows:

> If one may, one would like to point out that we are a gathering of serious people who are concerned with daily life. We are not concerned whatsoever with beliefs, ideologies, suppositions, theoretical conclusions or theological concepts, nor are we trying to found a sect, a group of people who follow somebody. We are not, let's hope, frivolous but rather we are concerned with what is happening in the world—all the tragedies, the utter misery, poverty—and our responsibility to it. . . .
>
> This is what is happening in the world—economic division, religious division, political division and all the religious, sectarian divisions. . . . One must have asked this question of oneself very often: what is one to do? Where should one begin?

As he proceeds to inquire into this issue, Krishnamurti introduces an imaginary interlocutor, a "Mr. X," who, he says, had come to visit him and raised some of these questions. He presents Mr. X as an actual person, but the individual he describes is so reasonable, earnest, and open-minded, it seems unlikely that he actually existed; or perhaps he represented a composite of various people. In any case, Krishnamurti soon puts his listeners in the position of Mr. X. He begins in this manner:

> May I, may the speaker, inform you of a conversation he had with a Mr. X which continued for several days? Mr. X has travelled all over

the world, more or less, he told the speaker. He is fairly well read, has been to various institutions, sometimes joining them, and with a rush getting out of them. He followed one guru or another and gave them up. . . .

And he looked at the various political parties, at the whole spectrum of political activities, and at last he said, "I have come to talk with you. . . . Let's talk things over together like two friends, you and I—like two friends who have lived together in the world, been through every kind of travail. What is it all about? Why is man born like this? Why has he become after many, many, many millennia what he is now—suffering, anxious, lonely, despairing, with disease, death and always the gods somewhere about? Let's forget all about those gods and talk together as two human beings. . . .

Why does each human being everlastingly, from the moment he is born till he dies, live in this conflict?

The rest of this talk consists of Krishnamurti's reply to the questions Mr. X has raised:

Where does one start to understand the whole movement of conflict? How does one feel one's way into all this? One way, the speaker said to Mr. X, is to analyse very carefully all the factors of conflict, one after the other. . . . But will analysis bring about the discovery of the cause, though it may bring you certain intellectual conclusions? . . . Or is there a different approach to the question?

Krishnamurti casts doubt upon "this whole attitude toward analysis." He specifically rejects "what the professionals, including those people who come from Vienna, or the latest American psychologists, say about analysis."

I analyse myself. I have been angry, or greedy, or sexual, whatever it is, and in analyzing it, that is, breaking it up and looking at it very carefully, step by step, who is the observer? Is not the observer, the analyser, all the accumulated past remembrances? . . .

And then the observer breaks it up into the observer and the observed, so that very division in analysis creates conflict. Are we together? You are Mr. X, I am the speaker. Are we taking the same journey together? The speaker says that the moment there is a division between the analyser and the analysed there must inevitably be conflict of some kind.

The investigation into the nature and sources of conflict leads in the second talk into a consideration of order and disorder. If we wish to take any responsibility for the world, to create a new kind of society and culture, without endemic conflict and "such terrible disorder and cruelty," we must understand how to bring about order. For that purpose,

> Must there not be order first in our house—not only in the outer walls of the house and garden, but also in the inward world in which we all live, the subjective world, the psychological world? . . .
>
> Where the mind, the brain is in disorder, which is the essence of conflict, that brain can never be orderly, simple, clear. That can be taken for granted as a law, like the law of gravity, the law that the sun rises in the east and sets in the west: where there is subjective or inward conflict there must be disorder. Look into it, please, carefully. . . .
>
> We live in disorder, that is certain. Why bother about order? Let us see if we can clear up disorder. If you can clear it up then there is order.

Krishnamurti's exposition leads into a discussion of the nature and characteristics of thought. He acknowledges that thought is essential to carry out ordinary acts of daily living and that it has achieved extraordinary success in the scientific and technological world. But as an instrument for understanding ourselves and ending psychological disorder, thought is the source of our difficulties, rather than the solution:

> So, can we, each one of us, feeling the responsibility that we have created this society in which we live, which is monstrous, immoral beyond imagination—can each one of us, living in this world, in this society, be utterly free from disorder? . . .
>
> So can thought bring about order? Because thought itself, being limited, may be the source of disorder. I wonder if you capture this? You understand my question? Very interesting. Go into it. Anything that is limited must create disorder; if I am a Muslim, which is very limited, I must create disorder; if I am an Israeli, I must create disorder, or a Hindu, Buddhist, a Christian, and all the rest of it. So is thought the very root of disorder?

The examination of thought continues in the third talk with a discussion of the origin of fear, which brings in the element of time. Krishnamurti's concern is not with any particular fear, but with fear per se—"why human beings, which is all of us, have put up with fear for thousands of years?" Here, as elsewhere, his intention is to understand the problem, and let the understanding itself lead to a resolution.

> Is time a factor of fear? Please inquire. . . . I am afraid because of something I have done, which I don't like you to know. Which is what? Thought, isn't it? . . . So thinking and time are together. There is no division between thought and time.
>
> Thought is the very root of fear. Do we see that? Not how to end thought, but see actually that thinking is the root of fear, which is time? Seeing, not words, but actually seeing.

The fourth talk represents an elaboration upon the themes already developed in the context of self-interest, sorrow, and beauty. "Is there beauty where there is self-conscious endeavor? Or is there beauty only when the self is not—when the me, the observer, is not?" At the end of this talk, Krishnamurti opens the door to consider whether there is a state of mind beyond thought and time:

> We will deal with it next Sunday . . . what is religion, what is meditation, and if there is something that is beyond all words, measure and thought—something not put together by thought, something that is inexpressible, infinite, timeless. We will go into all that. But one cannot come to it if there is fear, or lack of right relationships, you follow? Unless your brain is free from all that you cannot understand the other.

Krishnamurti's fifth talk in Saanen in 1985 was his final one there, after twenty years. As such, it had a special poignancy. In this talk, he examines the nature of love and of death, which leads in turn to his concluding reflections regarding meditation. Since these are his final remarks in all the talks at Saanen, they merit quotation here in their entirety:

> What is meditation? The word means ponder over, according to the dictionary. To think over. It also has a different meaning in Sanskrit

and in Latin, which is to measure. And to measure means comparison, of course. There is no measurement without comparison.

So can the brain be free of measurement? Not measurement by the yard-stick, by kilometers, miles, but the measurement of becoming and not becoming, comparing, not comparing. You understand? Can the brain be free of this system of measurement? I need to measure to get a suit made. I need measurement to go from here to another place. Distance is measurement, time is measurement. Oh, come on.

Can the brain be free of measurement? That is, comparison—have no comparison whatsoever so that the brain is totally free. This is real meditation. Is that possible, living in the modern world, making money, breeding children, sex, all the noise, the vulgarity, the circus that is going on in the name of religion? Can one be free of all that? Not in order to get something. To be free.

So meditation is not conscious meditation. You understand this? It cannot be conscious meditation, following a system, a guru—collective meditation, group meditation, single meditation, according to Zen or some other system. It cannot be a system because then you practice, practice, practice, and your brain gets more and more dull, more and more mechanical. So is there a meditation which has no direction, which is not conscious, deliberate? Find out.

This requires great energy, attention, passion. Then that very passion, energy, the intensity of it, is silence. Not contrived silence. It is the immense silence in which time, space is not. Then there is that which is unnamable, which is holy, eternal.

This brief review of Krishnamurti's philosophy is intended to suffice only as an introduction, a preliminary orientation to the content and substance of his teachings. As such, it is necessarily somewhat superficial and cannot convey the depth, nuance, and richness of a complete series of talks, much less of the teachings as a whole. Moreover, Krishnamurti emphasized that a merely verbal or intellectual grasp of his message has only a limited value; what matters far more is for the listener to see for oneself the truth or actuality of the dynamics of consciousness to which he was pointing. For that purpose, there is no substitute for an exposure not only to the actual teachings, but to the choiceless awareness of one's own processes of thought, feeling, and action.

Chapter Six

THREE DIARIES

Krishnamurti's stated philosophy from the public platform is assiduously secular. He scrupulously avoids any suggestion that he has personal access to or special knowledge of another dimension, spiritual, supernatural, or otherwise. On the contrary, his public philosophy, expressed on countless occasions, on several continents, over the course of decades, is limited almost entirely to the delineation of the dynamic nature and structure of ordinary consciousness, as it is experienced by virtually everyone. His stated concern is to serve as a mirror to the mind of the individual listener, in order that each one might become "a light to oneself," and in so doing bring about psychological freedom, the elimination of conflict, and an end to sorrow. His references to God and religion are almost uniformly disparaging; he maintains that God is merely a concept, a comfortable invention, and organized religion a trap in which most of mankind is imprisoned. To be sure, he does suggest that an orderly mind, a mind that is attentive, might come upon something that is sacred, something that is not merely the product of thought. References to the sacred, however, are few and far between, and accompanied always by the admonition that no form of seeking or desire can possibly bring one into contact with it.

Against this philosophy, however, there exists another current in Krishnamurti's life and work that stands in contrast to his statements from the public platform. As he often pointed out, he himself was not what mattered to his audience; he was not their guru, he said over and over again; he was not speaking as the voice of authority—psychological, spiritual, or otherwise. In keeping with that attitude, he kept his inner life private and not a matter for public display; to do so was wholly consistent with his insistence on his own insignificance. Nevertheless, Krish-namurti did indeed enjoy an extraordinary inner life, one that he allowed to become a matter of record only as he approached his eightieth year. By that time, his stated philosophy had fully matured and taken on a life of its own, with little possibility of any distortion or distraction from the revelation of his personal experiences. This inner life was described in an authorized biography, as well as in three volumes of a kind of diary he kept for occasional periods beginning in 1961. Although these experi-ences did not represent the content of his message to the world, they are in some sense not entirely separable from it; and, in any case, no de-scription of his outlook on life is complete without including them.

Krishnamurti and his brother came to Ojai in 1922, when he was 27 and Nitya was 24. They had been invited there by A.P. Warrington, then head of the American section of the Theosophical Society, who travelled with them to a property owned by a local Theosophist, Mary Gray, where the brothers could stay for an indefinite period of time. Shortly after ar-riving there, Nitya described the Ojai Valley in the following terms:

> In a long and narrow valley of apricot orchards and orange groves is our house, and the hot sun shines down day after day to remind us of Adyar, but of an evening the cool air comes down from the range of hills on either side. Far beyond the lower end of the valley runs the long, perfect road from Seattle in Washington down to San Diego in Southern California, some two thousand miles, with a ceaseless flow of turbulent traffic, yet our valley lies happily, unknown and forgotten, for a road wanders in but knows no way out. The American Indians called our valley the Ojai or the nest, and for centuries they must have sought it as a refuge.

After they had settled in Ojai for a few weeks, Krishna began to med-itate for half an hour each morning and again in the evening. As he wrote in a letter to a friend,

> I could, to my astonishment, concentrate with considerable ease, and within a few days I began to see clearly where I had failed and where I was failing. Immediately I set about, consciously, to annihilate the wrong accumulations of the past years.

Two weeks after he commenced to meditate in this manner, Krishna began to complain of a pain in the nape of his neck, and Nitya observed there a knot or swelling about the size of a marble. This initial symptom developed in the next day or two into something systemic, involving intense pain in the head, neck, and spine, accompanied by episodes of shivering, alternating with a burning sensation. Krishna complained bitterly of the dirt of his surroundings, even though his room was immaculate. At times he was not his normal self, and he reverted to a distinctly childlike persona. He was able to sleep the night through, but the symptoms resumed the next morning and continued for three days.

Present to observe these events were Nitya, Mr. Warrington, and Rosalind Williams, a nineteen-year-old American woman whose mother was friends with Mary Gray. Rosalind had struck up a friendship with the two brothers and made herself useful in the care of Nitya. She was the only person whose presence Krishna could tolerate when his symptoms became intense. When the pain was acute, he would sometimes cling to her and cry out for his mother, who had died when he was ten.

On the evening of the third day, Krishna was moaning and writhing in pain in his cottage as twilight fell, while Nitya, Mr. Warrington, and Rosalind sat on the porch outside. Nitya recorded these events in a long and detailed narrative. He wrote that, "Our lives are profoundly affected by what happened . . . our compass has found its lodestar."

> He would have none of us near him and began to complain bitterly of the dirt, the dirt of the bed, the intolerable dirt of the house, the dirt of everyone around, and in a voice full of pain said that he longed to go to the woods. . . . Suddenly he announced his intention of going for a walk alone, but from this we managed to dissuade him, for we did not think that he was in any fit condition for nocturnal ambulations.

Warrington noted that he knew Krishna's bed was perfectly clean, for he had personally changed the linen that morning. Nitya continued:

> Then as he expressed a desire for solitude, we left him and gathered outside on the verandah, where in a few minutes he joined us, carrying

a cushion in his hand and sitting as far away as possible from us. Enough strength and consciousness were vouchsafed him to come outside but once there again he vanished from us, and his body, murmuring incoherencies, was left sitting there on the porch. . . .

The sun had set an hour ago and we sat facing the far-off hills, purple against the pale sky in the darkening twilight.

A young pepper tree stood at the entrance to the cottage, "with delicate leaves of a tender green, now heavy with scented blossoms." Warrington suggested to Krishna that he might like to go sit under the tree, and after a moment's hesitation, he did so. Presently, those on the veranda heard a sigh of relief, and Krishna called out to ask why they had not sent him there much earlier. Then he began to chant an ancient song, one familiar to the brothers from their childhood. A few moments later, according to Nitya, something occurred outside the parameters of ordinary reality. He claimed there was an unusual light in the sky, and he had an overwhelming sense of the arrival of some transcendent personality or intelligence. "The place seemed to be filled with a Great Presence," he wrote, and, "In the distance we heard divine music softly played."

After this evening, the strange process ended. A few days later, Krishna recorded his own impressions of what had transpired:

> There was a man mending the road; that man was myself; the pickaxe he held was myself; the very stone which he was breaking up was a part of me; the tender blade of grass was my very being, and the tree beside the man was myself. I almost could feel and think like the roadmender, and I could feel the wind passing through the tree. . . . I was in everything, or rather everything was in me, inanimate and animate, the mountain, the worm, and all breathing things.

Krishna invoked images of nature to convey what occurred under the pepper tree. His experience there is not easy to correlate with the days of pain and semi-consciousness that led up to it:

> There was such profound calmness both in the air and within myself, the calmness of the bottom of a deep unfathomable lake. Like the lake, I felt my physical body, with its mind and emotions, could be ruffled

on the surface but nothing, nay nothing, could disturb the calmness of my soul. . . .

I have drunk at the clear and pure waters at the source of the fountain of life and my thirst was appeased. Never more could I be thirsty, never more could I be in utter darkness. I have seen the Light. I have touched compassion which heals all sorrow and suffering; it is not for myself, but for the world.

As dramatic as these events may have been, they turned out to be merely a prelude to a much longer series of somewhat related experiences. The pain in Krishnamurti's head and neck began to resume in subsequent months, although now the episodes were confined to one or two hours in the evening. In his letters to Annie Besant, Nitya described these events as Krishna's "process," and that name has been employed for this purpose ever since. The process continued to recur at regular intervals, sometimes daily, throughout the remainder of his life. He never sought treatment for it, although he once consulted a Theosophical doctor who observed the process for a week and agreed it was not a condition requiring medical intervention.

The meaning and significance of the process and of the experience under the pepper tree remain somewhat obscure to the present day. What is not unclear is that Krishnamurti avoided any mention of these personal experiences in his public talks. He sent accounts of these events to a few close associates, but he insisted that they not be shared with others. He evidently regarded it as a private matter, unrelated to the truth or validity of his teachings, but a potential source of distraction or confusion for his audience. Only toward the end of his life did he allow these experiences to become known.

An even more insightful avenue into Krishnamurti's inner life is contained in a diary he composed over a period of seven months beginning in April 1961. *Krishnamurti's Notebook* was published in 1975, almost simultaneously with *Years of Awakening*, and, although it did not receive as much attention as the biography, it is in many respects a more extraordinary document. It consists of approximately two hundred entries, each one a page or two in length. These entries have several recurrent and interrelated themes. In order of the sheer number of words devoted to each theme, they are as follows: descriptions of scenes observed in nature; comments on the psychological characteristics of humanity; the quality of a mind in meditation; the intermittent presence of an unusual force or energy that envelops him with a sense of the sacred; and the ongoing, occasional pressure and pain in the head and neck, sometimes intense, that he still refers to as "the process."

Taken together, these themes represent a kind of panorama of the scope or landscape of Krishnamurti's daily consciousness. Considered not in terms of the number of words devoted to each, but rather in terms of their apparent significance to him, their order of importance might be construed as follows: the presence of the sense of something sacred; the beauty of nature; the mind of man, coupled with the transformative quality of meditation; and the process. After about the first thirty entries, he discontinues any further mention of the process, as if its description requires no further elaboration, although presumably it continued on almost a daily basis. In some respects, it appears as though the entire diary exists mainly for the purpose of bringing to light the sacred quality; the other themes are important in their own right, but somewhat similar material is described elsewhere in Krishnamurti's work. Here the other themes seem to serve as a kind of context for the introduction of the sacred element.

Among the salient characteristics of the sacred quality is its essential unknowability. Krishnamurti uses a variety of terms to refer to it, none of them entirely equal to the task. He most commonly refers to it simply as "the other," or "that otherness." Additional appellations he employs include "the benediction" and "the immensity." He ascribes to this quality a sense of overwhelming power, something impenetrable, vast, innocent, and untouchable. The manner in which the sacred element is woven into the diary can perhaps be gleaned somewhat from two of the briefer excerpts.

On September 27, 1961, Krishnamurti was in Rome, and he wrote as follows:

> Walking along the pavement overlooking the biggest basilica and down the famous steps to a fountain and many picked flowers of so many colors, crossing the crowded square, we went along a narrow

one-way street, quiet, with not too many cars; there in that dimly lit street, with few unfashionable shops, suddenly and most unexpectedly, that otherness came with such intense tenderness and beauty that one's body and brain became motionless.

For some days now, it had not made its immense presence felt; it was there vaguely, in the distance, a whisper, but there the immense was manifesting itself, sharply and with waiting patience. Thought and speech were gone and there was a peculiar joy and clarity. It followed down the long, narrow street till the roar of traffic and the overcrowded pavement swallowed us all. It was a benediction that was beyond all image and thoughts.

The following month, Krishnamurti was in Bombay. On October 24, he wrote:

The dark leaves were shining and the moon had climbed quite high; she was on the westerly course and flooding the room. Dawn was many hours away and there was not a sound; even the village dogs, with their shrill yapping, were quiet. Waking, it was there, with clarity and precision; the otherness was there and waking up was necessary, not sleep; it was deliberate, to be aware of what was happening, to be aware with full consciousness of what was taking place. Asleep, it might have been a dream, a hint of the unconscious, a trick of the brain, but fully awake, this strange and unknowable otherness was a palpable reality, a fact and not an illusion, a dream. It had a quality, if such a word can be applied to it, of weightlessness and impenetrable strength.

Again these words have certain significance, definite and communicable, but these words lose all their meaning when the otherness has to be conveyed in words; words are symbols but no symbol can ever convey the reality. It was there with such incorruptible strength that nothing could destroy it for it was unapproachable. You can approach something with which you are familiar; you must have the same language to commune, some kind of thought process, verbal or nonverbal; above all there must be mutual recognition. There was none. On your side you may say it is this or that, this or that quality, but at the moment of the happening there was no verbalization for the brain was utterly still, without any movement of thought.

Even for someone schooled in the intricacies of Krishnamurti's philosophy, it is hard to know what to make of the "otherness." He hardly
seems to know what to make of it himself. However, he is adamant that
what he is witness to is not a matter of imagination or invention; the
other is far beyond any possible creation of thought or ideation. It is not
something that can be brought about by any act of intention, desire, or
will; it comes and goes of its own accord; indeed, an attitude of indif-
ference to whether or not it occurs is essential for it to take place. And
yet it represents a kind of healing, transformative energy, without which
life seems somewhat barren and meaningless.

Krishnamurti's Notebook is confined to a period of seven months, and
he offers no explanation for why he started it or stopped. In a brief
foreword, Mary Lutyens claims he does not know himself what moved
him to compose it. It is the only record we have, however, of his experience of the otherness. In subsequent years, he composed two additional
diaries of a somewhat similar nature, but without any references to the
sacred quality or energy. It seems reasonable to assume that the otherness
continued to come and go, but there is no way to know for certain, or
even whether it matters.

Krishnamurti's Journal is a shorter work than the *Notebook*, com-
mencing for some six weeks in 1973 and resuming for the month of April
1975. Like the *Notebook*, the *Journal* is occupied largely with vivid descriptions of scenes from nature, coupled with observations about ordinary
consciousness and about meditation. No reference is made to his process,
or to the otherness or benediction. The psychological observations closely
parallel his statements from the public platform, although in a somewhat
condensed and, if possible, a more immediate form. In reading the *Journal*,
one has the impression that he is being a little more direct than in his
public talks, stating facts bluntly, without any compromise. The descriptions of nature and of a mind in meditation serve to soften and offer some
relief from the realities of ordinary consciousness.

Krishnamurti to Himself was the last of the three diaries. It consists
of just 27 entries, composed in 1983 and 1984. These entries are a little
longer, on average about four pages each, perhaps in part because they
were dictated into a recorder rather than written out in longhand. In

this final journal, he introduces an imaginary interlocutor, a visitor who comes to inquire about certain points raised in the teachings. Krishnamurti finds this format conducive to elucidating various issues, and it resembles the pattern of individuals who came to seek his counsel throughout his life.

The three diaries taken together represent a remarkably comprehensive exposition of the inner quality of Krishnamurti's daily life and consciousness. The journals span a period of two and a half decades and reflect a consistency of style, theme, and content. The depictions of nature are stunning in their fine detail, suggestive nuance, and variety. The observations about consciousness and about meditation are at one with the teachings as they were articulated to the public. Only the references, confined to the *Notebook*, to the process and to the otherness, suggest a kind of experience and a depth of awareness not evident elsewhere in his work. In his dialogues with David Bohm, Krishnamurti broached some issues that bear a relationship to these experiences. These issues are the subject of more detailed discussion in subsequent chapters of this volume.

Chapter Seven

THE MIRROR OF RELATIONSHIP

Among the central themes animating Krishnamurti's work is the nature and quality of human relationship. His exposition encompasses the sources of conflict in relationship as well as love, violence, jealousy, envy, and attachment. The question therefore arises whether, or in what manner, his observations and insights regarding relationship were made manifest in his own life, personality, and interactions with others. Relationship, of course, is a two-way street, and no one, no matter how sensitive, considerate, and insightful they may be, can be immune to disharmonious interactions. Nevertheless, the quality of Krishnamurti's personal relationships warrants examination, not only for what it may suggest about his teachings, but also on its own merits. Was conflict endemic in his personal life, or absent altogether, or something in between? When conflict arose, how did he deal with it? Were his actions consistent with his philosophy?

Among the wealthy Theosophical families that looked after the future World Teacher and his brother during their early years in England was that of Edwin and Emily Lutyens. He was a distinguished architect who was responsible for much of the skyline of New Delhi. She was a friend of Annie Besant and an ardent Theosophist, and she and her daughters formed a close bond with the young Krishna. Emily composed an affectionate memoir of her relationship with Krishnamurti entitled *Candles in the Sun*. Her daughter, Mary, subsequently wrote her own memoir of those early days, *To Be Young*.

As he approached his eightieth year, Krishnamurti evidently felt it would be worthwhile for someone to compose a complete and authentic record of his life, perhaps in order to correct any misimpressions about

him that might arise after he was gone. He asked Mary Lutyens if she
would assume this responsibility, and she agreed. She had previously
published some seventeen novels, as well as biographies of her father and
of the art critic John Ruskin.

Lutyens wrote the story of Krishnamurti's life in three volumes, as
well as a fourth, supplementary volume that served as a summary of
the previous three. Her work is largely devoid of any rich or vivid descriptions or anecdotes that would give readers a sense of the character
and quality of Krishnamurti's relationships and manner of interaction.
It serves rather more as a record of the development of his philosophy,
his extensive travels, and of individuals prominent in the adminis-
tration of his work.

A warmer and more vital portrait of the man and his life was composed by Pupul Jayakar and published shortly after his death. Jayakar was
the woman primarily responsible for the management of Krishnamurti's
work in India after World War II. Her own work centered upon a revival
of traditional Indian arts and handicrafts, and in that capacity, she served
in the administrations of Jawaharlal Nehru, Indira Gandhi, and Rajiv
Gandhi. She "presided colossus-like over the country's cultural scene for
nearly 40 years," according to a quotation in Wikipedia, and she was the
author of a dozen books, including *The Earth Mother: Legends, God-
desses, and Ritual Arts of India* (Penguin Books, 1989). She is best known,
however, for her biographies of Indira Gandhi, with whom she was very
close, and of Krishnamurti, published by Harper and Row in 1986. *Krishnamurti: A Biography* is 500 pages of masterful prose. The comprehensive
portrait Jayakar paints is of a man whose life and work are seamless,
without contradiction, and overflowing with insight and originality.

A few excerpts from her work may provide some sense of the immediacy of Krishnamurti's personality and presence. In 1957, her husband
suffered a severe heart attack. Her relationship with him had been ". . .
intensely difficult for some time; he could not tolerate a wife who lived a
life and had interests independent of his own. He struck out where he
knew it would wound, but in the process the conflict shattered him and
his body broke down." When Jayakar next saw Krishnamurti, she spoke
to him of her sorrow and pain.

His compassion contained me. He made me face the fact that no relationship existed between me and the man I had married. I was not prepared to see this. The pain came in waves, drowning me, making clear sight impossible. He put the two palms of his hands swallow-like round my face. He made me look into his eyes and see my sorrow reflected in them. He was the father, the mother, the friend, and the teacher, providing to my anguished spirit toughness and tenderness; but he would not let me look away. Like a pillar of fire, his seeing annihilated the memories, the loneliness, the lack of affection that were the root of pain. I was brought face to face with the emptiness of sorrow. A perception was generated that burnt away the scars of what had been.

On a lighter note, Jayakar mentions that Buckminster Fuller was acquainted with Krishnamurti, and she describes an evening in 1963 when he came for dinner:

"Bucky," as his friends called him, was a designer who had revolutionized structures and designed for a future culture and way of life; he was at once a philosopher, a scientist with vision, creative vitality, and a holistic view of people and their needs. I knew Bucky well, and he telephoned me when he heard Krishnaji was in Delhi to suggest a meeting with "that marvelous, beautiful, wise person." I arranged a dinner at which both men were present. Bucky entered the room bouncing a yo-yo. Krishnaji was shy and a little withdrawn, his response in those days when he met a formidable intellect. Bucky started to talk. He talked before dinner, he talked at dinner, he talked after dinner. Krishnaji listened, hardly saying a word. Still Bucky talked. After Krishnaji left to return to Kitty Shiva Rao's house, where he was staying, Bucky turned to me and thanked me for the meeting and commented, "What a marvelous, wonderful, wise person Krishnaji is."

In 1975, the High Court in India overturned the re-election of Indira Gandhi, and she responded by declaring a state of emergency, suspending civil liberties and arresting some of her political opponents. The situation was extremely tense and volatile. Krishnamurti cancelled his annual visit to India that year for fear that his views on freedom would not be well received, and he might risk imprisonment. Jayakar spoke with Gandhi

about the possibility of Krishnamurti returning to India and was assured
that he would be most welcome there. In October 1976, he did return,
and Jayakar invited Gandhi to her home for dinner with him and several
guests. Gandhi arrived at 7:30 and mentioned that it was her birthday
"according to the Indian calendar."

> She expressed a desire to speak with Krishnaji, and was with him in
> his sitting room until nine. . . . After dinner, when everyone had left,
> Krishnaji took me to his room and told me that Indira was going
> through a very difficult period. For a long time after they met, they had
> sat silently. He could feel that she was very disturbed. She told him that
> the situation in India was explosive. Krishnaji had sensed something
> very fine within her, which politics was destroying. He also hinted at
> a current of violence that surrounded her.

Gandhi asked to meet with Krishnamurti again the following morning.
She "spent over an hour with Krishnaji. She came out of the room visibly
moved, and tears were streaming down her face." A few years later,
Gandhi described to Jayakar some of their conversation:

> Krishnaji and she had spoken of the events in India over the last few
> months, and Indira had said, "I am riding the back of a tiger, but I do
> not know how to get off its back." Krishnaji replied, "If you are more
> intelligent than the tiger, you will know how to deal with the tiger." She
> had asked him what she should do. He refused to tell her, but said that
> she should look at the conflicts, the actions, the wrongs as one problem,
> and then act without motive. He said he did not know the facts, but
> that she should act rightly, without fear of consequence.

Another vivid portrait, but one with a decidedly negative cast, was
composed by Radha Rajagopal Sloss, the daughter of Krishnamurti's
longtime associate, D. Rajagopal. Radha's mother was Rosalind, who had
befriended Krishnamurti and Nitya when they first came to Ojai in 1922.
After the birth of Radha in 1931, Rosalind and Rajagopal no longer lived
together, and their marriage was little more than a social fiction. In these
circumstances, Rosalind and Krishnamurti developed an intimate relationship that lasted for some fifteen years.

This relationship had remained a private matter until it was revealed by Radha in her book, *Lives in the Shadow*, a title that played on Emily Lutyens' title, *Candles in the Sun*. Radha writes with a pen dipped in vindictiveness. Her mother evidently developed a jealous antagonism toward Krishnamurti, and Radha's attitude is infected with a similar animus. Krishnamurti had to go to court against Rajagopal to recover large quantities of property and funds donated in support of his work, and the humiliation Rajagopal must have suffered as a result may also have colored Radha's attitude.

Mary Lutyens responded to *Lives in the Shadow* with a short book devoted to refuting its many errors and false implications. *Krishnamurti and the Rajagopals: A Personal Reply* recounts in meticulous detail the actual facts, including Krishnamurti's view of the affair, never previously published. During the course of the lawsuits, Krishnamurti had dictated a lengthy letter to Rajagopal recounting the history of their relationship. On the advice of his lawyers, the letter was never sent, but it was preserved by Mary Zimbalist, and Mary Lutyens includes it as an opportunity for Krishnamurti to reply to *Lives in the Shadow*. In this letter, Krishnamurti claims that Rajagopal encouraged and maneuvered him into conducting the affair with Rosalind in order to maintain a "hold" over him. He accuses Rajagopal of blackmail and of embezzlement to the extent of millions of dollars for his personal gain. He states that Rajagopal had abandoned every shred of decency.

No other account of Krishnamurti remotely approaches the negative judgment expressed by Radha Sloss, and numerous sympathetic testimonials and memoirs have been composed by others. In September, 1910, when he was fifteen years old, Krishna and Nitya accompanied Annie Besant on a trip to Benares, in northern India, where she had founded the Central Hindu College. On the faculty at that time was E. A. Wodehouse, professor of English and brother of the popular novelist P. G. Wodehouse. He subsequently served as one of Krishna's tutors for five years, and he recorded his impressions of him:

> What struck us particularly was his naturalness. . . . Of his "occult" position he seemed to be entirely unconscious. He never alluded to it—never, for a single moment, allowed the slightest hint of it to get into his speech or manner. . . . Another quality was a serene unself-

ishness. He seemed to be not the least preoccupied with himself. . . .
We were no blind devotees, prepared to see in him nothing but per-
fection. We were older people, educationalists, and with some experience of youth. Had there been a trace in him of conceit or affectation,
or any posing as the "holy child," or of priggish self-consciousness, we
would undoubtedly have given an adverse verdict.

In the early 1930's, Krishnamurti escaped the heat of the Ojai summers
with occasional trips to Carmel, along the California coast, where he
became friendly with the distinguished poet Robinson Jeffers. In 1934,
he also spent several days there in the company of Rom Landau, who
had travelled from England for that purpose. Landau was the author of
thirty books in several genres. He was an authority on the people and
culture of Morocco and served as professor of Islamic and North African
Studies at the University of the Pacific. In 1935 he published
God is My Adventure, a record of his interviews with Rudolf Steiner, P.D.
Ouspensky, Gurdjieff, and Krishnamurti.

When Landau visited Carmel, Krishnamurti picked him up from the
train station and drove him to his hotel. They began their conversations
that afternoon and continued for a week, as they walked among the pine
forests on the bluffs overlooking the Pacific. The two men discussed
everything from the nature of love and truth to the books Krishnamurti
had read. He said that he read "everything that seems interesting—
Huxley, Lawrence, Joyce, Andre Gide"—but never works of philosophy.

Toward the end of his stay in Carmel, Landau visited Robinson Jeffers
in the cobblestone house the poet had built with his own hands overlooking the sea.

Jeffers was reserved and shy. "For me," he said in a slow and hesitant
manner, "there is nothing wrong in Krishnamurti's message—nothing
that I must contradict."

"Do you think his message will ever become popular?"

"Not at present. Most people won't find it intelligible enough."

"What struck you most when you met him for the first time?"

"His personality. Mrs. Jeffers often makes the remark that light seems to enter the room when Krishnamurti comes in, and I agree with her, for he himself is the most convincing illustration of his honest message."

In their final meeting together, Landau asked Krishnamurti how he had arrived at his understanding of life. He quotes him in these terms: "My inner awareness was always there, though it took me time to feel it more and more clearly; and equally it took time to find words that would at all describe it. It was not a sudden flash, but a slow yet constant clarification of something that was always there." At the end of their week together, Landau's impression was that ". . . here was a man who lived his teaching even more convincingly than he preached it."

Sidney Field, a writer for Disney Studios, met Krishnamurti when he was nineteen and Krishnamurti was twenty-nine, and they remained friends for some sixty years. Field's parents were prominent in the Theosophical Society in Costa Rica, but his relationship with Krishnamurti, described in his memoir *The Reluctant Messiah*, was personal and direct. They could talk as easily about cars or the women Field was dating as about the possibility of life after death. (An appendix to his book recounts a long conversation on this subject conducted after the death of Field's brother.) Field quotes Krishnamurti as saying his life would have unfolded on similar terms even without the intervention of Annie Besant, although it would have been more difficult and taken longer. Field also offers an illuminating, independent perspective on the conflict with Rajagopal. As a witness to Krishnamurti's personality and character over the course of many years, Field's voice conveys a sense of authenticity, colored with anecdotes about the impact of Krishnamurti's philosophy on his own inner life.

The Kitchen Chronicles, by Michael Krohnen, is an affectionate memoir composed by Krishnamurti's chef in Ojai for the last ten years of his life. My friend Michael's position required the confluence of multiple skills, including the preparation of delicious and nutritious vegetarian fare on a reasonable budget for lunch guests numbering from half a dozen to twenty or more, on a daily basis, throughout the period of Krishnamurti's annual visit to Ojai. Michael usually sat near Krishnamurti at lunch and was often called upon to deliver the news of the day, gleaned from the Christian Science Monitor and the BBC. His memoir is replete with observations of Krishnamurti and the many guests who shared the lunch table. His book represents a light-hearted counterpoint to my account of Krishnamurti's involvement in the Oak Grove School during the same period of time.

Among the finest memoirs of Krishnamurti is *The Beauty of the Mountain*, composed by Friedrich Grohe, a wealthy, retired industrialist. Grohe's innocent nature, his warmth and generosity of spirit, and his passion for long, daily walks in natural settings, evidently endeared him to Krishnamurti, and the two men became rather close. On one occasion, he told Grohe, "We are brothers." His book, beautifully adorned with his sensitive nature photographs, is among the best for describing the unique quality of Krishnamurti's personality.

Additional memoirs continue to be produced, including ones by Mary Zimbalist, Mark Lee, and Professor P. Krishna. Lee and Krishna were close associates of Krishnamurti who worked with him in connection with his schools in India and the United States. Zimbalist was Krishnamurti's secretary and companion during the last two decades of his life. Each of these authors was captivated by and enamored of Krishnamurti and regarded him with the highest respect.

The consensus, then, regarding the nature of Krishnamurti's personal relationships is favorable, notwithstanding one voice of dissent. What remains to be seen are the course and quality of his relationship with David Bohm. The two men were collaborators in the process of psychological inquiry and dialogue, but their compatibility in that endeavor could not have materialized were it not for their mutual respect and affection on a more personal level. To what extent was that personal friendship sustained on an even footing throughout the more than twenty years of their relationship? In addition to the content of their exploration into psychological issues, it will be relevant to the present inquiry to consider as well the quality of their more personal interactions.

Chapter Eight

OJAI

I first heard Krishnamurti give a public talk in 1972, at the Civic Auditorium in Santa Monica, California, a few miles from where I lived at the time. The auditorium held nearly two thousand people, and the talk was well attended. No admission fee was required, although a donation was requested. A single, simple, straight-backed chair was placed onstage while the members of the audience filtered in and took their seats.

I had been studying Krishnamurti's published talks for several months and felt I had acquired a reasonably good introduction to his philosophy, but I had no idea what to expect upon observing him in person. The talk was scheduled to begin at 10:00 a.m., and he walked onstage punctually and took his seat. No one had introduced him. When he appeared there was a smattering of applause, but he discouraged it with a gesture of his hand. He was meticulously dressed in a suit and tie. He waited quietly, observing the audience, while everyone took their seats and settled down. Then he began to speak, without notes, without teleprompter, and evidently without anything memorized. He continued for about ninety minutes.

There was an unusual quality of seriousness and authenticity in the manner in which he spoke. There was nothing remotely entertaining about it, and yet it was rather fascinating. He addressed fundamental issues of daily life, and he did so in a way that was at times crystal clear and at other times elusive. At some levels his presentation was lucid and insightful, but as he progressed to deeper levels, it became more difficult to follow. This left a listener with a yearning to understand more.

At one point, Krishnamurti was examining some issues of human relationship, and he touched briefly upon the role played by sexual desire. At this point a heckler in the balcony behind me called out so all could hear: "Are you getting any?" Krishnamurti did not seem disturbed or fazed by this interruption. He paused for a moment to let the rudeness of the heckler's remark sink in; then he looked toward him and replied quietly, "If you are really interested, come see me afterwards." Then he proceeded with his talk and was not interrupted again.

Seeing him in person intensified my desire to penetrate the meaning of what Krishnamurti was expressing. He gave talks on consecutive weekend mornings, and he took a few questions from the audience after each one. After the first two talks, I prepared a question that seemed to me to expose a paradox in the logic of his presentation. During the question and answer period at the end of the third talk, I stood up in the cavernous auditorium and put my question to him. Some forty years later, I had long since forgotten the substance of my question and his answer; but, by sheer coincidence, while I was in the process of preparing this manuscript, the Krishnamurti Foundation selected for its online newsletter the video recording of that very question and answer and publicized it prominently. Although the camera at the event was trained on Krishnamurti, the audio was able to pick up my voice, and a friend who subscribes to the newsletter recognized it and brought the video to my attention.

My question brought a smile to Krishnamurti's face and evoked a slight ripple of laughter in the audience, but his reply was serious and thoughtful:

> **David Moody:** It seems to me that, to be free, one must be able to see what actually is. And yet, to see what actually is, it seems that one must be free. Is that not a paradox?

> **Krishnamurti:** It's not a contradiction. First, to investigate anything, especially into oneself, there must not only be great sensitivity, but freedom. Freedom from your prejudices, about yourself. How beautiful you are, or how good you are, or how ugly you are. Freedom, to look. That's all. So— listen to this—so, the first step is the last step! You understand? The first step: which is to look at myself without *any* prejudice, without any conditioning, just to see actually what is. That is the first step, and the last step!

There is no contradiction. To see clearly into myself and the world, there must be no 'me' who says, "I am right, you are wrong. My opinion is this, I am this"—you know.

Which doesn't mean you become vague, indifferent, or casual. But to see, there must be absolute clarity. And you cannot have clarity if there is no freedom.

So, when you look at yourself, you will see that you are looking at yourself with a formula, with an image. So, what is important is, not what you will see, but to be free of your image. Free of your *image*. Why you have images!

Which is, you have images because you protect yourself, you resist. You think you are better than what you are, or inferior than what you are.

So, all these images are a form of resistance and a form of defense, which prevent the actual looking. So, your first concern is not what you find, but whether you can look without prejudice. And therefore, that is the first step, and therefore it is the last step.

At the time of this event, I was enrolled as a graduate student in the Department of Political Science at UCLA. I had tried for years to find an avenue for penetrating the depths of psychology and human nature. My interest was spurred in part by the emotional disturbance that my mother suffered, beginning when I was about ten. Her troubles not only gave impetus to my interest in the psychological field, but also imbued me with skepticism regarding socially sanctioned authority figures, inasmuch as the medical profession did nothing but exacerbate her disturbance.

My high school years were successful in many respects, academically, athletically, and socially. But my years as an undergraduate at UC Berkeley were not so rewarding. I tried in vain to find a field where I could explore the depths of human nature. I majored in psychology for two years, but the psychology department at Berkeley at that time was under the sway of behaviorism, which—remarkably, for a field of psychology—considered studies of the human mind unnecessary and irrelevant. All that mattered, in this view, were the observable stimulus and response that governed the behavior of any organism—rat, pigeon, or human.

In my junior year, I took a course required for psychology majors in the field of neurophysiology. At first I found this rather interesting, a welcome relief from the sterile philosophy of behaviorism, until I ran across a series of experiments conducted by R. W. Sperry, a psychologist celebrated for his "split-brained" studies with cats. The brain of every mammal is divided into two hemispheres or lobes, and they communicate with one another by means of a thick band of neural tissue called the corpus callosum. Sperry had the idea to surgically sever the corpus callosum in some experimental cats and to observe the consequences. This research was considered at the time to represent the pinnacle of scientific respectability in the field of psychology. Sperry won a Nobel prize for this work, but it represented the last straw for me. I have a fondness for cats, and the idea that this kind of research could give any insight into actual daily problems of life seemed to me beyond the pale of reason.

By 1971, I was halfway through the doctoral program in political philosophy at UCLA. The theories of Hobbes, Rousseau, Marx, Freud, and others represented the nearest I could find to any penetrating examination of the fundamental contours of human nature and consciousness. In addition, I had been reading beyond the confines of political philosophy, including Wittgenstein, Ouspensky, and Alan Watts, and had been developing ideas of my own, with particular attention to the way the thinking process can distort our actions and perception. At the same time, my interest in Krishnamurti's philosophy had been kindled, for I felt I had finally found someone who addressed all the important issues of life and relationship in a direct and comprehensive manner. I did not know where this interest would lead, but I knew I had to pursue it in one way or another.

My home in West Los Angeles was a ninety-minute drive from Ojai, where Krishnamurti gave a series of public talks every year. I attended most of these in 1972, 1973, and 1974. In the summer of 1972, I participated in a group tour to Saanen, Switzerland, where he gave a more extended series of talks every year. In the spring of 1975, an announcement was made in Ojai that Krishnamurti intended to establish an elementary school there the following fall. This news electrified me. I had no experience in the classroom, but I had been teaching math and reading for a tutorial service for two years, and I held out hope that this background, along with my interest in Krishnamurti's work, might suffice to earn me a teaching position there. As it happens, my hopes were rewarded, and I was the first academic teacher hired at the Oak Grove School.

Krishnamurti had been establishing schools for several decades. There were two schools in India that had been thriving since the 1930's, and three additional schools had been started there since that time. In 1969, he founded the secondary-level boarding school Brockwood Park in Hampshire, England, with which David Bohm was closely associated. Oak Grove was among the last of his endeavors of this kind, and it was to be his only school in the United States. The general intention of all these schools was not only to provide a sound academic program, but to educate students at a broader and deeper level. There was no ideology designed to be absorbed, nor any expectation that students would adhere to a preconceived blueprint for dealing with issues of life and relationship. Nevertheless, it was considered crucial to awaken students to the nature of the challenges that would face them as adults and to prepare them to deal with these challenges intelligently and with an open mind. This entails objective observation of oneself and of the conditioning process that society imposes upon all of its members.

My involvement with Oak Grove initiated my more direct and personal observations of Krishnamurti. He wanted to meet me soon after I was hired, and in the first year of the school he conducted fifteen meetings with faculty, staff, and parents, describing the essential purposes of the school and inviting comments and dialogue in an open-ended manner on any and all relevant issues. In these interactions, his commitment to the purposes of the school was evident; he was congenial and courteous, but very serious about the nature and the significance of what we were undertaking together. Nothing I observed disturbed my sense of an individual imbued with extraordinary insight and authenticity.

In this context I first met David Bohm. It was spring of 1976, the first year of the school, and by this time I had had numerous opportunities to witness the manner of Krishnamurti's interaction with participants in the school. In general, he was warm, friendly, and relaxed, and he exuded a sense of good will. But on the more serious occasions of discussions of education, he had a tendency to be somewhat austere. He was careful in his language, and he expected the same from those with whom he was speaking. The questions he raised were focused and direct, and if the answers offered were wide of the mark, as they often were, he responded forthrightly but could not suppress, at times, a critical attitude.

On the day that Bohm was arriving in Ojai after travelling from his home in England, a half dozen members of the faculty and staff were meeting in the living room of Pine Cottage, Krishnamurti's living quarters, situated behind the pepper tree described in a previous chapter. As soon as Bohm arrived, I could sense a difference in the manner with which Krishnamurti treated him. Gone was any sense of severity; the two men were on an equal footing and their mutual respect was manifest. This was fascinating in its own right, quite apart from the substance of their conversation. I had at that time little understanding of Bohm's background, but I realized, as I watched Krishnamurti interact with him, that I had formed an assumption that Krishnamurti would treat everyone in the same manner. Clearly, that assumption was no longer tenable.

My initial impressions of Bohm were not entirely favorable. I could sense at once the quality of his intellect as well as his dedication to exploring the meaning of Krishnamurti's work. On the other hand, I felt there was something slightly unworldly about him. However trivial it may seem, I recall the image of his socks falling loosely around his shoes, revealing ankles so white they seemed never to have seen the light of day. After his more serious conversation with Krishnamurti concluded, they began talking about the school and its prospects. Bohm asked, "Do you think you can find good teachers in southern California?" Krishnamurti answered in the affirmative, but I felt the question was a little insensitive, in view of the fact that I was sitting right there. (In his defense, he probably had no idea who I was or where I was from.) It would be a few years before I fully appreciated Bohm's subtle and sensitive awareness of people, as well as the generous quality of his interactions. He would always be somewhat shy, but that never stopped him from engaging with anyone who wanted to inquire with him about serious issues.

Over the course of the next fifteen years, my involvement with Krishnamurti, the Oak Grove School, and with Bohm was sustained and intense. Every dimension of personality and commitment was required to navigate the currents of the school, especially after I assumed the role of director. These challenges, however, enabled me to witness both men in many contexts and situations, and to assess the quality of their character in multiple circumstances. These experiences are described in my book, *The Unconditioned Mind: J. Krishnamurti and the Oak Grove School* (Quest, 2011), and they inform the background for the present narrative.

What most distinguished Bohm, I felt, was the manner in which he was able to elucidate some of the more obscure points in Krishnamurti's philosophy. One could follow Krishnamurti regarding the danger of a nationalistic or tribal sense of identity and the falseness of organized religion. Also fairly accessible were his observations about the nature of conditioning and the imperative to understand and free oneself from it. Krishnamurti became more obscure, I felt, at the crucial point of explaining his key insight that "the thinker is the thought; the observer is the observed." Bohm's exposition of these issues in subsequent years made it somewhat clearer, in my view, than Krishnamurti ever succeeded in doing.

Another issue that Krishnamurti emphasized throughout his career was the nature of intelligence. He considered it vital for each human being to understand intelligence and allow it to function, but he invested that concept with a different meaning than we ordinarily associate with it. This was another element of Krishnamurti's philosophy that I found more accessible; and, as it happens, it was the subject of the first of the published dialogues between Krishnamurti and Bohm. For these reasons, it is the subject of the chapter that follows.

Chapter Nine

THE NATURE OF INTELLIGENCE

The idea that intelligence is a quantity that can be measured, like pounds of potatoes or the distance from here to Mars, is relatively recent in origin. It does not appear in the works of Aristotle, nor among the medieval scholars, nor among those who ushered in the Renaissance. It is not an idea that occurred to Newton, or to Kant, or to John Stuart Mill, or to anyone else until the idea was first proposed by Frances Galton in the 1860's and was endorsed by Darwin, among others. The concept was refined by Alfred Binet and achieved an apex of practical significance during World War I, when a team of American psychologists devised a series of tests to sort recruits into various categories for wartime purposes. The result was a measure of intelligence designated as a "quotient"—that is, the result of a process of division. It attempted to measure the "mental age" of each individual, and proceeded to divide that figure by the person's actual, chronological age, to produce the Intelligence Quotient, or IQ.

The concept of a measureable IQ was plagued by uncertainty and controversy from its inception. The foremost difficulty revolved around the means employed to measure an individual's mental age. Psychologists devised a collection of sub-tests for this purpose, but each one raised questions regarding whether, or to what extent, an individual's score represented actual native ability, or rather simply his or her degree of educational achievement.

Implicit in the concept of the IQ was the notion that intelligence is a unitary capacity, more or less determined at birth. If the means of measuring intelligence were significantly influenced by educational or cultural experiences, could they be considered reliable reflections of actual native ability? The idea that intelligence is unitary, determined at birth and more or less immutable thereafter, was enshrined in the concept of "g," psychological jargon for a pervasive, all-purpose intellectual ability unique to each individual. Once the concept of IQ had gained currency, the search for new and improved ways to measure "g" became the principal focus of investigations into the nature of intelligence.

Somewhat curiously, this objective was advanced by the onset of World War II, just as the previous developments had been spurred by the previous world war. At that time, psychologists developed an entirely new form of measuring mental ability. Rather than relying on an individual's vocabulary, mathematical skills, reading comprehension, or general knowledge—all of which are heavily influenced by culture and education—a test was devised that relied strictly upon evidence available to the naked eye at the time of testing. The Raven's test of intelligence is based upon a series of visual displays. Each display in the sequence shows a certain configuration of visual pattern, including lines, crosses, circles, ellipses, semi-circles, triangles, and so on. The person taking the test is asked to determine the logic of the progression from one display to the next. The correct choice is one of four alternatives given.

This test was designed to eliminate all cultural or educational influences from the measurement of "g." Although the skill tested might seem rather narrow, the test correlated well with other measures, and so was considered a reliable, efficient, and culture-free indicator of innate mental ability. More than half a century later, the Raven's test and the concept of "g" are still alive and well. There have been some new developments in the academic study of intelligence, but the concept of IQ retains pride of place, not only in the cultural imagination, but also in scientific studies. Even so, I was surprised to see an article in the *New York Times* in 2009 that claimed that an individual's intelligence quotient can be increased by practicing certain exercises designed to train short-term memory.

The *Times* article was predicated upon a study that had been published in the prestigious journal of the National Academy of Sciences. With such an imprimatur, it had to be taken seriously. Even so, I was skeptical. How could such a fluid and insightful capability as intelligence be influenced by something so mundane as exercises designed to train the mechanical process of short-term memory? I read the original article in the journal *Science*, as well as the referenced articles on which it was based. I discovered that the authors had relied upon a highly truncated version of the Raven's test, but had buried that fact in a footnote at the end of their article. On this basis, as well as several others, I wrote a critique that was published in the professional journal *Intelligence* and has since been cited many times by others interested in this issue.

The claim that exercises designed to promote short-term memory could actually improve intelligence failed to take into account, among other things, the work of educational psychologist Howard Gardner. Gardner developed the idea that intelligence is not a unitary capability but rather has a variety of manifestations. His theory of multiple intelligences effectively nullified the concept of "g," but the notion of a unitary IQ has become so deeply ingrained that it still persists in spite of all evidence to the contrary. Gardner showed that there exist not only cognitive intelligence, measureable by reading comprehension, for example, but also musical, mathematical, visual, emotional, social, and other forms of intellectual ability. Intelligence is not a unitary factor, measureable by any single form of test, no matter how cleverly devised or culturally-free it may be.

Against this background, it is interesting to consider the observations of Krishnamurti and David Bohm regarding the nature of intelligence. Their views are independent of this background but best understood in that context. In this way, we can see how unique is their contribution to this basic issue in psychology and human nature.

By 1972, Krishnamurti and Bohm had been acquainted with one another for over a decade, and during that time they had formed a close bond. In 1968, Krishnamurti had founded the Brockwood Park School in Bramdean, England, some eighty miles southwest of London, and Bohm was instrumental in the establishment and early years of the school. Brockwood Park is a private secondary school located on a dozen acres of gardens and trees surrounding an old English mansion, with a massive kitchen and dining hall, multiple wings and endless rooms. Krishnamurti had previously founded several schools in India and one in the United States, but this was his first school for European students. He must have been grateful and rather impressed that Bohm and his wife drove down from London almost every weekend to visit the school and to conduct meetings with students and staff.

By this time, Bohm and Krishnamurti had engaged in numerous dialogues with one another, seventeen of which were recorded. These dialogues consisted of small group conversations or discussions with students or staff at which both men were present. On October 7, 1972, however, there occurred the first recorded dialogue consisting of only the two men talking with one another. An edited transcript of this conversation appears as the final chapter in *The Awakening of Intelligence*, which includes a selection of Krishnamurti's public talks as well as some of his dialogues with various other individuals.

When this conversation occurred, Krishnamurti was 77 years old and Bohm was 54. Their dialogue commences with Krishnamurti joking that the two men are about to engage in a kind of "game of ping-pong." Bohm is more serious, wondering whether the recording device has been turned on and how to begin the conversation. Krishnamurti allows him to take the lead. Bohm begins by mentioning that he had been sent a collection of some of the transcripts that were going to be made into *The Awakening of Intelligence*, and Krishnamurti remarks that it is a "very good title." Bohm agrees and proceeds to offer some observations about the nature of intelligence. He implicitly asks Krishnamurti to confirm the validity of his suggestions.

Fundamental to Krishnamurti's philosophy is a radical distinction between the intellect, which is a function of thought, and intelligence. According to Krishnamurti, thought is a mechanical process, a product of knowledge and experience, and not to be confused with observation, perception, insight, or intelligence. Intelligence represents the capacity to discern truth, the ability to apprehend what is actually the case, rather than the mechanical products of intellect or what has been programmed by society, culture, and conventional wisdom. Bohm begins by following up on this distinction. He suggests that thought is like the information in a book, and that intelligence reads the meaning of the information. He points to the etymological source of the word "intelligence," which is *inter-legere*, from the Latin, "to read between." Krishnamurti rounds out this distinction by saying intelligence "reads between the lines" of thought.

The remainder of the seventy-minute dialogue consists of an exploration of the various ways in which thought or intellect can be distinguished from intelligence. The most basic distinction is that thought is matter, or rather, as Bohm preferred to put it, "a material process." According to Bohm, science has amply proven that all of thought is a "physical, material, electro-chemical process." Later in the dialogue, it emerges that intelligence is a form of pure energy. Perhaps most crucial to the distinction that Bohm and Krishnamurti attempt to draw is that thought is an activity of the brain, whereas intelligence depends upon the inactivity, or the quietness of the brain. The two men agree that the brain is essential for intelligence to operate, but the brain is "only an instrument," and its function for intelligence to awaken is to cease the activity of thought. As Bohm puts it, the quietness of the brain is itself the operation of intelligence.

Needless to say, this view is radically removed from the ordinary understanding of the nature of intelligence. Bohm attempts to place this perspective within the context of conventional scientific views:

> **David Bohm (DB):** I think it would be useful to go back into questions which tend to be raised in the whole of scientific and philosophical thinking. We could ask the question: is there some sense in which intelligence exists independently of matter? You see, some people have thought that mind and matter have some separate kind of existence. . . . I think the question should be considered in order to help to make the mind quiet.

> **Krishnamurti (K):** But you see, Sir, when you say, "help to make the mind quiet," will thought help the awakening of intelligence? It means that, doesn't it? Thought and matter, and the exercise of thought, and the movement of thought, or thought saying to itself, "I will be quiet in order to help the awakening of intelligence."

> **DB:** You might perhaps say the condition for it to awaken is the non-operation of thought.

> **K:** Yes.

On another occasion, Bohm refers to the intelligence inherent in mathematics. He suggests that the theorems of geometry, for example, may be based upon the ability of intelligence to read and verify the conclusions of thought.

DB: We have the static products of thought that seem to have a certain relative harmony. But that harmony is really the result of intelligence, at least it seems so to me. In mathematics we may get a certain relative harmony of the product of thought, even though the actual movement of thought of a mathematician is not necessarily in harmony, generally won't be in harmony. Now that harmony which appears in mathematics is the result of intelligence, isn't it? . . . . It is not perfect harmony because every form of mathematics has been proved to have some limit; that is why I call it only relative.

K: Yes. Now, in the movement of thought is there harmony? If there is, then it has relationship with intelligence. If there is no harmony, but contradictions and all the rest of it, then thought has no relationship with the other.

DB: Then would you say that we could do entirely without thought?

K: I would put it round the other way. Intelligence uses thought.

Krishnamurti points out that thought is constantly seeking security, but that intelligence is secure within itself.

K: Thought, the intellect, dominates the world. And therefore intelligence has very little place here. When one thing dominates, the other must be subservient.

DB: One asks, I don't know if it is relevant, how that came about.

K: That is fairly simple.

DB: What would you say?

K: Thought must have security; it is seeking security in all its movement.

DB: Yes.

K: But intelligence is not seeking security. It has no security. The idea of security doesn't exist in intelligence. Intelligence itself is secure, not, "It seeks security."

In seeking security, thought has created nationalism, for example, although nationalism is in fact a great danger to the individual. Intelligence, by contrast, is capable of seeing that danger and therefore can use thought to create an entirely different kind of world.

DB: Now would you say that when intelligence understands the activity of thought, then thought is different in its operation?

K: Yes, obviously. That is, if thought has created nationalism as a means of security and then sees the fallacy of it, the seeing of the fallacy of it is intelligence. Thought then creates a different kind of world in which nationalism doesn't exist.

About halfway through the dialogue, Krishnamurti takes the conversation in another direction. He suggests that intelligence is an essential attribute of life and not a quality given to each individual in a pre-determined amount, according to genetic inheritance. Rather, it is something that is discoverable and accessible by anyone. This raises the question, what is the state of mind that is capable of discovering or allowing intelligence to operate? In this context, Krishnamurti remarks that religious philosophers have pointed to God as the source of this kind of intelligence.

K: As a human being I would be concerned only with this central issue. I know how confused, contradictory, disharmonious one's life is. Is it possible to change that so that intelligence can function in my life, so that I live without disharmony, so that [I am] guided by intelligence? That is perhaps why the religious people, instead of using the word "intelligence," have used the word "God."

DB: What is the advantage of that?

K: I don't know what the advantage is.

DB: But why use such a word?

K: It came from fear, fear of nature, and gradually out of that grew the idea that there is a super-father.

DB: But that is still thought functioning on its own, without intelligence.

K: Of course. I am just recalling that. They said trust God, have faith in God, then God will operate through you.

DB: God is perhaps a metaphor for intelligence—but people didn't generally take it as a metaphor.

K: Of course not, it is a terrific image.

The question remains, what kind of psychological action or understanding can open the door to the operation of intelligence? Any activity of thought, according to Krishnamurti, cannot bring it about. Only the quietness of the mind can allow intelligence to operate. Even if thought realizes this fact, it will be to no avail. Thought may say to itself, "I must be quiet in order to allow intelligence to operate," but that is just a form of desire and not the action required for intelligence actually to function.

Only the action of insight, he maintains, can bring about the quietness of the mind that will allow intelligence to operate. Insight is a kind of perception or seeing that is independent of thought. Thought is inherently fragmentary in nature, whereas insight has as its essential quality the ability to see the whole; as such, insight alone is capable of bringing about the state of a quiet mind, within which intelligence can function.

K: Because a human being lives in this disharmony, he must enquire into this. And that is what we are doing. As we begin to enquire into it, or in enquiring, we come to this source. Is it a perception, an insight, and has that insight nothing whatsoever to do with thought? Is insight the result of thought? The conclusion of an insight is thought, but insight itself is not thought. So I have got a key to it. Then what is insight? Can I invite it, cultivate it?

DB: You can't do any of that. But there is a kind of energy that is needed.

K: That is just it. I can't do any of that. When I cultivate it, it is desire. When I say I will do this or that, it is the same. So insight is not the product of thought. It is not in the order of thought. Now, how does one come upon this insight? [Pause.] We *have* come upon it because we denied all that.

DB: Yes, it is there. You can never answer that question, how you come upon anything.

K: No. I think it is fairly clear, Sir. You come upon it when you see the whole thing. So insight is the perception of the whole.

During the course of this dialogue, Bohm offers a number of observations that Krishnamurti acknowledges and agrees with, but then moves on. This is unfortunate, because Bohm's perspective is much closer to that of the listener than is Krishnamurti's, and his comments warrant closer attention. He mentions at one point, for example, that the instinct to follow the dictates of pleasure and security makes perfect sense within the animal kingdom. In humanity, however, the activity of thought has seized upon and elaborated the role of pleasure and security and so has overwhelmed the instincts and produced a dysfunctional world. Elsewhere, Bohm points out that it is not effective to tell the conscious mind to look, rather than to think, because thought already feels it is looking. Krishnamurti agrees but does not elaborate upon this crucial point.

This dialogue cannot be fully appreciated without being listened to several times. It is like a sonata by Beethoven, so full of nuance and unexpected developments that it cannot be grasped entirely on the first or second exposure. Krishnamurti's voice expresses a kind of measured passion, whereas Bohm is more cerebral and precise, the perfect counterpoint to Krishnamurti's enthusiasm. The harmonious quality of their interaction is almost as remarkable as the substance of their conversation.

Chapter Ten

WHOLENESS
AND FRAGMENTATION

As we have seen, Krishnamurti associates intelligence with insight, and insight with the perception of a whole. Wholeness is also a crucial element in Bohm's understanding of both physics and consciousness. As such, it represents a major point of contact between their respective points of view and so warrants more detailed attention here.

Krishnamurti maintains that thought inadvertently introduces fragmentation into our perception of ourselves and of the world. He says thought is inherently fragmentary in itself, and so whatever it thinks about will also be in fragments. Consider, for example, his observation that "you are the world." He maintains that the individual separates himself from the rest of mankind by identifying with a particular group, such as his or her family, neighborhood, or nation. These divisions, introduced into perception by thought, are fundamentally false. Human beings, he maintains, are everywhere essentially the same: they all suffer; they all desire; they all experience a common set of psychological circumstances that is more fundamental than the superficial distinctions of race, nationality, ideology, or religious affiliation.

A corresponding outlook is apparent in Krishnamurti's insistence that, in the psychological field of thought, emotion, and motivation, the observer is the observed. The entity who observes his or her own anger or jealousy is not in reality separate from what he or she is observing. The distinction between the two is introduced into consciousness by the very nature of the thinking process. This artificial distinction, moreover, is by no means benign or inconsequential; on the contrary, it engenders conflict and confusion. The failure of thought to understand its own essential nature is the origin of much if not most psychological disturbance.

These themes appear in various forms in virtually all of Krishnamurti's talks and dialogues. The series of talks he gave in Saanen in 1967 provides a somewhat representative sample of the manner in which he expressed these views. Near the beginning of the second talk that year, he said, "To understand the problems which each one of us has is to understand the problems of relationship in society—for we have only one problem really and that is the problem of relationship in this social, psychological structure." As the investigation proceeds, he raises the question, "Does one see the whole picture or does one see only a part of the picture, a detail?" This question leads to a consideration of ways in which thought functions in fragments, and finally to the conclusion that thought is "inevitably" fragmentary:

> This is a very important question to ask oneself, because one sees things in fragments and thinks in fragments—all one's thinking is in fragments. . . . with good opposed to evil, hate and love, anxiety and freedom. One's mind is always thinking in duality, in comparison, in competition, and such a mind, functioning in fragments, cannot see the whole. If one is a Hindu, if one looks at the world from one's little window as the Hindu, believing in certain dogmas, rituals, traditions, brought up in a certain culture and so on, obviously one does not see the whole of mankind.
>
> So to see something totally, whether it is a tree, or a relationship or any activity that one has, the mind must be free from all fragmentation, and the very nature of fragmentation is the center from which one is looking. The background, the culture as the Catholic, as the Protestant, as the Communist, as the Socialist, as my family, is the center from which one is looking. . . .
>
> One sees that one is dependent psychologically on so many things and one has discovered intellectually, verbally, and through analysis, the cause of that dependence; the discovery is itself fragmentary because it is an intellectual, verbal, analytical process—which means that whatever thought investigates must inevitably be fragmentary. One can see the totality of something only when thought doesn't interfere; then one sees not verbally and not intellectually, but factually, as I see the fact of this microphone, without any like or dislike; there it is.

According to David Bohm, a corresponding set of relationships occurs within physical reality. Drawing upon the findings of relativity and quantum mechanics, he saw signs of wholeness in the physical fabric of the universe. He felt there was another "order" of reality, beyond what we observe on the face of things. Observable reality is explicit, on the surface—the "explicate order" of things—but relativity and quantum mechanics suggest the possibility of a deeper kind or level of reality, what Bohm called "the implicate order."

In the implicate order, wholeness prevails. On the surface of reality, everything seems to exist independently: atoms, people, planets—everything is a separate entity unto itself. But relativity and quantum physics, according to Bohm, indicate that in fact everything is connected and whole. In 1980, he expressed these views comprehensively in *Wholeness and the Implicate Order*, perhaps his most profound and revolutionary work. He introduces some of the essential themes in this book as follows:

> Order in its totality is evidently ultimately undefinable, in the sense that it pervades everything that we are and do (language, thought, feeling, sensation, physical action, the arts, practical activity, etc.). However, in physics the basic order has for centuries been that of the Cartesian rectilinear grid (extended slightly in the theory of relativity to the curvilinear grid). Physics has had an enormous development during this time, with the appearance of many radically new features, but the basic order has remained essentially unchanged.
>
> The Cartesian order is suitable for analysis of the world into separately existent parts (e.g., particles or field elements). In chapter 5, however we look into the nature of order with greater generality and depth, and discover that both in relativity and in quantum theory the Cartesian order is leading to serious contradictions and confusion. This is because both theories imply that the actual state of affairs is unbroken wholeness of the universe, rather than analysis into independent parts.
>
> Nevertheless, the two theories differ radically in their detailed notions of order. Thus, in relativity, movement is continuous, causally determinate and well defined, while in quantum mechanics it is discontinuous, not causally determinate and not well defined. Each theory is committed to its own notions of essentially static and fragmentary

modes of existence (relativity to that of separate events, connectable by signals, and quantum mechanics to a well-defined quantum state).

One thus sees that a new kind of theory is needed, which drops these basic commitments and at most recovers some essential features of the older theories as abstract forms, derived from a deeper reality in which what prevails is unbroken wholeness.

If this were merely a matter of theoretical interest, it could perhaps be dismissed as speculative. In the best tradition of science, however, Bohm's point of view bore empirical fruit. He was the theorist, but his student Yakir Aharonov noticed a way in which Bohm's insights into the quantum world could be observed in an entirely unexpected and yet quantifiable manner. What is now known at the Aharonov-Bohm effect represents a demonstration of "non-locality," in which the behavior of an atomic particle is affected by electromagnetic fields even in areas where the fields do not exist. Non-locality suggests the possibility of an intrinsic wholeness of reality. *New Scientist* magazine included the Aharonov-Bohm effect as one of the "seven wonders" of the quantum world.

As Bohm makes clear, science is largely based upon a mechanistic, reductionist vision of reality. The role of science is to understand what causes what, to add up all the empirical facts and fit them into a model or theory that makes them coherent. This endeavor often consists of an effort to explain facts and phenomena in terms of their constituent parts. The basic assumption underlying this process is called reductionism, the principle that the larger is explained by the smaller. Reductionism means we explain behavior by motivation; motivation by physiology; physiology by genetics; genetics by chemistry; and so on. But there is another way in which to view the principles and dynamic causes that bring about the world in which we live. Holism is organic, not mechanistic, and it emphasizes the property of emergent characteristics—things that cannot be anticipated or deduced from the sum of their parts.

The English chemist James Lovelock described in the biological world a somewhat similar set of relationships as Krishnamurti did in the psychological field and Bohm did in the physical universe. Lovelock's Gaia hypothesis encompasses chemistry, biology, geology, and paleontology in order to present a vision of a unified earth system. Lovelock and his co-author Lynn Margulis proposed that life exerts an overarching effect upon the climate and chemistry of Earth in a direction favorable for the continued propagation of life. This idea was revolutionary at the time it was first proposed, in the late 1960's and early 1970's, and it soon came under fire from Richard Dawkins, C. Ford Doolittle, and other defenders of biological orthodoxy.

So long as science remains wedded to reductionist thinking, holistic perspectives such as the Gaia hypothesis are at a disadvantage in terms of gaining acceptance in the scientific community. Gaia entails a willingness to entertain the possibility that the entire ensemble of living and non-living elements of Earth functions collectively in a systemic, unified fashion. At first glance, it is not clear whether this proposal is compatible with conventional biological theory. Darwin's principle of natural selection is rooted in the struggle of one individual against another, and subsequent developments in evolutionary biology have emphasized the role of genes, molecular units of DNA, as the crucial actors in the progressive development of species. Even in cases where organisms such as bees, ants, and termites behave so that individuals sacrifice their own welfare for the benefit of the nest, all is explained in terms of genes furthering their own propagation.

There is little room in this picture for life as a whole to exert any influence in a consistent direction. Nevertheless, the fact is that Earth has remained a reasonably comfortable place for life to persist for well over three billion years. The magnitude of that period of time defies any easy comprehension. Although life is tenacious within certain limits, it is easily extinguished by significant changes in temperature or chemistry, such as the salinity of the ocean or the composition of the atmosphere. Since life has unquestionably had a hand in the development of the conditions on Earth for such an immense period of time, it is difficult not to conclude that some emergent, homeostatic influence may well be at work.

Science proceeds by means of paradigms, overarching themes and theories that tend to define the nature and meaning of empirical evidence. Over time, however, evidence tends to accrue that does not conform with the expectations of the prevailing paradigm. These "anomalies," as Thomas Kuhn called them, eventually accumulate to a critical mass that succeeds in overturning the existing paradigm and ushering in a new one. Something of this kind appears to be taking place with respect to the Gaia hypothesis. Although it was initially met with scorn by the established guild of scientists, Gaia remains a challenge to a new generation, what are now called Earth system scientists, to explain in what manner life does or does not exert a positive (in the sense of beneficial to life) influence on the environment. The key insight that life significantly influences Earth's physiology is no longer considered controversial. What remains open to question is whether that influence occurs in a direction consistently favorable to life.

The Gaia hypothesis is comparable in its scope and assumptions to what Bohm proposed regarding the implicate order of the physical universe and what Krishnamurti proposed regarding the psychological world. In each case—physical, biological, and psychological—there exists a prevailing outlook that proceeds by analysis of things and events into discrete, separate units. But Bohm, Lovelock, and Krishnamurti have each proposed an alternative perspective in which wholeness prevails and fundamentally alters the relationships among the parts. These three alternative perspectives themselves constitute a kind of interlocking whole, a consistent outlook across otherwise disparate fields of inquiry. In this manner, each one illuminates and subtly reinforces the others.

In 1975, Bohm and Krishnamurti engaged in an extended series of recorded dialogues in which they explored the issue of wholeness, among many other topics. In one of these dialogues, Krishnamurti brought into focus why thought is inherently fragmentary. He began by asking, "Why has mankind given such tremendous importance to thought?" In pursuing this question, Bohm mentioned that the process of thinking is essentially mechanical in nature.

> **Krishnamurti:** But does thought realize that it is mechanical?... Why does thought not realize it is mechanical? Why does it suppose that it is something different from a machine?

> **David Bohm:** Yes, it may in some sense suppose it has intelligence

and feeling and that it's a living thing, rather than mechanical.

K: I think that's the root of it, isn't it? It thinks it's living. And therefore it attributes to itself the quality of non-mechanical existence. Thought is clever, giving itself qualities which basically it does not have.

This led into a discussion of perception, which is not mechanical, and which sees things in their totality. That contrast precipitates the investigation into fragmentation, which leads to the observer, the center of the thinking process.

K: Does this answer why thought is fragmentary? . . . . Thought has created the 'me', and the 'me' has apparently become independent of thought, and the 'me', being still part of thought, is the psychological structure. And perception can only take place when there is no 'me'. . . .

So there is a center. Is that center independent of thought?

DB: It would seem the center *is* thought.

K: That's it. That's why it is fragmented. . . . You see the basic reason for fragmentation is that we function from a center.

DB: Physically we are forced to function from a center because the body is the center of our field of perception. Psychologically we form an imitation of that, we have the thought of the center. That form is useful physically, but then it was extended psychologically.

K: Right, that's why thought is fragmentary. . . .

DB: It's not clear to me why thought had to form a center. We knew there was a center but why did we give the center such importance psychologically?

K: Because thought never acknowledges to itself that it is mechanical. . . .

DB: Yes, thought attributes to the center the quality of being a perceiver, as well as a thinker and an actor. . . . I think even from the beginning, thought mistook itself for something living and creative and then it established the center in order to make that permanent.

K: Quite right. So, now we've seen why thought is fragmentary.

DB: But why is it fragmentary?

K: Because of the center. Thought created the center as a permanency, and that center forms a unit to pull everything together. . . .

DB: It doesn't quite explain why it is fragmentary.

K: Because it has separated itself from the thing it has created.

DB: That's the point, so let's make that very clear. It has attributed to itself a center which is separate from itself, whereas in fact it has created the center and it is the center.

K: It *is* the center.

DB: But it attributes to that center the property of being alive and real, and so on. And that is a fragmentation.

K: That's the basic thing. All existence has to be made to fit that center.

DB: For example, if somebody attributes to the center the quality of being a certain nation, then you must distinguish another nation as not belonging to this center. So it fragments mankind in order to hold the center together. Therefore the entire world is fragmented indefinitely, shattered into fragments.

From this perspective, the dynamic disparity between wholeness and fragmentation is not merely an abstract, speculative, or philosophical issue, but rather one with major ramifications for daily life and consciousness. Endemic, inexorable conflict, on both an individual and a global scale, rests upon a foundation of psychological division, the sources of which are identifiable in the thinking process and are fundamentally false. Similarly, the radical shift in perspective entailed by the implicate order and by the Gaia hypothesis carries deep-seated consequences for our stewardship of the planet. Gaia locates all of human endeavor within a larger, inescapable biological context, one that imposes immeasurable responsibility as well as humility. The recovery of wholeness, therefore, holds open the opportunity for a new way of living, one in which harmony may prevail, in the individual, in society, and with the world of nature.

Chapter Eleven

BOHM'S RESERVATIONS

Over the course of two decades, beginning in 1964, Krishnamurti and Bohm engaged in 144 recorded dialogues. Many of these conversations occurred with one or two other individuals present and participating, or with small groups. Some of the dialogues, however, were conducted with Krishnamurti and Bohm exclusively. Among these were the dialogues mentioned in the preceding chapter, a dozen conversations conducted over a period of five months in 1975. At that time, Krishnamurti's work was organized and managed by foundations located on three continents, in America, England, and India. All publication issues were handled by a committee organized by the foundation in England. That committee regarded the 1975 series of dialogues as sufficiently interesting to warrant publication as a book. As a result, the dialogues were transcribed, edited, and prepared for presentation to the world.

This series of dialogues featured an effort by Bohm to elaborate upon a new vocabulary he had introduced into his conversations with Krishnamurti. Bohm was fascinated by the root, etymological meanings of words, and he considered it important to correlate these with the other elements of the overall philosophy the two men were exploring together. Among the terms he regarded as crucial were *truth*, *reality*, and *actuality*. By means of his analysis of the roots of these words—for example, *reality* is based upon the Latin *res*, or "thing"—he invested them with meanings that we do not ordinarily ascribe to them, but which he felt corresponded with Krishnamurti's work. In this perspective, *reality* no longer represents the familiar meaning of what is the case, or the way things actually are. Instead, reality is a construction of thought, and may or may not correspond with the world as it is. Bohm prefers to reserve the term *actuality* for what is in fact the case; and *truth* represents a kind of distillation or special instance of actuality. He goes to some lengths to elucidate these distinctions, and Krishnamurti is receptive to his efforts. Partly for this reason, Bohm at times appears to be taking the initiative and guiding the course of the conversation. Anyone familiar with the two men and their work together would realize that Bohm is offering his ideas to Krishnamurti for their mutual exploration. But to an outside observer, this might not have been so clear.

Among the trustees of the Krishnamurti foundation in England, as well as a member of the publications committee, was Mary Lutyens, his official biographer, whose relationship with Krishnamurti is described in a previous chapter. In 1977, the edited transcripts of Bohm's dialogues with Krishnamurti, all set for publication, came to her attention. As she was a member of the publications committee, it is not clear why she had not seen the transcripts earlier. Perhaps, as she was not actively involved in the editing process, it was simply passed along to her and to others for final approval. In any case, when she read the edited transcripts, she objected strongly to their publication.

According to private correspondence I have received from a reliable source, Lutyens felt that the dialogues presented Krishnamurti in a manner that was not authentic. They were overly intellectual, in her view, and the vocabulary that Bohm was promulgating was not familiar to her and did not correspond with her sense of Krishnamurti's work. Above all, perhaps, she felt the dialogues presented Krishnamurti in the role of a student being instructed by Bohm, which would present a false image to the public of their actual relationship. She went so far as to count the number of lines spoken by each man, and she objected to the fact that Bohm spoke more than Krishnamurti. Among the members of the publications committee, Lutyens was alone in her objections, but she was adamant. She threatened to resign from any further role if the book went forward. More to the point, perhaps, she spoke with Krishnamurti and expressed her concerns to him. As a result, in the end, her opinion won the day. Portions of three of the dialogues were published in 1978, but some twenty years elapsed before additional portions were published, and about half of the material is still not available in printed form.

There remained the delicate task of informing Bohm of what had transpired. Only Krishnamurti could do so, and he was evidently somewhat careless in the manner in which he handled it. Rather than sitting down with Bohm and discussing the matter thoroughly, he mentioned it rather casually at the end of a lunchtime conversation in the large dining hall at Brockwood Park. He offered as a kind of compensation that he and Bohm would conduct another series of conversations, and he assured Bohm that these would in fact be published. Krishnamurti's promise was carried out, and the ensuing series of dialogues, published under the title *The Ending of Time*, represents perhaps the most deep and comprehensive of all their conversations together. Nevertheless, Krishnamurti failed to grasp the impact upon Bohm of the decision not to publish the existing set of dialogues. He clearly miscalculated, for he seemed to think that Bohm was comfortable with this decision. But that was not the case.

It is probably no longer possible to understand fully the outlook of the two men with regard to this issue. However, I can confirm from my conversations with Bohm that the issue continued to bother him more than a decade later. Krishnamurti's philosophy devotes a good deal of attention to the inherent falseness of the image we each construct about ourselves. But was Mary Lutyens' objection to the dialogues that they suggested an incorrect image of Krishnamurti? Did she succeed in conveying this concern to him? If so, and if he was concerned about his image, was this not a contradiction with a central element of his teaching? For his part, Krishnamurti probably regarded it all as a somewhat secondary matter. His concern was not with what was published, but rather with what people actually understood. Moreover, he need not have had an image of himself to be concerned about how his work was presented to the public. It would be consistent with his stated philosophy not to be dependent upon anyone for his observations and insights, and if the dialogues somehow suggested otherwise, they would have been misleading.

A period of two or three years elapsed between the time Krishnamurti informed Bohm of the decision not to publish the series of dialogues they had held, and the time he was able to make good on his promise to conduct a subsequent series that would in fact be published. During this interval, Bohm evidently developed a rather negative view of Krishnamurti and his work. These views were expressed in a few letters to a friend whom Bohm had reason to believe shared this attitude. The first of these letters is dated June, 1979, and the other three in January and February, 1980. The letters were written to Fritz Wilhelm, a fellow physicist, who was also quite familiar with Krishnamurti and his work.

Wilhelm had met Krishnamurti at the annual talks given in Saanen, Switzerland, and he was subsequently invited to come to Ojai to serve as director of an Adult Educational Center under the auspices of the Krishnamurti Foundation of America. The Center was formed almost simultaneously with the opening of Oak Grove School in 1975, and Wilhelm served as its director until 1980. Upon his departure, the Center closed and was not re-opened. The general intention of the Center was to provide a place where people could stay and explore Krishnamurti's teachings in a congenial atmosphere with someone who was thoroughly familiar with Krishnamurti's work. It was a rather challenging assignment, not one I would have been willing to assume. Wilhelm, however, did not seem daunted by it.

Since the Center operated in a manner ancillary to the school, I was fairly well acquainted with him and had numerous opportunities to observe him in casual as well as working circumstances. The school attracted a variety of interesting and intelligent teachers, and I was usually receptive to those who shared my interest in Krishnamurti's work and often formed close bonds with them. Wilhelm was not among those with whom I felt a sense of rapport. I took a sabbatical from the school from 1978 until 1980, but as I prepared to return, I was not surprised to learn that Wilhelm was leaving Ojai for a position elsewhere in California. Whether he left on his own initiative or was asked to leave was not clear to me, but Krishnamurti privately expressed to me some reservations about him.

Bohm, on the other hand, developed a close bond with Wilhelm, and so it is not surprising that he turned to him to express his reservations about Krishnamurti. In his letters to Wilhelm, Bohm leveled a series of criticisms that were surprising not only for their attitude and substance but for the manner in which they targeted Krishnamurti personally. The overall theme of these letters is that Krishnamurti held a distorted and conditioned image of himself. Bohm maintained that Krishnamurti regarded himself as the embodiment of truth, so that his words and deeds were essentially infallible. Bohm suggested that Krishnamurti had absorbed the Theosophical notion that he was the World Teacher and uniquely unconditioned, ideas that Bohm dismissed as "nonsense." (In the excerpt below, "that boy" represents Krishnamurti's way of referring to himself in his youth):

> The difficulty is, that if K is like all of us, a mixture of what is true and what is not, then we are compelled to treat K's false aspects as inseparable from the living truth and thus we become deeply confused and enter into deep inner conflict. . . .
>
> I would say that K was conditioned in a different way from most people, and this made certain insights possible to him, while he is even more caught in nonsense than most people in certain other areas (especially, when he thinks about "that boy") . . . .
>
> At present, one must say that the teachings do not go far enough so that a person who lives them will change fundamentally (and in fact this has happened to no one, not even to K, who is caught in his own nonsense).

In these letters, Bohm refers to the dialogues that were not published, and it is apparent how deeply he was wounded or offended by this decision. He makes it clear that he was apprised of the circumstances that led to this decision, including the fact that Mary Lutyens was instrumental in bringing it about. At one point he complains that he had "no opportunity" to discuss the decision with Krishnamurti, but that is difficult to understand, since his opportunities to interact with Krishnamurti were numerous. Elsewhere he acknowledges that the failure to address the matter more forthrightly was at least as much his own responsibility:

> I accept, at the very beginning, that part of the responsibility for the breakdown of the communication is my own. One way in which this has happened is that I feel that K has dismissed and tried to push aside

my own work in science and philosophy in a way that is not justified, because I think it makes a significant contribution to what is being attempted by all of us.

Another issue that Bohm alluded to in these letters was a chronic pain he was experiencing in his chest. He attributed this pain to the "crushing" weight of conflict he felt due to his devotion to Krishnamurti and his work, coupled with the kind of reservations he was expressing in these letters:

> K dismisses everybody and frequently says that nobody is doing anything—not at Brockwood, nor in Ojai, nor in Canada, nor in India. . . . For example, in India, he gave a talk in which he dismissed physics as "limited," saying that he was glad that I was not present to hear him say it. . . . I have fears that the attempt to limit myself to what K says and to the work he wants to do is "crushing" me (literally, the pain in the chest).

As one who worked with Krishnamurti for ten years during this time period, it seems to me that Bohm was exaggerating in his assertion that K "dismisses everybody," and so on. Moreover, the pain in his chest may have had little to do with Krishnamurti. A few months after the last of these letters was composed, Bohm experienced what was probably a heart attack, although it was misdiagnosed at the time. The following year, his symptoms became more acute, and angioplasty revealed that he required triple bypass surgery. Bohm underwent this surgery in England, in April 1981.

In a letter also written in February 1980, a few weeks subsequent to those already mentioned, Bohm repudiated, to some extent, his earlier criticisms of Krishnamurti, and he specifically asked Wilhelm to destroy those letters:

> I think that some of my recent letters will give a somewhat distorted impression, as they emphasize the questions that I have been raising, and do not adequately convey my positive feelings toward K. A letter is always dangerous, as there is no way to correct false impressions, at least for a very long time. May I suggest that you destroy those letters, as there is, in any case, nothing in them that needs to be preserved.

The fact that Wilhelm did not destroy the letters, as Bohm requested, and instead made them available for publication, is a story in its own right.

The only available biography of Bohm was composed by his friend, the science writer F. David Peat. It appeared in 1997, five years after Bohm died, under the title *Infinite Potential: The Life and Times of David Bohm*. The book is well written and researched, especially with regard to Bohm's scientific work. In composing the present volume, I have relied upon Peat's work extensively. Shortly after the hardback copy of the book was published, Wilhelm sent Peat excerpts from the correspondence in which Bohm had expressed his criticisms and reservations about Krishnamurti. Peat considered these letters to be important and revealing, and he arranged for them to be published as an afterword to the paperback edition of his book, which was then in the process of preparation. In the afterword, Peat confesses his own misgivings about the personality of Krishnamurti and about Bohm's involvement with him, and he seems to regard the letters as a kind of confirmation of his own views.

What was not included in Peat's afterword was Bohm's subsequent letter to Wilhelm, stating that the letters gave a distorted impression and asking Wilhelm to destroy them. Bohm's final letter only came to light after it was discovered in a file sent by Wilhelm to Bohm's wife, Saral. I was engaging in an email correspondence at that time with Saral, Peat, and others involved in this work, and I will quote from Saral's description (March 26, 1998) of how the final letter was discovered, and why Peat did not include it in his afterword:

> Now about David Peat's ignoring the contents of the letter from Dave where he asks for the letters to be destroyed. I have just spoken with David P. on the phone and he said that Fritz [Wilhelm] did not send all the letters to him but only a disk with excerpts. Fritz sent me the same disk and I can assure you that that letter was not on it. However when Fritz sent me the original letters for the archives there it was. . . . [ellipsis in original] it was a big shock to me.
>
> I cannot understand, if Fritz had not wanted that letter to be seen why did he send it to me? I can only think that he had the letters in a file and he sent the whole file without looking through them. In any

case I phoned David Peat when I saw the letter and also I spoke to Basil Hiley [Bohm's colleague and collaborator at Birkbeck College] and David told me that the publishers were printing the paperback by then. The whole business is not very pleasant. It would be good to let it drop and let the extraordinary work the two men did, both together and separately, stand for itself.

There is no sense in commenting upon or interpreting this sequence of events; the facts speak for themselves. There is one final point, however, that merits emphasis. In one of the letters to Wilhelm, dated January 28, 1980, Bohm wrote:

> Part of the trouble is that K and I have not really been communicating for about six years. [This statement is not accurate. In addition to other recorded conversations, the last of the dialogues that Bohm wanted published occurred about four years prior to the date of this letter.] When we had the dialogues which they decided not to publish, I felt at last that things were changing. But with the decision not to publish, and with no chance for us to discuss this decision things got even worse.

In the concluding paragraph of his afterword—and therefore the last paragraph of his book—Peat seizes upon this statement and writes as follows:

> Whatever the case, while the two men did meet again on cordial terms, they never discussed together as before. But then Bohm's letter of January 28, 1980 suggests that the intensity and attention to truth had disappeared from their interactions several years before.

The fact of the matter, however, is that the most extensive and profound of all the dialogues between Bohm and Krishnamurti had yet to occur. This was the series that Krishnamurti had promised Bohm at the time the earlier publication was cancelled, and is the subject of the following four chapters. There were in addition numerous other dialogues between the two men subsequent to 1980, including a final pair of conversations in 1983, published in 1986 as *The Future of Humanity*. Evidently the idea that the two men "never discussed together again as before" played into Peat's preferred narrative about the relationship between them. Either Peat was unaware of the subsequent dialogues, or he deliberately omitted them from consideration. In either case, this oversight represents a serious lapse of scholarship.

Nevertheless, Bohm's letters do suggest a certain limitation in the nature of his relationship with Krishnamurti. Why did he not bring his concerns and criticisms to Krishnamurti directly and resolve them in a more forthright fashion? Surely he had no shortage of opportunities to do so. Notwithstanding the exceptional quality of their explorations into consciousness, it appears something was missing in their personal interaction, at least insofar as Bohm was able to express himself. This issue was evidently never resolved, as subsequent events made clear.

Chapter Twelve

THE ENDING OF TIME I

An interval of five years elapsed between the series of dialogues conducted in 1975 that were not published in full and the subsequent series that Krishnamurti had promised Bohm would in fact be published. During that interval, the two men engaged in numerous other conversations, many of them recorded, with other participants involved. Among these was a videotaped series with David Shainberg, a psychiatrist from New York, that was published under the title *The Wholeness of Life*. In this series, Shainberg plays the role of everyman, responding to the radical pronouncements of Krishnamurti from the perspective of an ordinary listener, one somewhat naïve or unschooled in the depths of this philosophy, although Shainberg was in fact very familiar with it. Bohm and Krishnamurti coach him and bring him along as well as they can, but his presence anchors them and prevents their dialogue from taking full flight. No such impediment prevails in the series of fifteen conversations conducted in April, June, and September 1980, published in 1985 as *The Ending of Time*.

Before examining the substance of these conversations, it is helpful to understand the context in which they occurred. The initial series of eight dialogues took place in Ojai over a period of three weeks beginning April 1. Krishnamurti's annual visit to Ojai typically occupied the interval from February through April, and on February 21, five weeks before the commencement of his dialogues with Bohm, he dictated a statement regarding an exceptional experience he had recently undergone. It was unusual for him to record a statement reflecting upon his personal experiences, but the content of it suggests why he felt it was necessary in this case. He referred to himself in the third person or as "K":

For a long time he has been awakening in the middle of the night with that peculiar meditation which has been pursuing him for very many years. This has been a normal thing in his life. It is not a conscious, deliberate pursuit of meditation or an unconscious desire to achieve something. It is very clearly uninvited and unsought. . . . Sometimes it is so intense that there is pain in the head, sometimes a sense of vast emptiness with fathomless energy. Sometimes he wakes up with laughter and measureless joy. These peculiar meditations, which naturally were unpremeditated, grew with intensity. Only on the days he travelled or arrived late of an evening would they stop, or when he had to wake early and travel.

With the arrival in Rishi Valley [India] in the middle of November 1979, the momentum increased, and one night in the strange stillness of that part of the world, with the silence undisturbed by the hoot of owls, he woke up to find something totally different and new. The movement had reached the source of all energy. . . . Desire cannot possibly reach it, words cannot fathom it, nor can the string of thought wind itself around it. One may ask with what assurance do you state that it is the source of all energy? One can only reply with complete humility that it is so.

All the time that K was in India until the end of January 1980, every night he would wake up with this sense of the absolute. . . . The whole universe is in it, measureless to man. When he returned to Ojai in February 1980, after the body had somewhat rested, there was the perception that there was nothing beyond this. This is the ultimate, the beginning and the ending and the absolute. There is only a sense of incredible vastness and immense beauty.

In his 1980 dialogues with Bohm, Krishnamurti introduced this material somewhat tentatively, but it forms the center of gravity of the entire series. As a result, the conversations assume a somewhat metaphysical orientation, one that probes the fundamental nature of the universe; indeed, the first two conversations are largely given over to exploring this dimension of reality. Soon enough, the more familiar themes of human nature and ordinary consciousness take center stage and occupy the lion's share of time and attention. Even then, however, this series of dialogues is distinguished by the manner in which the more familiar themes are woven around and directed toward the quality of the universe as a whole.

The first dialogue opens on a note that prefigures the wide perspective that is a hallmark of the series of conversations. Krishnamurti begins, "I would like to ask if humanity has taken a wrong turn." It soon becomes apparent he is considering mankind in its entirety, the whole of the human race, not only in its contemporary manifestation, but far into the past. Bohm replies in the affirmative—"It must have, a long time ago" —but at first he is thinking only in terms of the last few thousand years. Krishnamurti makes it clear that his question pertains to man's development through evolutionary time, over the course of a million years or more. Has something occurred in the development of the human brain that has set the whole of humanity on a wrong course?

What precipitates such a question? Everywhere human beings live in a state of conflict, according to Krishnamurti, not only in the form of endless wars, but also inwardly, within themselves. Why do people tolerate this? The pervasiveness of conflict throughout human history cries out for explanation. What is at the root of it? Has the human brain taken a wrong turn in its development?

Krishnamurti maintains that the root of conflict is the psychological process of "becoming": the incessant urge of each individual to be something more or better than what he or she already is—"always trying to become more and more and more and more." He asks why this psychological process has assumed such central importance. Bohm replies that the impulse to improve things, to make things better, began outwardly, in the effort to improve one's environment or material circumstances. In the outer world, that impulse is reasonable and can have a successful outcome because matter can yield and change its form or shape. But when a similar impulse is applied inwardly, in an effort to improve oneself or one's nature, it leads to conflict. "Inwardly, I want to be what I am," Bohm maintains, "and at the same time I want to be what I should be." These contradictory impulses represent the essence of inner conflict.

Krishnamurti presses the issue further. The process of psychological becoming can only occur in the context of time. Here he draws a sharp distinction between ordinary, chronological time, and what he refers to as "psychological time." Ordinary time refers to the sequence of events in the physical world, whereas psychological time refers to the past and future of the self or ego, the entity at the center of consciousness. The impulse to improve oneself psychologically, to transform from what one is to what should be, can only take place, he says, in psychological time. But that kind of time, he insists, is illusory. We don't ordinarily recognize any distinction between chronological and psychological time, but Krishnamurti maintains there is a deep difference between the two and that the difference is crucial.

"I want to abolish [psychological] time," he says, almost impetuously. Bohm replies with ironic humor, "Well, go ahead." Time is movement, Krishnamurti declares, the movement from here to there, or from what is to what should be. What happens, he asks metaphorically, to a man who has been going north all his life and suddenly realizes that direction leads nowhere? Suppose he turns east or even stops moving altogether? The quality of his brain will have changed. If there is no movement, out-wardly or inwardly, then there occurs another kind of movement, one which is not from here to there. It is not a movement in time.

By means of this sequence of exploratory steps, at about thirty minutes into the dialogue, the stage has been set for Krishnamurti to reveal the events that occurred a few months prior to this dialogue. The following excerpt from the transcript of their conversation is almost verbatim and therefore differs slightly from the edited version that appears in *The Ending of Time*.

> **Krishnamurti:** First of all: Conscious meditation is no meditation, right?
>
> **David Bohm:** What do you mean by "conscious meditation"?
>
> **K:** That is, deliberate meditation. Deliberate, practiced meditation, which is really premeditated meditation. Is there a meditation which is not premeditated—which is not the ego trying to become some-thing?
>
> **DB:** Before we go ahead, could we suggest what meditation should be? Is it an observation of the mind observing?

K: No, no, no. It has gone beyond all that.

DB: All right. But you are using the word "meditation."

K: I am using the word "meditation" in the sense in which there is not a particle of endeavor, of any sense of trying to become, consciously reach a level, and so on.

DB: The mind is simply with itself, silent.

K: That is what I want to get at.

DB: It is not looking for anything.

K: Yes. You see, I don't meditate in the normal sense of the word. What happens with me is—I am not talking personally, please—what happens with me is, I wake up meditating.

DB: All right. In that state.

K: And—one night at Rishi Valley in India, I woke up. A series of incidents had taken place; meditation for some days. I woke up one night, in the middle of the night. It was a quarter past twelve; I looked at the watch. [Laughs.] And—I hesitate to say this, because it sounds extravagant and rather childish—the source of all energy had been reached. And that had an extraordinary effect on the brain, and also physically.

Sorry to talk about myself, but [pause] literally, any sense of—I don't know how to put it—any sense of the world and me, and that—you follow?—there was no division at all. Only this *tremendous* source of energy! I don't know if I am conveying something.

DB: So the brain was in contact with this source of energy?

K: Yes. Now, coming down to earth, and as I have been talking for sixty years, I would like another to reach this—no, not "reach" it. You understand what I am saying? Because I think all our problems are resolved—political, religious—every problem is resolved. Because it is pure energy from the beginning of time.

This revelation leads back into a discussion of time as a factor of conflict. Bohm points out that we normally feel that "time exists independently of us. We are in the stream of time, and therefore it would seem absurd for us to deny it, because that is what we are." Krishnamurti agrees that to deny time is "tremendous." Thought itself is based on "experience, knowledge, memory, and response, which is the whole of time." If there were no thought, no psychological time, the sense of individual identity would dissolve, and then what would remain? "Most people would say, 'What a horror this is. You've led us to an empty wall.'" But because there is nothing left, he maintains, rather paradoxically, there is "everything"— and everything is energy. Such energy, we may reasonably infer, is what he was referring to when he described what had occurred in Rishi Valley a few months previously. (It should be noted that in physics as well, what we perceive as empty space or nothingness is in fact filled with energy.)

Needless to say, perhaps, this dialogue left a great deal of territory still to be explored. Much of what had been introduced so far required more detailed examination. The second of the fifteen conversations occurred the following day and picked up at the point where the previous one left off.

Krishnamurti began by referring again to psychological time as the origin of conflict:

K: Time is the enemy of man. And that enemy has existed from the beginning of man. And we asked, why has man from the beginning taken a wrong turn, a wrong path? And, if so, is it possible to turn man in another direction in which he can live without conflict?

The conversation proceeds by supposing that it is in fact possible for an individual to free himself from the illusion of psychological time, which entails the ending of the ego, the self, because the ego requires time in order to exist. When time in this sense has come to an end, what then takes place? Here Krishnamurti introduces a refinement of his observations about the source of all energy. He suggests that once the sense of individual identity has been dispelled, that particular mind no longer exists as it had before, and the brain comes into contact with another kind of mind, a "universal mind," which encompasses not only all of nature, but the universe. He maintains he is just exploring, "groping after" words to express his insight, and Bohm allows him free rein, not challenging or questioning too deeply, but rather seeking to clarify Krishnamurti's meaning. The universal mind is part of the energy he has been referring to, and that energy is alive, "enormous," and has a kind of intelligence.

> **DB:** You are bringing in the whole universe as well as mankind. What makes you do this? What is the source of this perception?

> **K:** To put it very simply, division has come to an end. Right? The division created by time, created by thought, created by this education, and so on—all that. Because it has ended, the other is obvious.

In subsequent dialogues, more attention is given to whether or how it is possible for others to become aware of or to confirm these observations about energy and the universal mind. But for the moment, Krishnamurti is concerned to open up still more territory. What happens next forms the foundation for all the succeeding conversations:

> **K:** I would like to push it a little further; which is, is there something beyond all this?

> **DB:** Beyond the energy, you mean?

> **K:** Yes. We said nothingness; that nothingness is everything; and so it is that which is total energy. It is undiluted, pure, uncorrupted energy. Right. Is there something beyond that?

After some clarification of the language, the conversation continues:

> **DB:** This pure energy you talk about is emptiness. That is, it is not felt as some thing.

> **K:** No.

> **DB:** Now beyond that emptiness—are you suggesting there is that which is beyond the emptiness, the ground of the emptiness?

> **K:** Yes. . . . What is beyond emptiness? Is it silence? Or is silence part of emptiness?

> **DB:** Yes, I should say that.

K: I should say that too. If it is not silence—[pause]. Could we—I am just asking—could we say it is something absolute? You understand?

Bohm's use of the term "ground" in this exchange is significant for all that follows. Later Krishnamurti expresses some reluctance to use this term, but for the moment he accepts it. First he wants to know if Bohm is willing to follow him up to this point.

K: So if I say there is something greater than all this silence, energy, would you accept that? Accept in the sense that up to now we have been logical.

DB: We will say that whatever you speak of, there is certainly something beyond it. Silence, energy, whatever, there is always room logically for something beyond that. But the point is this: even if you were to say there is something beyond that, still you logically leave room for going again beyond that.

This point in the conversation seems to reveal that Bohm's relationship to the issues Krishnamurti is raising is based not on observation or direct experience, but rather represents simply an acceptance of what may logically be possible. Krishnamurti, by contrast, is introducing material from a sense of immediate awareness or perception. Thus, when Bohm says that logically there is always room for something to exist beyond whatever has already been posited, Krishnamurti is emphatic: "No. No."

DB: Well, that's the question.

K: That's the point, that's the point.

DB: Why is that? You see, whatever you say, there is always room for something beyond.

K: That's what I—there is nothing beyond.

DB: Well, that point is not clear, you see.

K: There is nothing beyond it. I stick to that—not dogmatically or obstinately. I feel that is the beginning and ending of everything. Yes, sir, I see something in this.

Krishnamurti asks if Bohm would agree that the ending and the beginning can be the same. Here Bohm reintroduces the language of the "ground," and their exchange is revealing, since this term recurs so often subsequently.

K: Sir, just in ordinary parlance, the ending and the beginning are the same, right?

DB: In which sense? In the sense that you are saying the beginning of everything is the ending of everything?

K: Yes. Right? You would say that?

DB: Yes. If we take the ground from which it comes, it must be the ground to which it falls.

K: Falls, that's right. That is the ground. Upon which—not "upon"—

DB: Well, it's a figure of speech.

K: Yes, figure of speech. Upon which everything exists—space –

DB: energy—

K: energy, emptiness, silence—all that is on that. Not "ground," you understand?

DB: No, it is just a metaphor.

K: There is nothing beyond it.
   [Pause.]

DB: This ground has no cause.

K: No cause. If you have a cause, then you have –

DB: You have another ground.

K: No, no. That is the beginning and the ending. Yes, sir. That's right.

DB: It is becoming more clear.

As he does so often, Krishnamurti wants to know how such a conversation would be perceived by an ordinary man. What relationship could he have to the ground? What meaning could it have to him? Bohm suggests the notion of the ground is similar to what others have called God.

K: Ah, no, this isn't God.

DB: Yes, it is not God, but it is plying the same—it has—you could say that "God" is an attempt to put this notion a bit too personally perhaps.

K: Yes. Yes.

But still Krishnamurti wants to know who would even listen to this.

K: You are a scientist. You are good enough to listen because we are friends. But who will listen among your friends? [They would say,] "What the hell are you talking about?" [Pause.] I feel that if one pursues this, we will have a marvelously ordered world.

After exploring the stratosphere, as it were, the metaphysical height and depth of the universe, the third conversation comes emphatically back down to earth. The dialogue begins with Bohm asking whether or not the ground that Krishnamurti has pointed to is indifferent to humanity. Bohm observes that science has attempted to find the ground of the universe through the investigation of matter, but this has led to the sense that the universe is fundamentally without meaning, in the sense that it is indifferent to man.

DB: Not only physicists but geneticists, biologists, have tried to reduce everything to the behavior of matter—atoms, genes, DNA. And the more they study it, then the more they feel it has no meaning, it is just going on. Though it has meaning physically, in the sense that we can understand it scientifically, it has no deeper meaning than that. . . . You see, the universe appears to be totally indifferent to mankind. It is immense vastness; it pays no attention to us; it may produce earthquakes and catastrophes; it might wipe us out; it is essentially not interested in mankind.

He contrasts this state of affairs with what occurred before science, when people "felt that the ground of our existence was in something beyond matter—God or whatever they wished to call it." But with the advent of science, that perspective is becoming less and less tenable, "because the story told by the religious people is not plausible."

DB: Now, I think the point is, would *this* ground be indifferent to mankind?

K: Quite. How would you find out? What is the relationship of this ground to man, and man's relationship to it? . . . . Suppose one says it has [some significance for man]—otherwise life has no meaning, nothing has any meaning. How would one—not prove—how would one find out?

Suppose you say this ground exists, as I said the other day. . . . How would one discover or find out or touch it—if the ground exists at all? If it doesn't exist, then really man has no meaning at all. I mean, I die and you die and we all die, and what is the point of being virtuous, what is the point of being happy or unhappy—just carry on? How would you show the ground exists? In scientific terms, as well as the feeling of it, the nonverbal communication of it?

The remainder of the conversation is devoted primarily to answering this question. Krishnamurti maintains that to show "scientifically" that the ground exists requires that a number of people—ten or more, not just one individual—come into contact with it. But, "The ground has certain demands, which are: there must be absolute silence, absolute emptiness. Which means no sense of egotism in any form. . . complete eradication of the self."

Here, then, is where the difficulty begins. Bohm points out that most people will not be able to follow to this point, even if they are interested, because so much of what Krishnamurti is saying is foreign or contrary to the ordinary point of view:

DB: Also his whole background is against it. You see, the background gives you the notion of what makes sense and what doesn't. Now, when you say, for example, one of the steps is to not bring in time –

K: Ah, that's *much* more difficult.

DB: Yes, but it is fairly crucial.

K: But wait. I wouldn't begin with time. I would begin at the schoolboy level. [Laughs.]

What Krishnamurti means by "the schoolboy level" are such principles as not to live with any form of theory or belief, including belief in God, or an afterlife, or the superiority of one's own nation or race. Beliefs and theories prevent observation of facts, he maintains, and introduce an element of irrationality in daily life. Somewhat remarkably, Bohm takes issue with Krishnamurti on this point. After following and apparently accepting the exposition into the ground of the universe and the source of all energy, he challenges the "schoolboy" principle that one can live entirely without theories. Science, he maintains, proceeds by means of theories; it is not possible to organize facts or even establish what qualifies as a fact without the guidance of theories. After some discussion, Krishnamurti yields on this point insofar as it applies to the study of outward things—"I wouldn't know"—but he insists that theories are not necessary for purposes of inward observation.

A little later in this dialogue, Krishnamurti introduces the factor of insight, which plays a crucial role in the network of issues with which he is concerned. What is the dominant element in consciousness, he asks, as it presently exists? He declares that "obviously" it is thought. He then inquires why man has "enthroned" thought and given it supreme importance. Thought is based on memory, he maintains, and therefore thought and time are intimately interconnected; time is the matrix in which thought operates. Insight, by contrast, is not based on memory and occurs outside of time; insight is a form of perception and has the quality of immediacy. A mind that has freed itself of psychological time is capable of insight into the whole structure of thought and consciousness, and is therefore able to come into contact with the ground.

Perhaps two dozen people were present during these dialogues, and a few of them interposed questions or observations as the conversations proceeded. The most frequent interpolations were offered by Fritz Wilhelm, Bohm's correspondent of a few months previously. I was also present at these meetings, although Krishnamurti evidently did not notice me at first, for early on in the fourth dialogue he provided for my benefit a summary of the preceding conversations:

> **K:** You were not here the other day. We were having a dialogue about the ending of time. . . . We went into that quite a bit, and we say it is possible for a human being who will listen to find out through insight the ending of time. Because insight is not memory. Memory is time—memory as experience, knowledge, stored up in the brain, and so on. As long as that is in operation there is no possibility of having insight into anything.
>
> Is it possible to have a total insight? Which is the ending of the "me," because the "me" is put together by thought; thought is time; "me" is time. . . . It is only when that ends there is total insight.
>
> And the question then arises: If the "me" ends, what is there? . . . If one is investigating without any sense of reward or punishment, then there is something. We said that something is total emptiness, which is energy and silence. . . . And we pushed it further: Is there something beyond all this? Right, sir? And we said there is.

> **David Moody (DM):** The ground.

> **K:** The ground. You were perhaps here. And the last thing, if I remember rightly—will people listen to this? Is it that the beginning of this inquiry is to listen?

Krishnamurti's summary indicates the direction of the remainder of this dialogue. Is it possible for the self to end completely? What will enable a human being to break out of the pattern of a self-centered, egotistic way of living? Bohm proposes that when there is a great crisis, people are able momentarily to drop their customary patterns of thinking and behavior, but once the crisis is over, they go back to their familiar ways.

Krishnamurti suggests that insight will allow someone to break out of the pattern of egotistical activity. But what will enable someone who has this insight to convey it to someone who does not have it?

> **K:** Because if you have that insight, it is a passion. It is not just a clever insight, to sit back and be comfortable. It is a passion. This passion

won't let you sit still. . . . You have that passion of this immense insight. And that passion must, like a river with a great volume of water, go over the bank. In the same way, that passion must move.

Now, I am a human being, ordinary, fairly intelligent, well read, experienced. I have tried this, that, and the other thing, and I meet someone, X, who is full of this. Why won't I listen to him?

As one who had participated in many meetings with Krishnamurti and listened rather carefully, I could not let this question pass without replying.

DM: Sir, I think one does listen.

K: Does one? Do you?

DM: Yes, I think so.

K: Just go very, very slowly. Do you so completely listen that there is no resistance, no saying, "Why, what is the cause, why should I?" You follow what I mean? . . . . X comes along and says, "Look, there is a different way of living, something totally new"—which means, "please listen." Will you? Completely?

Finally, he maintains that all "explanations" are useless in this regard. Insight has no cause, he says, and to accumulate knowledge or explanations about the self or the ending of the self will not bring about insight.

K: You see, explanations have been the boat in which to cross to the other shore. And the man on the other shore says there is no boat. He says, "Cross!" He is asking me something impossible. Right?

DB: If it doesn't happen right away, then it's impossible.

K: Absolutely. He is asking something impossible for me to do.

Nevertheless, in listening to X, one becomes more sensitive, alert, and "allergic" to any word of explanation. The process of listening completely, without resistance, therefore becomes the catalyst that opens the door to a solution to the impossible question.

Throughout these four dialogues, the interaction between Bohm and Krishnamurti is balletic in its grace and subtlety. Their art consists of maintaining a balance on a razor's edge, with respect and even deference to one another on one side, and rigor and objectivity on the other. Krishnamurti has taken the lead and introduced a wealth of material that Bohm could hardly have anticipated, yet Bohm participates as an equal partner, correcting, challenging, and clarifying as the inquiry proceeds. In subsequent dialogues, he takes an even more active role in terms of initiating topics and elaborating issues as needed.

From beginning to end, their conversation is enveloped in warmth and an implicit feeling of mutual support, rather like two mountain climbers roped together. There is no sign or trace of any element of animosity, however brief, even when they disagree. The issues Bohm raised in his letters to Wilhelm are entirely foreign to this quality of relationship. Indeed, their mutual compatibility is manifest, and it forms a foundation that supports their exploration and allows it to unfold.

Chapter Thirteen

THE ENDING OF TIME II

In the fifth dialogue in the series of fifteen that were published as *The Ending of Time*, Bohm begins by asking whether "we could go further into the nature of the ground, whether we could come to it and whether it has any interest in human beings." By this stage in the development of the exploration, it would be helpful if the discussion were framed in terms of the ground *of* something—the ground of the universe, or of existence, or of reality, or whatever is really meant by that word. However, the dialogue proceeds as if the meaning of "the ground" has already been sufficiently well developed; and, in the absence of further clarification, perhaps it is best to think of it simply as the ground of everything, including matter, mind, and all of nature.

Krishnamurti replies to Bohm's question by reframing it in terms of ideas: "Is the ground an idea? That is what I want, first, to be clear. Why have ideas become so important?" Bohm replies that we often fail to distinguish between ideas and what they represent:

> **DB:** Ideas are often taken to be something more than ideas; we feel they are not ideas but a reality.

> **K:** That is what I want to find out. Is the ground an idea, an imagination, an illusion, a philosophic concept? Or is it something that is absolute in the sense there is nothing beyond it?

As the conversation develops, Krishnamurti suggests the ground can only be approached by a mind that is "free from all knowledge, except that which is technological." He recognizes that such a suggestion is radical and unlikely to be easily received or readily accepted. Nevertheless, he puts himself in the position of a "fairly educated, thoughtful man," one who "sees vaguely that this understanding, or coming upon this ground, gives an immense significance to life." In the following passage, he puts himself in the position of that man who is listening to someone tell him about the ground:

> K: Here is a person who says there is such a thing. And I listen to him, and not only does he convey it by his presence; he conveys it also through the word, although he tells me to be careful; the word is not the thing.
>
> But he uses the word to convey something to me which I vaguely capture—that there is something so immense that my thought cannot capture it. And I say, "All right, you have explained that very carefully, and how am I, whose brain is conditioned that way, disciplined, in knowledge—how is it to free itself from all that?"

Bohm points out that the aim of most of the major religions has consisted of an effort to create such a ground precisely by means of thought. "Through knowledge and thought, people created what they regarded as the ground. And it wasn't."

A little later, Krishnamurti returns to one of his most frequent refrains, that the psychological self, the center of psychological knowledge, represents a basic impediment to contact with the ground. He articulates this view with passion:

> K: All that I want is this center to be blasted! You understand? The center not to exist. Because I see that the center is the cause of all the mischief, all the neurotic conclusions, all the illusions, all the endeavor, all the effort, all the misery—everything is from that core.

The individual self is not only illusory but far too petty to come into contact with something so immense as the ground. To realize that "is a tremendous shock. It is as if you have knocked me out!" For purposes of establishing some relationship with the ground, "All you have done or not done is absolutely of no value."

In the end this very realization opens the door to contact with the ground.

> K: So there is only one thing, and that is to discover that all I have done is useless—ashes! You see, that doesn't depress one. That is the beauty of it. I think it is like the phoenix.

DB: Rising from the ashes.

K: Born of ashes.

DB: In a way, it is freedom, to be free of all that.

K: Something totally new is born.

DB: Now, what you said before is that the mind *is* the ground, it is the unknown.

K: The mind? Yes. But not this mind.

DB: In that case, it is not the same mind.

K: If I have been through all that and come to a point when I have to end all that, it is a new mind.

DB: That's clear. The mind is its content, and the content is knowledge, and without that knowledge, it is a new mind.

The sixth dialogue takes place after an interval of a weekend, and during that period Bohm travelled to San Francisco where he met with a group of students and discussed what he had been talking about with Krishnamurti. He mentioned to them that Krishnamurti had said that insight has the capacity to affect or transform the very structure of the cells of the brain. The group had expressed considerable interest in this idea, but Bohm felt unable to develop it, and he asks Krishnamurti to go into it more fully.

The dialogue unfolds by means of an examination of the difference between thought and insight, and what relationship each has with the other. The first major distinction between the two follows from Krishnamurti's observation that thought is matter. His view is that thought is the action or response of memory, based on knowledge and experience stored up in the brain cells as a form of matter. Bohm introduces an interesting and useful refinement of this view by distinguishing between matter per se and a material process, a process that takes place within matter. He points out that water, for example, consists of matter, but that waves within water are not matter itself, but rather a process, a material process. Krishnamurti agrees that it would be more accurate to refer to thought as a material process, rather than matter, and that becomes the language they use in what follows.

Insight, by contrast, is neither matter nor a material process; it is instantaneous, a flash of light, a form of pure perception. Bohm points out that it is not clear how something nonmaterial can have any effect upon a material process; and if it does not, how does thought become aware of or capture the light of insight? To complicate matters, Krishnamurti insists that insight occurs without a cause, material or otherwise; in other words, it is not the result of thought. Therefore, it would appear there is a one-way relationship between insight and thought: insight can affect thought, but thought cannot have any effect upon insight.

Krishnamurti maintains that insight does indeed have an effect upon the material process of thought; in fact, it brings about a kind of mutation in the brain cells. He adds that he is referring to "total insight," not the kind of partial insight that may occur to a scientist or an artist in the course of their work. Total insight represents a perception of "the total human activity," by which he evidently means to include the self and its role in consciousness. The ordinary mind functions in darkness, and the self is the center of darkness. Insight illuminates thought and the self and so dispels the darkness. Bohm asks whether such insight persists after it occurs, or whether it is like a flash of lightning, momentarily illuminating the landscape, which subsequently falls back into darkness. It is not like that, Krishnamurti declares: once the flash of insight occurs, its effect upon consciousness is pervasive and lasting.

In the course of reflecting upon these issues, Krishnamurti asks why insight is not the natural, normal function of everyone. He indirectly refers to himself as one for whom insight was present from childhood, naturally and without effort. If this can occur in one brain, why does it not occur in all brains? He seems genuinely puzzled by this question, and it carries over to become the point of departure for the following conversation.

The seventh dialogue is framed at the outset in terms of animal instincts. It is evidently instinctual to respond to hate with hatred. Is humanity acting largely or entirely in terms of animal instincts? Bohm suggests not only that this is the case, but also that the instincts are now intertwined with thought, which tends to exacerbate the overall situation. But the man who has insight does not fall into that pattern, according to Krishnamurti. His insight enables him not to respond to hate with hatred, but rather to act rationally, in a manner not dictated by instinct. Why is that not the general condition of mankind? Is the man with insight just an anomaly, almost unnatural by virtue of his independence from acting out of instinct?

Posing the issue in this manner leads to the question of whether there is a division of some kind between the man with insight and everyone else. By this means, division becomes a key element in this dialogue. The most basic division in consciousness originates in the self, whose inherent nature is to be divided from everything else. Other forms of division, such as those based upon religion or nationalism, are also ubiquitous throughout society. In fact, thought is inherently divisive and so generates darkness within the mind of the individual and in relationship to others.

But the ground has no division within it, and the mind that is in contact with the ground is similarly undivided. The insight that dispels the darkness of division generated by thought therefore opens the door to a state of mind in which no fundamental division exists of any kind. Most remarkably, according to Krishnamurti, there is then no psychological division between life and death. Of course the physical organism inevitably comes to an end, but that, he says, is a trivial matter. The ending of the psychological division between life and death must have an extraordinary effect upon the brain, he maintains, since it removes all the fear and anxiety commonly associated with death. The brain that lives without fear of death has undergone the essential equivalent of "a surgical operation."

The eighth dialogue is the last in the series that occurred over a period of three weeks in Ojai, and it brings this initial set of conversations to some degree of closure or resolution. The first two dialogues introduced the source of all energy and the ground, and the next five revolved in various ways around whether or how it is possible for any given listener to have a comparable insight and come into relationship with the ground. In the eighth dialogue, instead of asking what understanding the ordinary man can have of this material, Krishnamurti turns the issue around and asks what is the role or responsibility of the man with insight towards those who live in darkness.

> **K:** I think if we could find out the quality of a mind that has been through everything from beginning to the end—all that we have talked of in our recent discussions—that man's mind is entirely different, yet he is in the world. How does he look upon it?
>
> You have reached and come back—these are approximate terms—and I am an ordinary man, living in this world. So what is your relationship to me? Obviously none, because I am living in a world of darkness and you are not. So your relationship can only exist when I come out of it—when darkness ends.

Krishnamurti refers to the man with insight as "X," and the ordinary man as "Y." What relationship has X to Y? Of course X has to live in this world, live in society, but his relationship with society is rather superficial. X is not engaged in the process of becoming, the movement from what is to what should be. His mind is in touch with another kind of movement altogether, a movement without time, the movement that is the ground. And so society will inevitably realize that X is unusual or extraordinary: what will society do with him? Krishnamurti says society will either worship him, or kill him, or neglect him altogether.

If society neither worships nor kills him, how does X live or function in society? Does he need to acquire some skill in order to earn a livelihood? At first Krishnamurti argues that skill of any kind may be unnecessary. Bohm points out that even if X were to live in a cave, he would have to develop some rudimentary skill to acquire food; and to live in civilization, he would need at least the skill to drive a car and so on. Krishnamurti concedes this point, but he concludes that the role of X in society is to work to dispel the darkness in which others live. His role is to teach, to write, and to speak, and by that means he will earn his livelihood. "What's wrong with it?" he asks.

> **DB:** It's perfectly all right as long as it works. Of course, if there were a lot of people like X, there would have to be some limit.

> **K:** No, sir. What would happen if there were lots of people like X?

DB: That is an interesting question. I think there would be something revolutionary.

K: That's just it.

DB: The whole framework would change.

K: That's just it. If there were lots of people like that, they would not be divided. That is the whole point, right?

DB: I think that even if ten or fifteen people were undivided, they would exert a force that has never been seen in our history.

K: Tremendous! That's right.

DB: Because I don't think it has ever happened, that ten people were undivided.

K: That is X's job in life. He says that is the only thing. A group of those ten Xs will bring a totally different kind of revolution. Right? Will society stand for that?

DB: They will have this extreme intelligence, and so they will find a way to do it, you see.

K: Of course.

DB: Society will stand for it, because they will be intelligent enough not to provoke society, and society will not react before it is too late.

K: Quite right. You are saying something which is actually happening.

But is that all, Krishnamurti asks. If his role is limited to that, it seems to him to be a rather small affair. X is in contact with something immense, something much greater than can be contained in such a role.

K: Suppose X is you, and you have an enormous field in which you operate, not merely teaching me but you have this extraordinary movement which is not of time. That is, you have this abounding energy, and you have reduced all that to teach me to come out of darkness. You follow what I mean?

Bohm asks why the ground needs to act through a particular man, rather than acting directly upon the consciousness of mankind. "Oh, yes,

that I can easily explain," Krishnamurti replies. "That's part of existence, like the stars." It is not the case that the ground "needs" X; but if
X exists, the ground will "use" him in the sense that it operates through
his mind. "X is doing something totally different to affect the consciousness of man."

Such a function may not manifest itself in any conspicuous way. The
action of the ground through X may not resemble any specific activity
ordinarily recognized by others. Nevertheless, by his very presence, X
must have an effect upon the consciousness of humanity, an effect that
supersedes and is independent of his role as one who writes and speaks.

> **K:** X has that immense intelligence, that energy, that something, and
> he must operate at a much greater level than one can possibly conceive.
> Which *must* affect the consciousness of those who are living in
> darkness. . . .
>
> So the ground is using him, let's call it; is employing him. . . . Why
> should he do anything? Except this?

> **DB:** Well, perhaps he does nothing.

> **K:** That very doing nothing may be the doing!

> **DB:** Well, in doing nothing, he makes possible the action of the
> ground.

> **K:** Yes.

> **DB:** In doing nothing which has any specified aim –

> **K:** That's right. No specified content which can be translated into
> human terms.

> **DB:** Yes, but still he is extremely active in doing nothing.

> **K:** Yes.

A little later, Krishnamurti returns to the prospect of a group of people
who share the insight of X:

> **K:** All right, let's leave the vastness and all that. X says, perhaps
> there will be ten people who will join the game, with this insight,

and that might affect society. It will not be communism, socialism, this or that. It might be totally different, based on intelligence and compassion.

DB: Well, if there were ten, they might find a way to spread this much more.

K: That's what I am trying to get at. . . .

DB: Are you saying that if the whole of mankind were to see this, that would be something different?

K: Oh, yes, of course! It would be paradise on earth.

Chapter Fourteen

THE ENDING OF TIME III

The next two dialogues in the *Ending of Time* series occurred several weeks later at Brockwood Park, the secondary school Krishnamurti founded in Hampshire, England. For anyone interested in penetrating the meaning of Krishnamurti's overall philosophy, these conversations are of pivotal importance. Gone are any references to the ground or the source of all energy; perhaps ironically, the reader or listener therefore feels on much more familiar and solid ground.

Previous dialogues in this series made repeated reference to psychological knowledge and psychological time, without pausing to examine these terms with care. One almost has the impression that Bohm may have been just hanging on, trying to keep up with Krishnamurti's more metaphysical observations, and therefore partially abdicated his role of clarifying terms as needed for the ordinary listener. Since the next two conversations take place on more familiar territory, Bohm is more conscientious about prompting Krishnamurti to elucidate the meaning of his language and observations.

In keeping with the broad perspective that characterizes the series of conversations, Krishnamurti opens up the ninth dialogue by inquiring about the human brain, considered from a holistic perspective, much as we might inquire about the elephant brain or the dolphin brain.

> **K:** We have a civilization that is highly cultivated and yet at the same time barbarous, with great selfishness clothed in all kinds of spiritual garb. . . . Man's brain has been evolving through millennia upon millennia, yet it has come to this divisive, destructive point, which we all know.
>
> So I am wondering whether the human brain—not a particular brain but the human brain—is deteriorating. Whether it is capable of

revival, renewal, or is just in a slow and steady decline. Or whether it is possible in one's lifetime to bring about in itself a total renewal from all this, a renewal that will be pristine, original, unpolluted.

After some clarification of the question, Bohm replies from the perspective of a scientist who might attempt to alter the structure or function of the brain from the outside.

DB: Some people who do biofeedback think they can influence the brain, connecting an instrument to the electrical potentials in the skull and being able to look at the result; you can also change your heartbeat and blood pressure and other things. These people have raised the hope that something could be done.

K: But they are not succeeding.

DB: They are not getting very far.

K: And we can't wait for these scientists and biofeedbackers—sorry!—to solve the problem. So what shall we do?

DB: The next question is whether the brain can be aware of its own structure.

K: Yes. That's the first question. Can the brain be aware of its own movement? And the other question is, can the brain not only be aware of its own movement but can the brain itself have enough energy to break all patterns and move out of them?

Bohm points out that science has discovered that the brain begins to shrink as it ages. He associates this shrinkage with mechanical activity, such as being engaged for many years in a routine job. This is a relatively recent development in evolutionary terms because "before man was organized into society, he was living close to nature, and it was not possible to live in a routine."

Krishnamurti suggests that knowledge itself may be a factor in the deterioration of the brain, and Bohm agrees, up to a point: "Yes, when it is repetitious and becomes mechanical." Krishnamurti persists in doubting the value of knowledge until Bohm forces him to clarify what he means.

K: I want to question the whole idea of having knowledge.

DB: But, again, it is not too clear, because we accept that we need some knowledge.

K: Of course, at a certain level.

DB: So it is not clear what kind of knowledge it is that you are questioning.

K: I am questioning the experience that leaves knowledge, that leaves a mark.

DB: Yes, but what kind of mark? A psychological mark?

K: Psychological, of course. . . .

DB: What do you mean by psychological knowledge? Knowledge about the mind, knowledge about myself?

K: Yes. Knowledge about myself and living in that knowledge and accumulating that knowledge.

DB: So if you keep on accumulating knowledge about yourself or about relationships—

K: Yes, about relationships.

DB: But one should see what it is about this knowledge that makes so much trouble.

K: If I have an image about someone, that knowledge is obviously going to impede our relationship. It becomes a pattern. . . . Can the brain, in psychological matters, be entirely free from this kind of knowledge?

As the dialogue develops, the accumulation of knowledge is contrasted with perception and immediate action from that perception. Krishnamurti suggests this is what is needed for the brain to break out of its pattern. The contrast between knowledge, which is bound by time to the past, and perception, which is immediate and therefore, in a sense, outside of time, precipitates an extended discussion of the meaning of psychological time. Because this concept is crucial for the entire series of dialogues, this passage does not lend itself to summarization.

DB: Perhaps we could discuss what it means to be free of time. You see, at first sight it sounds crazy, but, obviously, we all know that you don't mean that the clock stops.

K: Science fiction and all that!

DB: The point is, what does it really mean to be psychologically free of time?

K: That there is no tomorrow.

DB: But we know that there is tomorrow.

K: But psychologically—

DB: Can you describe better what you mean when you say "no tomorrow"?

K: What does it mean to be living in time? Let's take the other side first, because then we come to the other. What does it mean to live in time? Hope; thinking and living in the past, and acting from the knowledge of the past; images, illusions, prejudices—they are all an outcome of the past. All that is time, and that is producing chaos in the world.

Although Krishnamurti has begun to address the issue more fully, Bohm remains persistent, and he hammers his point home in an amusingly ironic fashion:

DB: Well, can we say that if we are not living psychologically in time, we may still order our actions by the watch? The thing that is puzzling is if somebody says, "I am not living in time, but I must keep an appointment." You see?

K: Of course. You can't sit here forever.

DB: So you say, I am looking at the watch, but I am not psychologically extending how I am going to feel in the next hour. . . .

It should be made clear why this necessarily produces suffering. You are saying that if you live in the field of time, suffering is inevitable.

K: Inevitable.

DB: Why?

K: It is simple. Time has built the ego, the "me," the image of me sustained by society, by parents, by education. All that is the result of time. And from there I act.

DB: Towards the future psychologically. That is, towards some future state of being.

K: Yes. Which means that the center is always becoming.

DB: Trying to become better.

K: Better, nobler. So all that, the constant endeavor to become something psychologically is a factor of time. . . .

DB: Are you saying that through time the self is set up, and then the self introduces division and conflict and so on? But that if there were no psychological time, then perhaps this entire structure would collapse, and something entirely different would happen?

K: That's it. That is what I am saying.

A little later in the dialogue, Bohm astutely brings out a relationship between time and the sense of individuality. Krishnamurti has made the point that psychological time is an illusion, and also that the ego or sense of self is illusory. Bohm shows the manner in which these two illusions are related to one another, and therefore helps illuminate them both.

DB: Time and separation as individuality are basically the same structure.

K: Of course.

DB: Although it is not obvious in the beginning. It might be worth discussing this. Why is psychological time the same illusion, the same structure as individuality? Individuality in the sense of being a person who is located here somewhere.

K: Located and divided.

DB: Divided from others. He extends out to some periphery; his domain extends out to some periphery, and also he has an identity which extends over time. He wouldn't regard himself as an individual if he said, "Today I am one person, tomorrow I am another." So it seems that we mean by "individual" somebody who is in time.

Finally, the conversation comes around to the point of departure. What will bring about a renewal or rejuvenation of the brain? Not surprisingly, the answer is insight.

K: We have said that perception is out of time, is seeing the whole nature of time. Which, to use a good old word, is to have an insight into the nature of time. If there is that insight, the very brain cells which are part of time break down. The brain cells mutate, bring about a change in themselves.

You may disagree; you may say, "Prove it." I say this is not a matter of proof; it is a matter of action! Do it, find out, test it. . . .

DB: Are you saying that this psychological content is a certain structure, physically, in the brain? That in order for this psychological content to exist, the brain over many years has made many connections of the cells, which constitute this content?

K: Quite, quite.

DB: And then there is a flash of insight, which sees all this, and that it is not necessary. Therefore all this begins to dissipate. Then whatever the brain does is something different.

The tenth dialogue in the series and the second one that took place at Brockwood Park begins from a new point of departure. Krishnamurti asks whether the mind or brain can not only be free from all illusion or self-deception, but "whether it can have its own order—an order not introduced by thought, or effort, or any endeavor to put things in their proper place. . . . Is there an order which is not man-made?"

This question plays to one of Bohm's many strengths. The concept of order is central to his work in physics, especially as it developed in his later years. The most fundamental and characteristic idea of the latter part of his scientific career was that of the "implicate order," and his most profound scientific work was *Wholeness and the Implicate Order*, published that very year. In the process of developing the concept of the implicate order, he reviewed in depth the various different forms of order, not only in the scientific field but in ordinary life. Although Krishnamurti posed an unusual question, Bohm was well equipped to address it.

He opens up the question by introducing several observations. If one is interested in an order that is not man-made, one may consider the order of nature, or even of the entire cosmos. According to the mathematician von Neumann, mathematics can be considered the study of the relationship of relationships, which Bohm interprets as "order working within the field of order itself, rather than working on some object." It may also be helpful to consider what is disorder, but Bohm maintains "it is not possible to give a coherent definition" of disorder, precisely because disorder is "inherently what violates order." However, within any given framework, something outside the framework may be construed as disorder. He elaborates this point by considering the case of cancer:

DB: If the body is not functioning rightly, even if cancer is growing, there is a certain order in the cancer cell; it is just growing according to a different pattern, which tends to break down the body. Nevertheless the whole thing has a certain kind of order.

K: Yes, yes.

DB: It has not violated the laws of nature, although relative to some context you could say it is disorder; because, if we are talking of the health of the body, then the cancer is called disorder. But in itself—

K: Cancer has its own order.

DB: Yes.

K: Quite. [Laughs.]

DB: Yes, but it is not compatible with the order of the growth of the body. . . . The whole point of order is not to have contradiction. That's the whole purpose of mathematics.

K: But the brain is in contradiction.

DB: Yes, in some way something has gone wrong. We said it took a wrong turn.

K: Yes, we have said that the brain took a wrong turn.

Against this background, Krishnamurti reframes his question as whether the brain can be free of any form of order which is "imposed or self-imposed." If it cannot, he maintains, "meditation has no meaning." This is a rather surprising development, but Bohm moves with it and extends it. If the brain cannot free itself from all impositions and patterns, "probably life has no meaning."

K: If it goes on as it has done, indefinitely, for millennia, life has no meaning. But to find out if it has a meaning at all—which I think there is a meaning—must the brain be totally free of all this?

DB: Well, what is the source of what we call disorder? It is almost like a cancer going on inside the brain, moving in a way which is not compatible with the health of the brain.

K: Yes.

DB: It grows as time goes on.

K: Accretion.

DB: Accretion, from one generation to another.

K: Each generation repeats the same pattern.

DB: It tends to accumulate through tradition with every generation. It's almost the same question as, how are we going to stop these cancer cells from taking over?

K: Yes, that's what I want to get at. How is this set, accumulated, generation-after-generation pattern to end, to be broken through? That is the real question at the back of my mind.

As the conversation develops, it emerges that the "accumulation" consists of the past, the psychological knowledge which has developed over time and which represents the content of the self. It contains all the background of memories about one's family, the society or nation in which one lives, religious traditions, as well as the individual experiences that collectively form the content of the ego. Krishnamurti acknowledges that to give up all that, especially with no promise of any reward in return, must be extraordinarily difficult.

K: Am I willing to face absolute emptiness?

DB: What will you tell somebody who is not willing, or feels unable, to face this?

K: I am not bothered. If somebody says, "I can't do all this nonsense," I say, "Well, carry on."

But suppose I am willing to let my past go completely. Which means there is no effort or reward or punishment, no carrot, nothing. And the brain is willing to face this extraordinary and totally new state to it, of existing in a state of nothingness. That is appallingly frightening.

But the individual who has insight into the nature of the past will by virtue of that insight be free of the past, and therefore,

K: . . . the brain is willing to live in nothingness. . . . Which means, there isn't a thing that thought has put there. There is no movement of thought, except for technical thought, knowledge, which has its own place. But we are talking of the psychological state of mind where there is no movement of thought. There is absolutely nothing.

DB: Yes, and perhaps no sense of the existence of an entity inside.

K: Absolutely, absolutely, of course. The existence of the entity is the bundle of memories, the past.

DB: But that existence is not only thought thinking about it, but also the feeling that it is there, inside. You get a sort of feeling.

K: Inside, yes. There is no being. There is nothing.

The conversation concludes in a rather remarkable fashion. Krishnamurti returns to the question of order, an order that is not man-made, but he does so now in the context of a mind that is in a state of meditation. Such meditation must be "totally uninvited, without conscious intention," but it represents the culmination of the process of insight into the past. Moreover, it leads to an unexpected observation about the state of mind, as it were, of the cosmos itself.

> **K:** For the man who is becoming or being, meditation has no meaning whatsoever. That is a tremendous statement. Now, when there is this not-being, or not-becoming, what is meditation? . . . Would you say—I hope this doesn't sound silly—that the universe, the cosmic order, is in meditation?

> **DB:** Well, if it is alive, then we would have to look at it that way.

> **K:** No, no. It is in a state of meditation. I think that is right. I stick to that. . . . The sunrise and sunset is in order. All the stars, the planets— the whole thing is in perfect order.

This leads to the question whether the universe is based on time. Bohm suggests it is not, although he acknowledges that is not the way science regards it: "Science itself has put time into a fundamental position." But time is the product of thought.

> **DB:** Thought has entangled the brain in time.

> **K:** All right. Can that entanglement be unraveled, freed, so that the universe is the mind? You follow? If the universe is not of time, can the mind, which has been entangled in time, unravel itself and so *be* the universe? You follow what I am trying to say?

> **DB:** Yes.

> **K:** That is order!

> **DB:** That is order. Now, would you say that is meditation?

> **K:** That is it. I would call that meditation. Not in the ordinary dictionary sense, but a state of meditation in which there is no element of the past. . . . Then life has an extraordinary meaning, full of compassion.

Chapter Fifteen

THE ENDING OF TIME IV

The final five dialogues in the series occurred more than three months after the initial ten. They were again held at Brockwood Park, and they took place over a period of two weeks. In spite of the lapse of time, these conversations blend seamlessly with the previous ones. Collectively, all fifteen conversations form a kind of mosaic, an arrangement of topics that is not strictly logical or consecutive, but rather follows an internal dynamic of its own, with topics sometimes overlapping, but also often breaking new ground. The last five dialogues, moreover, are sufficiently coherent with one another that they can be treated as a single unit, especially in the context of the material that has already been explored.

Krishnamurti initiates the eleventh conversation with a brief summary of all that has gone before.

K: I think we asked, if I remember rightly, what is the origin of this, of all human movement. Is there an original source, a ground—that's right, sir?

DB: That's right.

K: —a ground from which all this sprang—nature, man, the whole universe? Was it bound by time? Was it in itself complete order, and beyond which there is nothing more?

And, Dr. Bohm reminded me yesterday, we talked about order, whether the universe is based on time at all, and whether man can ever comprehend and live in that supreme order.

We wanted to investigate, not merely intellectually, but profoundly, how to comprehend or live from that ground, move from that ground, the ground that is timeless. There is nothing beyond it. And I think we better begin from there.

DB: Begin from the ground. [Laughs.]

K: Sir, I don't know if you would agree, as a scientist of eminence, whether there is such a ground, whether man can ever comprehend it, live in it—live in the sense, not as something he, living in it—but that itself, living. And whether we can, as human beings, come to that?

The conversation continues to unfold in terms of order, whether man-made or otherwise. Bohm suggests that science has explored order in the physical universe, and has implicitly attempted to find a ground of the universe by studying matter. But this approach has not brought any sense of meaning to life. Krishnamurti points out that nature is always in order, even though it may not seem so from a human perspective. The eruption of a volcano is order, as is the killing of a deer by a tiger. He maintains that "any serious man" can bring order into his own life, and to do so is necessary because

K: . . . society as it is is disintegrating and destructive, and it destroys human beings. It's a machine that is destructive in itself. And if a human being is caught in that, it destroys him. And any intelligent human being says, "I must *do* something."

This is not the level of order that really interests him, however. It is merely man-made order as a response to man-made disorder. Bohm elaborates on this point with an amusing example: "The order we see in this room, the microphone, the TV, is man-made; and also the disorder, the terrible programs put on the television. [Laughs.]" But the kind of order Krishnamurti envisions is of another dimension altogether, and it brings about a new quality of mind.

K: Can the mind, conditioned by man, uncondition itself so completely that it's no longer man-made? Can the man-made mind liberate itself completely from itself?

DB: That is the question.

K: That is the question.

DB: Of course that's a somewhat paradoxical question.

K: Of course it's paradoxical; but it's actual, it is so.

One of the new elements that appears in the final dialogues is the distinction between the particular and the general. This distinction may seem rather abstract, but it is woven throughout the remaining exploration. The mind of any given individual is a particular mind, while the psychological features that are common to all is the general mind. One moment may be considered a particular time, whereas time in general encompasses the whole of the past, present, and future. Other similar examples are not difficult to discover.

Bohm and Krishnamurti suggest that the process of breaking free from the pattern of the man-made mind begins with the individual's awareness of his own particular mind, and moves from there to the recognition that his own mind is of the same form or structure as the mind of man in general. All the activity of the man-made mind, whether particular or general, occurs within a border, a certain limited field, which is essentially the field of knowledge, of what is known. This represents one kind of movement. But insight is also a kind of movement, one of another character altogether. It is a movement "beyond matter, a movement of energy." The man-made mind can expand and contract,

> **K:** . . . but the boundary is very, very limited, definite. Now, it is always moving within that limitation. Can it die away from that?
>
> **DB:** That's the point; that's another kind of movement. It's kind of in another dimension, I think you've said.
>
> **K:** Yes. And we say it is possible through insight, which is also a movement, a totally different kind of movement.
>
> **DB:** Yes, but then we say *that* movement does not originate in the individual nor in the general mind.
>
> **K:** Yes. It is not the insight of the particular or the general. We are then stating something outrageous.

DB: That violates most of the sort of logic that people use. Either the particular or the general should cover everything, in terms of ordinary logic.

Krishnamurti addresses this dilemma in terms of the nature of thought. Thought is the movement that is common to both the particular mind and the general mind. Since insight is not of the nature of thought, it is something outside both the particular and the general. As a result of insight, he maintains, "that movement which thought has created also comes to an end. Therefore time comes to an end."

Bohm hesitates here and says this represents "a jump." He acknowledges that there is a close connection between thought and time, but the precise relationship requires clarification.

K: Thought is time. . . . Thought is based on time; thought is the outcome of time.

DB: Yes, but then does that mean that time exists beyond thought? If you say thought is based on time, then time is more fundamental than thought. Is that what you want to say?

K: Yes. Yes. . . .

DB: Would we say that physically or in the cosmos time has a significance apart from thought?

K: Physically, yes.

DB: So then we're saying in the mind or psychologically.

K: Psychologically. As long as there is psychological accumulation as knowledge, as the "me," and so on, there is time. . . . So we're saying thought is time.

DB: Or time is thought.

K: Yes.

DB: The movement of time is thought—psychological time.

K: Psychological accumulation is thought and time.

DB: We're saying we happen to have two words when really we only need one.

K: One word. That's right.

DB: Because we have two words, we look for two different things.

K: Yes. There is only one movement, which is time and thought.

It should be clear that the accumulation Krishnamurti is referring to consists of all the ideas, images, memories, and other forms of knowledge that collectively comprise the sense of self. The aggregation of these images, he maintains, is inevitably the source of conflict. Bohm takes care to bring this point out:

DB: Can we make it clear why it does harm in the psychological realm?

K: Let's think it out. What is the harm in accumulating, psychologically? It divides.

DB: What does it divide?

K: The very nature of accumulation brings about a division between you and me and so on.

DB: Could we make that clear, because it is a crucial point? . . .

K: I have accumulated psychologically as a Hindu; another has accumulated as a Muslim. There are thousands of divisions. Therefore accumulation in its very nature divides people, and therefore creates conflict.

DB: Each person accumulates in his particular way. You cannot make a common way of accumulating. . . . Any attempt to accumulate will divide.

Bohm points out that knowledge of this kind carries a sense of necessity, a significance far beyond other forms of knowledge. "Knowledge about the nation to which you belong seems to have immense significance." Moreover, this form of knowledge is not even commonly recognized as being knowledge. We ordinarily consider knowledge to have an essentially passive character, as if it is merely something available to us, which we can pick up and use, or not, as we please. But knowledge about the self has another quality. It is "experienced as an entity which seems not to be knowledge but some real thing."

DB: I think the general difficulty is that knowledge is not just sitting there as a form of information but is extremely active, meeting and shaping every moment . . . although people don't generally think of it that way. They think it is just sitting there.

K: It is waiting.

DB: Waiting to act, you see. And whatever we try to do about it, knowledge is already acting. By the time we realize that this is the problem, it has already acted. . . .

And so it creates a state of the body which seems the very being of the self. And now the person doesn't experience it as mere knowledge. He feels something very powerful which doesn't seem to be knowledge.

This way in which the self is experienced is part of the general consciousness of humanity, but it is always experienced as a particular self, something that each individual considers unique. There is a deep irony in that what each person considers most special—his or her own individuality—is in fact the most common, fundamental feature of humanity. Bohm illuminates this point with an analogy drawn from science. The question has arisen whether love, properly understood, is ever something personal, in the sense of being confined to one individual's feeling for another.

DB: Perhaps we can see that love is not personal. Love does not belong to anybody, any more than any other quality does.

K: Earth is not English earth or French earth. Earth is earth!

DB: Yes, I was thinking of an example from chemistry: If a scientist or chemist is studying an element such as sodium, it's not that he's studying his sodium and somebody else is studying *his* and they somehow compare notes.

K: Quite. Sodium is sodium.

DB: Sodium is sodium universally. So we have to say that love is love universally.

K: Yes, but, you see, my mind refuses to see that, because I am so terribly personal, terribly "me and my problems" and all that. I refuse to let that go. When you say sodium is sodium, it is very simple; I can see that. But when you say to me that grief is common to all of us—

DB: It's the same grief.

K: Sodium is grief! [Laughs.]

DB: This can't be done with time. But, you see, it took quite a while for mankind to realize that sodium is sodium.

As this exchange suggests, Krishnamurti had introduced the element of love into the dialogue as representing an essential ingredient in breaking down the deeply ingrained patterns of the man-made mind. He hesitated to use that word because it has been made common, even somewhat vulgar at times, in its ordinary applications; but if those distortions could be removed, love perhaps represents the kind of energy necessary to precipitate insight. Compassion and care are roughly equivalent to the meaning he has in mind, and this kind of love is inseparable from intelligence.

In the final dialogues, Krishnamurti repeatedly raises the metaphor of a solid, blank wall, an enormous wall within which the man-made mind functions, a wall that seems insurmountable. What can dissolve this wall, or enable someone to break through it?

K: What is there that can be communicated, which will break through the wall that human beings have built for themselves? Is it love? That word has become corrupted, loaded, dirty. But cleansing that word, is love the factor that will break through all the clever, analytical approach? Is love the element that is lacking?

DB: Well, we have to discuss it; perhaps people are somewhat chary of that word. . . .

K: That is why I said it is rather a risky word.

DB: We were saying the other day that love contains intelligence.

K: Of course.

DB: Which is care as well; we mean by love that energy which also contains intelligence and care—all that.

In the last dialogue in the series, Krishnamurti begins by introducing a new factor, the tendency to think always in terms of problems to be solved. "We have cultivated a mind that can solve almost any technological problem, but apparently human problems have never been solved. . . . The whole of human existence has become a vast, complex problem." He suggests that it is possible to live another way entirely, such that every issue or challenge that arises is met and addressed immediately, and never allowed to linger as a problem.

K: You see, personally, I refuse to have problems.

DB: Somebody might argue with you about that and say, you might be challenged with something.

K: It's not a problem. I was challenged the other day about something very, very serious.

DB: Then it is a matter of clarification. Part of the difficulty is clarification of the language.

K: Not only of language, it's a question of relationship and action. A certain problem arose the other day which involved lots of people, and so on. And a certain action had to be taken. But to me personally it was not a problem.

DB: We have to make it clear what you mean, because without an example, I don't know.

K: I mean by a problem something that has to be resolved, something you worry about; something you are endlessly concerned with—questioning, doubting and uncertain; and you take some kind of action at the end which you will regret.

Krishnamurti maintains that what distinguishes a mind beset by problems from one that refuses to entertain or indulge any problem is the factor of attention. The nature of attention and inattention therefore occupies center stage as the series of dialogues approaches its conclusion. As the exploration unfolds, attention becomes indistinguishable from intelligence and love, and together these become the elements that will liberate the man-made mind from the "nice, cultured prison" in which it is confined.

K: Where there is attention, there is no problem. Where there is inattention, everything arises. Now, without making attention into a problem, what do we mean by it? So that I understand it. Not verbally, not intellectually, but deeply, in my blood, the nature of attention in which no problem can ever exist.

Obviously attention is not concentration. It is not an endeavor, an experience, a struggle to be attentive. But you show me the nature of attention, which is that when there is attention, there is no center from which "I" attend. . . . I feel that attention is the real solution to all this—a mind which is really attentive, which has understood the nature of inattention and moves away from it.

DB: But first, what is the nature of inattention?

K: Indolence, negligence, self-concern, self-contradiction—all that is the nature of inattention.

DB: Yes. You see, a person who has self-concern may feel that he is attending to the concerns of himself. See, he feels, I have got problems, and I am attending to them.

K: Ah—I see, you are using that word—quite, quite. Yes. If there is self-contradiction in me, and I pay attention to it in order not to be self-contradictory, that is not attention.

DB: But can we make this clear, because ordinarily one might think that this is attention.

K: No, it is not. It is merely a process of thought, which says, "I am this; I must be that."

DB: So you are saying that this attempt to become is not attention.

K: That's right. Because the psychological becoming breeds inattention.

That is the root of it. To end becoming. . . .

Psychologically, becoming has been the curse of all this. A poor man wants to be rich, and the rich man wants to be richer; it is all the time this movement of becoming, both outwardly and inwardly. And though it brings a great deal of pain and sometimes pleasure, this sense of becoming, fulfilling, achieving psychologically, has made my life into all that it is.

As the final dialogue comes to a close, Krishnamurti returns to the original point of departure.

K: We have asked whether man has taken a wrong turning and entered into a valley where there is no escape. That can't be so, sir, that is too depressing, too appalling.

DB: The mere fact that it is appalling does not make it untrue. I think you would have to give some stronger reason why you feel that to be untrue. Do you perceive in human nature some possibility of a real change?

K: Of course, sir. Otherwise—

DB: It would be meaningless.

K: We'd be monkeys, machines! . . . What is needed is to make the mind go very, very deeply into itself. . . .

From the particular move to the general. From the general move still deeper, and there perhaps is the purity of that thing called compassion, love, and intelligence. But that means giving your mind to this, your heart; your whole being must be involved in this.

We have gone on now for a long—have we reached somewhere?

DB: Possibly so, yes.

K: I think so.

It is a remarkably modest conclusion, in view of all the territory that the two men have traversed. It is rather as if they had climbed all the mountains in the Himalayas, and at the end of it one turns to the other and says, "Well, have we gotten anywhere?" And yet, in another sense, this conclusion is fitting, well within the spirit of the dialogue as a whole. As profound and penetrating as it is, the dialogue is conducted in a spirit that is modest, tentative, exploratory, and with complete humility. There is no sense of achievement or superiority, and no psychological becoming. The two men are simply companions, on a journey together without beginning or end, on a road that is paved with intelligence and love.

Chapter Sixteen

CONFRONTATION

In addition to their highly disparate backgrounds, Krishnamurti and Bohm exhibited substantial differences in personality. In their dialogues together, these differences were apparent, but they were secondary to the overall effect of harmony and compatibility. Outside the immediate context of their interaction with one another, the differences were sharper and may ultimately have contributed to a kind of crisis in their relationship. Some general observations about their working relationship and the way each man engaged with others may provide some context in which to consider the significance of the confrontation that eventually occurred.

Even with the benefit of hindsight, it is not easy to assess the relative contributions of Krishnamurti and Bohm to the overall work they were engaged in. Krishnamurti once asked me how I regarded this issue. I can't recall the terms in which he put it, but the meaning of his question was clear. I said that one was like the sun and the other like the moon— implying that both were exceptional and beautiful in their own right, but that one was the reflection of the other. To my surprise, Krishnamurti asked me to clarify which was which, and I said that he was the sun and Bohm was the moon. This seemed to satisfy him, and I have no doubt today that it is largely correct, although the metaphor does not do justice to Bohm, whose light was by no means merely a reflection of Krishnamurti or anyone else.

Moreover, it must be admitted that Bohm had certain talents that escaped Krishnamurti. Among other things, he was more verbally adept, more articulate. In addition, mired as he was within the structure of consciousness to which most of us are prey, he was able to see much better than Krishnamurti what points or issues might be confusing to most listeners. Bohm was one of us, not a man "on the other side of the river," in the metaphor that the two men employed in one of their conversations. No matter how skillful he may have been in articulating the contours of consciousness, Bohm was evidently not able himself to make that transition into another way of being.

In his interactions with friends and associates, Bohm displayed certain characteristics that remained constant throughout his life. Perhaps the foremost of these was his indefatigable appetite for serious conversation. It seemed as though the process of dialogue was the very means by which he worked out new ideas and arrived at fresh insights. To be sure, he also often walked alone and meditated upon the issues that interested him, not only in physics, but in consciousness and human nature. But in his conversations with Joseph Weinberg, at the home of the Kahlers in Princeton, and with many others (including my own interactions with him), Bohm's capacity for sustained dialogue was unparalleled.

Also noteworthy was his pure and unadulterated interest in science and human nature, uncorrupted by motives of profit or self-interest. He was not immune to detecting such motives in others, and sometimes he complained bitterly about them in letters to close friends. But he himself was driven by his fascination with truth. I sometimes tried to persuade him to write a popularization of his findings in quantum physics for a general audience—not only for his own financial well-being but for the public at large—but he refused. Only the ongoing process of discovery seemed to motivate him.

In his more casual interactions with people, Bohm was rather shy but always courteous and accommodating. He exuded a sense of good will. Also not to be overlooked was his fine sense of humor. He had a fondness not only for wordplay but for all the ironies of life and human nature. His intense devotion to serious issues was leavened, in other words, with modesty and an abiding awareness of the foibles and limitations of himself and others. For these reasons, Bohm was a wonderful companion for those who shared his passions. His interest in physics and philosophy was not confined to an abstract arena but permeated every aspect of his life. Perhaps the word that describes him best is authenticity; he was a man devoted to truth, no matter what the cost in personal or professional currency.

Interwoven with his warmth and authenticity, an element of vulnerability was also evident in Bohm's psychological make-up. At times he seemed almost fragile, notwithstanding his formidable intellect and powers of perception. It is difficult not to conclude that his intense interest in the psychological field may have been motivated in part by his awareness of his own susceptibility to anxiety or insecurity of various kinds.

In his conduct of group meetings, Bohm exhibited a persona very different from that of Krishnamurti. The latter had a tendency to be somewhat austere, even severe at times, in his interactions with the participants, as he strove to make a point or to elicit some degree of understanding. Bohm, by contrast, was like a shy and friendly uncle, endlessly tolerant of all the imperfections in the family. It was said by some who knew them both that Krishnamurti answered every question with "no," whereas Bohm answered every question with "yes."

I sometimes complained privately to Krishnamurti about the quality of his interactions with teachers and staff. I said he appeared to be angry at times when the participants in his meetings could not keep up with him or offer satisfactory answers to his questions. He said, no, he was not angry, he just wanted to *move*. On another occasion, he told me, "I cannot tame myself." Once I went so far as to directly contrast his style of interaction with that of Bohm. I said that Bohm was willing to explain everything, and I urged Krishnamurti to do the same. He reacted with what appeared to be scorn. "Is that what you want—explanations?" he replied. I chose not to press the matter further.

In his letters to Fritz Wilhelm in 1979 and 1980, Bohm expressed a somewhat similar set of concerns about the quality of Krishnamurti's interactions with teachers and members of staff at his schools. Bohm complained that Krishnamurti seemed rather dismissive of the efforts of everyone to understand what he was saying. He felt that this attitude engendered a sense of fear and uncertainty among the teachers and staff that was not conducive to the intention of the schools.

Had I not had other evidence available to consider, I probably would have sympathized with Bohm's complaint. However, after I left Oak Grove in 1988, I was intensely curious to listen again to the group meetings Krishnamurti had conducted and try to plumb the depth of their meaning. Those meetings had been recorded on high quality equipment, and, as the former director of the school, the audiotapes were made available to me. I created transcripts of these recordings with meticulous care. Most of the transcripts of Krishnamurti's talks and dialogues are edited to one degree or another, but I wanted to create transcripts that were verbatim, entirely faithful to the recorded words. Not a single syllable should differ, in my view, between what was heard on the recording and what appeared on the printed page. This was a labor of love, but it was very laborious. It required three or four hours of transcription for every hour of actual dialogue. In the end, I produced three volumes of these dialogues, encompassing fourteen meetings in all.

One of the things that struck me most forcefully in this endeavor was the courteous and accommodating manner of Krishnamurti's participation. The severe and at times impatient individual that I had anticipated listening to was rarely to be heard. On the contrary, his patience and abiding sense of good will were almost always on display, no matter how confused or misguided were the comments he had to deal with. I reflected at length upon the discrepancy between how I had perceived his manner when I was physically present in these meetings, and how he came across to me when I was transcribing the conversations from the comfort and security of the office in my home, many years later. There was finally only one explanation that made any sense. There was something about the quality of Krishnamurti's immediate presence that evoked a hyper-sensitivity to his responses among those interacting with him. An uncanny degree of order, presence, and acute awareness about him simply defied description, and was unlike anything one had observed before. This engendered in turn an acute reaction to the slightest expression of disapproval on his part. If he were to wince slightly at someone's comment, or pass his hand briefly over his eyes, or respond with any degree of sharpness in his voice, it felt like thunder and lightning.

I can only surmise that a somewhat similar reaction was taking place in Bohm when he wrote to Wilhelm. If so, it stands to reason that a much more pronounced reaction might well have occurred if Krishnamurti were to confront Bohm directly about the quality of his understanding of Krishnamurti's work. Krishnamurti often emphasized that a merely verbal, intellectual understanding was insufficient in and of itself; a direct and immediate perception was required, something that would actually transform the nature and structure of consciousness. After two decades of their mutual collaboration, Krishnamurti must have begun to suspect that Bohm's understanding of his work was more of an intellectual nature rather than the deeper perception that would precipitate transformation.

In 1981, at the age of 62, Bohm suffered a heart attack that resulted in multiple bypass surgery. At the time the surgery occurred, the outcome was not clear. Krishnamurti met with him in the days before and attempted to calm him and to impart a healing energy. The surgery was difficult, however, and even after he recovered, Bohm remained somewhat preoccupied with his health. In addition, as often occurs with patients who undergo heart surgery, there may have been some other psychological effects, including depression or simply a lack of confidence or joie de vivre. In any case, I was told by a reliable source some years later that Krishnamurti remarked at one point that he was no longer able to discuss with Bohm as he had done previously.

Nevertheless, he did recover sufficiently for Krishnamurti to agree to conduct another pair of videotaped conversations with him. These occurred in 1983 and were the last of the recorded dialogues featuring the two men alone together. These conversations were held at Brockwood Park and were published under the title *The Future of Humanity*. If *The Ending of Time* began with Krishnamurti peering into the evolutionary past and wondering whether mankind had taken "a wrong turn," *The Future of Humanity* looks forward with a somewhat similar concern. In his preface to this volume, Bohm writes as follows:

> The starting point for our discussions was the question: "What is the future of humanity?" This question is now of vital concern to everyone, because modern science and technology are clearly seen to have opened up immense possibilities of destruction. It soon became clear as we talked together that the ultimate origin of this situation is in the generally confused mentality of mankind, which has not changed

basically in this respect throughout the whole of recorded history and probably for much longer than this. Evidently, it was essential to inquire deeply into the root of this difficulty if there is ever to be a possibility that humanity will be diverted from its present very dangerous course.

These dialogues constitute a serious inquiry into this problem, and as they proceeded, many of the basic points of Krishnamurti's teachings emerged. Thus, the question of the future of humanity seems, at first sight, to imply that a solution must involve time in a fundamental way. Yet, as Krishnamurti points out, psychological time, or "becoming," is the very source of the destructive current that is putting the future of humanity at risk. To question time in this way, however, is to question the adequacy of knowledge and thought as a means of dealing with this problem.

But if knowledge and thought are not adequate, what is it that is actually required? This led in turn to the question of whether mind is limited by the brain of mankind, with all the knowledge that it has accumulated over the ages. This knowledge, which now conditions us deeply, has produced what is, in effect, an irrational and self-destructive program in which the brain seems to be helplessly caught up.

If mind is limited by such a state of the brain, then the future of humanity must be very grim indeed. Krishnamurti does not, however, regard these limitations as inevitable. Rather, he emphasizes that mind is essentially free of the distorting bias that is inherent in the conditioning of the brain, and that through insight arising in proper undirected attention without a center, it can change the cells of the brain and remove the destructive conditioning.

If this is so, then it is crucially important that there be this kind of attention, and that we give to this question the same intensity of energy that we generally give to other activities of life that are really of vital interest to us.

Although this pair of dialogues is a fine example of their mutual collaboration, the conversations turned out to be a prelude to a crisis in the relationship between the two men. The details are not entirely clear, but evidently Krishnamurti confronted Bohm, less than a year later, and challenged him regarding the depth of his understanding. Such an interpretation is supported by remarks recorded by Mary Zimbalist in her memoirs. She recounts a conversation that occurred shortly after Bohm's surgery in which Krishnamurti declared his intention to urge him to leave his work in physics and devote himself exclusively to psychological inquiry. Several factors probably entered into Krishnamurti's decision to finally take this step in 1984. No doubt he was acutely aware of his own mortality—in fact he died less than two years later. Who could carry on his work if not a man like Bohm? And yet Bohm was still wedded to his scientific career, and no matter how much time he devoted to understanding and articulating psychological issues, physics was still his day job, and he had no real intention of giving it up.

In addition, Krishnamurti could not help but notice certain tendencies in Bohm that ran somewhat counter to a deep understanding of his work. Among these was his reliance or dependence on his wife, Saral. Fundamental to Krishnamurti's philosophy was that psychological freedom entails freedom from attachment to any person or idea or ideal. How could Bohm be so familiar with Krishnamurti's work, and so adept at expressing it, often in novel ways, and yet remain caught in conventional traps of thought and feeling?

Whatever the nature of the confrontation that occurred, it was evidently deeply disturbing to Bohm. If it were difficult to accept the slightest indication of disapproval from Krishnamurti during the course of meetings and dialogues, this more direct evaluation or criticism must have been much more threatening. According to his biographer, Bohm began to take anti-depressant medication after this event, and whether he ever fully recovered from it is not clear. He continued to produce important work in the scientific and philosophical fields, but his psychological stability—rather than being enhanced, as Krishnamurti must have hoped—evidently took a turn for the worse, as events later in his life made manifest. Both his valuable work and his later instability are explored in the chapters that follow.

Chapter Seventeen

THOUGHT AS A SYSTEM

Krishnamurti died of pancreatic cancer at the age of 90 in February 1986, in Ojai, which he had considered his primary home since 1922. He emphasized on numerous occasions that no one was authorized to speak on his behalf or assume his mantle after he was gone. He wanted to make certain that there would be no priests to follow him, interpreting and distorting his message for the future. Nevertheless, at the time of his death, it was clear to many that Bohm was the individual who had the deepest perception of the meaning of Krishnamurti's work. As a result, although he was not in any sense Krishnamurti's spokesman or interpreter, it fell to Bohm to continue to articulate a similar understanding of consciousness.

Although he was not a successor to Krishnamurti, a sufficient number of people were impressed with Bohm's observations in the psychological field to support his annual six-week trip from England to Ojai for several years following Krishnamurti's death. A few of his closest friends in Ojai organized weekend seminars, attended by forty or fifty individuals, with fees sufficient to cover the Bohms' travel expenses. The Krishnamurti Foundation of America kindly provided them with living quarters while they were in Ojai. The apartment in which they stayed, less than 100 yards from Krishnamurti's Pine Cottage, eventually came to be known as the Bohm flat.

These seminars were recorded and transcribed and are available through UMI Dissertation Services. One seminar in particular seemed to rise above the others in its clarity and focus, and it was brought out in book form by Routledge, the publisher of most of Bohm's books. *Thought as a System* represents perhaps the most sustained and penetrating examination of the essential nature of thought in all the work of Krishnamurti and Bohm. Both men had a tendency to weave their observations about thought into a larger landscape, but in this volume, thought is pinned down, as it were, and examined at length on its own terms.

Bohm begins the seminar by reflecting upon the overall state of the world. He emphasizes the endemic national and religious divisions, the frequent wars, the seemingly inexorable deterioration of the environment, as well as the global economic situation—extreme poverty side by side with fabulous wealth, and economic growth ultimately the enemy of environmental stability. He suggests there is a common source to all these problems. We use thought in an effort to solve them piecemeal, but Bohm asks us to consider that thought itself may be inadvertently the source of these problems. The instrument that we consider to be our servant, and indeed the means of our very survival, may in fact be the underlying factor that is contributing to and even causing all these problems in the first place.

Bohm recognizes that this view goes against conventional wisdom or what is taken for common sense. Thought seems rather ephemeral and entirely in the service of our intentions and understanding. It appears to us that thought merely reports what is the state of affairs in the world around us, as well as inwardly. Thought is our ubiquitous tool for resolving every issue—scientific, technological, economic, personal, and so on. How could so useful a tool be the very source of the problems we are trying to solve?

> We can use the analogy of a stream, where people are pouring pollution upstream at the same time they are trying to remove it downstream. But as they remove it they may be adding more pollution of a different kind.
>
> What is the source of all this trouble? . . . I'm saying that the source is basically in thought. Many people would think that such a statement is crazy, because thought is the one thing we have with which to solve our problems. . . . It's like going to the doctor and having him make you ill. . . .
>
> I'm saying the reason we don't see the source of our problems is that the means by which we try to solve them are the source. That may seem strange to somebody who hears it for the first time, because our

whole culture prides itself on thought as its highest achievement. I'm not suggesting that the achievements of thought are negligible; there are very great achievements in technology, in culture and in various other ways. But there is another side to it which is leading to our destruction, and we have to look at that.

Bohm emphasizes that thought contains implicit assumptions about itself. Thought considers itself to be a servant, an agent on behalf of the ego, the self, the thinker. In fact, however, thought is participatory in the manner in which it reports upon the world. Thought introduces into our perception of the world distinctions which are not necessary or faithful to actual reality. One conspicuous example of this process is the boundary between nations. Thought is responsible for creating these boundaries; but, once created, the boundaries seem to us real, inevitable, and present of their own accord.

Thought introduces in addition the fiction that within the boundaries of a nation, the inhabitants are essentially unified by allegiance to the nation-state. But in fact the members of the nation are riven by numerous conflicts and divisions. So both the separation from all other people in the world, as well as the notion that the members of the nation are one, are images introduced by thought into our perception of reality. In short, while thought considers itself to be the impartial reporter of events, it is actually participating in the construction of the reality upon which it is reporting. Thought functions by making representations of the world, but "thought is affecting what you see. The representation enters into the perception. . . . That is crucial. And it is a tremendous source of illusion if we once lose track of the fact that this is happening."

Thought introduces false distinctions internally, psychologically, as well. It considers itself to be separate from emotion, but the two are intimately interconnected: thought engenders emotion, and emotion engenders thought. They are reflections of one another, intrinsically coupled, even while thought contains the assumption that it is separate, above and beyond the emotions that it observes and analyzes.

Suppose that somebody keeps you waiting for a couple of hours. You can get angry, thinking: "What does he mean treating me like this? He has no concern, no consideration for me." . . . By thinking that way you can get very angry. Then if he comes and explains that the train was late, the anger goes. This shows that the emotion was influenced by thought. By changing your thought, the anger fades.

The thought of something pleasant will make you feel good. The thought that you are doing great will make you feel good inside—all the good feelings will come out. . . . If somebody says you are guilty, which is a thought, then you can feel very miserable. Feelings are tremendously affected by thoughts. And obviously thoughts are tremendously affected by feelings, because if you are angry you don't think clearly.

In reality, therefore, thought and its various manifestations and consequences form an interconnected web best described as a *system*. A prime example of a system is any government, whether democratic or autocratic. Even where a dictator seems to be exclusively in charge, no government can function without a bureaucracy or network of actors who carry out the dictates of the man in charge. In democratic societies, the systemic nature of the government is more conspicuous, as a president or prime minister is required to interact with an elective body ostensibly representing the collective will of the people. Systems are apparent in nature as well. Climate is a system insofar as it is the product of numerous interacting elements, including atmosphere, temperature, ocean currents, topography, and so on. Any phenomenon, in short, consisting of a complex mixture of interacting elements to produce a unified effect may reasonably be characterized as a system.

> I would say that thought makes what is often called in modern language a *system*. A system means a set of connected things or parts. A corporation is organized as a system . . . also the body is a system. Society is a system . . .
>
> Similarly, thought is a system. That system not only includes thoughts and feelings, but it includes the state of the body; it includes the whole of society—as thought is passing back and forth between people in a process by which thought evolved from ancient times.

If there is a fundamental flaw in the operation of thought, therefore, it must be a systemic flaw, one which will infect the entire network of interrelated elements.

So we have this system of thought. Now, I say that this system has a fault in it—a systemic fault. It's not a fault here, there or there, but it is a fault that is all throughout the system. . . . You may say, "I see a problem here, so I will bring my thought to bear on this problem." But "my" thought is part of the system. It has the same fault as the fault I'm trying to look at, or a similar fault.

All of the foregoing leads to the conclusion that thought is not aware of the nature and consequences of its own operation; that is, thought is not entirely aware of itself. Bohm employs the term *proprioception* to make this point. Proprioception is a property of the body with which we are familiar. When a bird flies across my field of vision, I must use my eyes in order to see it. But when I move my arm, I don't need my eyes to tell me my arm has moved; the arm and all the parts of the body have within them neurological receptors which report directly on the movement and position of the parts.

We have with the body a very interesting situation called *proprio-ception*, which means 'self-perception.' If you move any part of your body, you know that you have moved it—the movement resulted from your intention. You know that immediately, without time, without an observer, without having to think. If you can't tell that, then you're in a very bad way. There are people who have lost it and they can't move coherently, because you must be able to distinguish between a movement that you have created and one that occurred independently.

In one of his many colorful metaphors, Bohm describes a woman who, due to some accident or illness, had lost the capacity for proprioception in her arms. One night she woke up to find herself being attacked by some assailant. Her efforts to defend herself only increased the assault. Finally she succeeded in turning on the light, and she found there was nobody there. She had been inadvertently hitting herself, but she could not realize it until she turned on the light, because she had lost the capacity for proprioception in her arms.

Of course we know that thought exists, and we have a general sense of its operation in our daily lives. But in its actual functioning, thought does not signal to us in the same way that our body does. The most important failure of this kind has to do with the nature of the self or personal identity. We consider ourselves to be the source, the originator of thought; we are the thinker. But in fact the self, the thinker, is a product of thought, the construction of thought. Thought creates the thinker, rather than the thinker creating thought. This illusion is brought about by the fact that thought lacks awareness of its own operation; it lacks proprioception.

The question arises whether thought can acquire the capacity for awareness of its own operation. To do so would be to open the door for the correction of a systemic flaw in the primary tool we use to apprehend the world. Bohm leaves this as an open question. He admits that perception and intelligence are modes of awareness that supersede the operations of thought; but whether these can be brought to bear upon or within thought itself remains unresolved. Bohm is open to this possibility, but he doesn't seem to be entirely convinced.

> So you can see that this is the way the system is working. And there are other features of this system which need going into. . . . But I think we have begun to see enough of it to see that there *might* be a way out—not to say there is, but there might be. Now, this requires that we see thought as one whole, with the entire chemical-physical system, and all that.

Bohm waits until the final hour of the weekend seminar to raise the issue of time. His discussion proceeds along lines familiar to those who have studied his conversations with Krishnamurti, but there are some points of contrast as well. He recognizes a distinction between physical, chronological time and psychological time, but the difference between the two is not as hard and fast as it had been characterized previously.

> Leibniz, the philosopher, has said that space is the order of co-existence. All that co-exists is in a certain order which we call 'space'. And time is the order of successive existence—the order of succession. The real basis of time is succession—things succeeding each other in a certain order. Time is a concept which is set up by thought to represent succession. . . . The seasons are the succession of process. Your body goes through a succession of rhythms. And that succession is the basis of the whole thing—that is a thing that's actual.
>
> Thought deals with that, puts it in order by means of the concept of

time. We may draw a line and call that 'time', but as I have said earlier, that's really representing time by space. You say the clock tells time, but it doesn't. What you actually see is the position of the hands of the clock, not the time. It means time; it's been set up in such a way that it should measure time. But we never actually see, perceive, or experience 'time'—it's inferred.

Bohm weaves his discussion of time into a subtle and nuanced account of Krishnamurti's aphorism "the observer is the observed." Although he takes pains to explain what this means, Krishnamurti's remarks on this matter never quite convey with precision what he is getting at. Bohm makes the issue more lucid and accessible by bringing in the element of time:

> We discussed the observer and the observed being perceived as separate, with a space between them. But we said that that is in the image. If it were not an image, that separation would imply that there would be time to act, that it would take time to cross the space. And, having that space in time, the observer would be independent enough so that he could think about the observed a little while and then do something.
>
> But if that separation is just simply an image, when in fact the observer and the observed are all one thought process, then whatever you call 'the observer' has already been affected by the thing he wants to observe. Namely, if he wants to observe anger he has already been affected by anger in a distorted way. So he doesn't have any time. There is no space. There is no time. There is nothing but thought, which has been affected by anger. And this requires an insight, which would free the whole process.

The sustained exposition of psychological issues that Bohm presents in this seminar reveals an interesting difference between his manner of presentation and that of Krishnamurti. Both men are describing a radical reconstruction of our understanding of the landscape of consciousness. But Krishnamurti's approach is that of an artist, meticulous in his language, but disparaging of a merely verbal or intellectual understanding of his observations; he wants his listeners to observe the territory of consciousness directly, immediately, with an authentic perception of their own. Bohm, by contrast, is content to remain for the time being at the intellectual level. He acknowledges that immediate perception or insight is ultimately required, but for purposes of the seminar he is content merely to draw a map of the terrain, rather than demanding that his listeners see the actual landscape for themselves. If Krishnamurti is an artist, fueled with creative vision, Bohm is the careful cartographer, painstakingly drawing a map that is intended to guide perception. Both approaches seem valid, within their respective spheres; and together, they each reinforce and illuminate the other.

Chapter Eighteen

PHYSICS AND METAPHYSICS

In my afternoon walks with Bohm, especially after I left Oak Grove, I sometimes urged him to compose a book for a general audience outlining his perspective on physics as a whole. With his gift for elucidation of obscure or difficult points, often on display in his work with Krishnamurti, I felt he could help the interested layman understand not only the central findings of twentieth-century developments in physics, but also the place of physics, its essential contribution as well as its limitations, within the overall scope of intellectual endeavor. In addition, I felt there were some underlying connections between his scientific work and his interest in the psychological field that warranted exploration.

My efforts to coax Bohm to undertake this task were not successful, so I eventually had recourse to another approach. Without warning him in advance, I brought a tape recorder with me one afternoon on one of my visits to his apartment and initiated a conversation along these lines. The result was all I could have hoped for: a concise but comprehensive perspective on the essence of physics and its place in understanding nature as a whole, including both its substance and its characteristic methodology, as well as some attention to the role of the observer in modern physics. The edited transcript of this conversation appears here as appendix 4, *Physics and the Laws of Nature*.

Anyone interested in exploring the relationship between Bohm's physics and his metaphysics—meaning by that word issues pertaining to mind, knowledge and the ultimate nature of reality—might find *Physics and the Laws of Nature* a useful introduction or point of departure. An earlier exposition of somewhat similar views appears in Bohm's 1965 book *The Special Theory of Relativity*. Although he did his most original work in quantum mechanics, Bohm was also an authority on relativity, and this book was reprinted as a classic in the field in 1990. In the first chapter and the appendix of this volume, Bohm makes clear his view that science does not deal in final knowledge or "eternal verities," but rather represents successive advancements and refinements in our perceptual capacities:

> We are finally led to suggest that science is mainly a way of extending our perceptual contact with the world, rather than of accumulating knowledge about it. In this way, one can understand the fact that scientific research does not lead to absolute truth, but rather (as happens in ordinary perception) an awareness and understanding of an ever-growing segment of the world with which we are in contact.

One can see in this statement, composed in January 1964, that Bohm was already, even in his approach to science, favoring perception over knowledge in a manner reminiscent of Krishnamurti's approach to psychological issues. It seems unlikely that this was a product of his work with Krishnamurti, which had begun three years earlier, but rather was the expression of views developed over a longer and independent period of incubation. Nevertheless, this perspective must have been among the salient points of contact that led Bohm to his attitude of receptivity toward Krishnamurti's outlook. Coupled with their common interest in the role of an observer, albeit in different fields, there was clearly fertile ground for the cultivation of their collaboration.

Our review of the content of their dialogues together suggests some other ways in which Bohm's background in physics prepared him to appreciate and participate in Krishnamurti's work. Not until *The Ending of Time* dialogues with Bohm did Krishnamurti give any sustained attention to the ground of all existence, but when he did so, Bohm seemed not at all caught off guard or unprepared to pursue that line of inquiry. On the contrary, it was he who suggested use of the term "ground," which Krishnamurti was at first hesitant to adopt, and Bohm was quick to grasp the implications of this notion and to pose appropriate questions about it. No doubt he was aware that an implicit feature of physics, and indeed of all of science, is to "get to the bottom" of things, to discover the most fundamental level of reality. Whether that reality was expressible as a physical law, as a mathematical formula, or as a form of metaphysical revelation, was perhaps a secondary matter to him; his own investigations had led him to examine the world of matter to its greatest depth, and had led to mystery and impenetrable questions. Krishnamurti's insights at this level were evidently not entirely surprising or inexplicable to Bohm.

In the catalogue of points of contact between Bohm's physics and his metaphysics, perhaps none looms larger than the issue of time. Relativity theory introduces a radically new understanding of time, supplanting the common sense or Newtonian notion that time is an absolute, an unalterable and invariant feature of the universe, a characteristic of reality that must be constant for all observers wherever they may be. Relativity overturns this comfortable notion in two respects. The passage of time is now no longer identical for everyone everywhere, but rather dilates or diminishes according to the velocity with which the observer may be moving. Thus we have the paradox of the identical twins who are no longer the same age after one of them travels in a spaceship at speeds approaching the velocity of light. No matter that present technology does not permit this experiment to be put to the test; the fact that our leading physical theory regards this effect as inevitable is sufficiently disturbing in itself to shake our sense of security in the absolute nature of time. Moreover, relativity couples time intrinsically with space; time is no longer independent, but rather is bound up in the fabric of space—so much so that, in some domains of physics, it is no longer reasonable to speak of space and time as separate, but rather as spacetime.

Familiarity with this background must have prepared Bohm to appreciate Krishnamurti's observations about time and to explore with him that dimension of his philosophy. Krishnamurti acknowledged that this was not a "schoolboy" issue, but when he denied the existence of psychological time, Bohm was not only prepared to entertain that notion, but was already steeped in skepticism regarding any conventional, received understanding of time. Indeed, when pressed on the matter by Krishnamurti, he acknowledged that even with regard to physical reality, he did not regard time as an inevitable or necessary feature of the actual universe, but rather as a construct superimposed for our convenience.

As a result, Bohm was highly receptive to Krishnamurti's insistence upon the essential equivalence of thought and time. In fact it was Bohm who suggested (in a manner reminiscent of spacetime), that perhaps we need only one word instead of two: thought-time.

Some have suggested, including Bohm himself (in his letters to Wilhelm), that Krishnamurti's philosophy was not entirely original, but was similar in some respects to various themes apparent in Hinduism and Buddhism. Certainly the notion that the sense of individual identity is illusory has been put forth by others, although the closely related assertion that the observer is the observed has never before been given the emphasis that Krishnamurti did. But Krishnamurti's radical distinction between chronological and psychological time and his categorical insistence that psychological time is illusory are unique to his philosophy. Bohm's willingness to endorse this view represents an important source of confirmation for it.

At the same time, it must be admitted that the meaning of this distinction is not necessarily entirely clear. For this reason, I initiated with Bohm a kind of dialogue by audiotape when I was in Ojai and he was at home in England. I posed a series of questions about both physical and psychological time, and he replied at some length, in a careful and comprehensive review of the issue as he understood it. This exchange occurred about four years after Krishnamurti's death and represents the most complete exposition of the issue of which I am aware. Most remarkable about it is the conclusion of Bohm's comments, in which he describes the close relationship among three of the most central issues in his account of consciousness: psychological time, proprioception of thought, and the role of the observer. Nowhere else, to my knowledge, are these three issues conjoined in quite this manner. The transcript of this exchange appears as appendix 2 of the present volume.

The most complete account of the manner in which Bohm's physics prepares for and dovetails with his metaphysics is given in his magnum opus, *Wholeness and the Implicate Order*, published in 1980, the same year as his conversations with Krishnamurti that became *The Ending of Time*. While *wholeness* and *order* are key constructs for Bohm, the general plan and objective of *Wholeness and the Implicate Order* is to examine the foundations of both quantum theory and relativity in an effort to bring into focus what they have in common and where they are incompatible. This entails examining, among other things, the roles of causality, determinism, and mechanism as underlying principles in both theories, as well as in earlier paradigms in physics. By this means, Bohm uncovers a new way of understanding the whole of physical reality in such a way as to encompass both quantum theory and relativity, in spite of their apparently irreconcilable features.

> As we have seen, relativity theory requires continuity, strict causality (determinism) and locality. On the other hand, quantum theory requires non-continuity, non-causality and non-locality. So the basic concepts of relativity and quantum theory directly contradict each other. It is therefore hardly surprising that these two theories have never been unified in a consistent way. Rather, it seems most likely that such a unification is not actually possible. What is very probably needed instead is a qualitatively new theory, from which both relativity and quantum theory are to be derived as abstractions, approximations and limiting cases.
>
> The basic notions of this new theory evidently cannot be found by beginning with those features in which relativity and quantum theory stand in direct contradiction. The best place to begin is with what they have basically in common. This is undivided wholeness. Though each comes to such wholeness in a different way, it is clear that it is this to which they are both fundamentally pointing.
>
> To begin with undivided wholeness means, however, that we must drop the mechanistic order. But this order has been, for many centuries, basic to all thinking in physics.

Bohm's proposal of an implicate order is not itself the qualitatively new theory that would embrace both relativity and quantum theory as limiting cases. Rather, it provides a context within which such a theory might emerge, just as the Cartesian order represented by a coordinate system provided the context for a mechanistic description of physical reality. The implicate order, moreover, has the additional feature that it embraces the emergence of consciousness as well, and so brings into a single coherent framework all the most salient features of the cosmos.

This point is brought out most clearly in the book's concluding section, "Matter, consciousness, and their common ground."

> Our overall approach has thus brought together questions of the nature of the cosmos, of matter in general, of life, and of consciousness. All of these have been considered to be projections of a common ground. This we may call the ground of all that is, at least in so far as this may be sensed and known by us, in our present phase of unfoldment of consciousness. Although we have no detailed perception or knowledge of this ground it is still in a certain sense enfolded in our consciousness, in the ways in which we have outlined, as well as perhaps in other ways that are yet to be discovered.

Where Bohm and Krishnamurti part company lies in whether "the ground of all that is" is the final and ultimate source of the universe, the end and the beginning, or whether additional levels or layers of reality may exist beyond it. Krishnamurti was emphatic in stating that the ground to which he was referring was final and ultimate. Perhaps because he was proceeding by means of direct perception, or insight, or what may be called revelation, his view differs from Bohm's, whose mode of procedure was more logical and analytical. Bohm subscribes to the view that the universe is infinite, not only quantitatively, in extent, but also qualitatively:

> Is this ground the absolute end of everything? In our proposed views concerning the general nature of 'the totality of all that is' we regard even this ground as a mere stage, in the sense that there could in principle be an infinity of further development beyond it. . . . Through the force of an even deeper, more inward necessity in this totality, some new state of affairs may emerge in which both the world as we know it and our ideas about it may undergo an unending process of yet further change.

The publication of *Wholeness and the Implicate Order* in the same year as occurred the dialogues which became *The Ending of Time* perhaps represents the pinnacle of Bohm's intellectual career. The following year he underwent major heart surgery, and three years later occurred the confrontation with Krishnamurti that he evidently found so disturbing.

Although he continued to produce important work, including the seminar that became *Thought as a System*, 1980 may reasonably be considered the annus mirabilis of Bohm's contribution to humanity.

In 1991, Bohm suffered an episode of severe psychological depression. Serious depression does not necessarily have a psychological source, but may be simply the result of specific forms of chemical imbalance in the brain whose origin is considered idiopathic, or without any identifiable cause. Nevertheless, there may be psychological factors that precipitate or contribute to the chemical condition, and these cannot be ruled out as possible participants in a complex mixture of events. Bohm must have been anticipating his own mortality, inasmuch as he was 72 years old and had undergone multiple-bypass heart surgery ten years earlier. He also felt that his scientific work remained incomplete; he had come to an impasse, to some degree, in his effort to compose the definitive textbook exposition of his interpretation of quantum reality. Although he did finally succeed in completing the textbook—*The Undivided Universe: An Ontological Interpretation of Quantum Theory*—this outcome was in doubt for many months.

Another contributing factor in his depression, according to his biographer and one or two close friends, was the publication in 1989 of *Lives in the Shadow*, by Radha Sloss, described in a previous chapter of the present volume. Sloss's revelation of Krishnamurti's long affair with her mother, and the attendant two abortions and miscarriage, evidently was disturbing to Bohm, although he did not read the book himself. Had he done so he might have been relieved to learn that the abortions were obtained not for reasons of appearances, but rather to protect the life of the mother. Bohm's biographer maintains that Bohm was also disturbed by the revelation that Krishnamurti had not been celibate, although this claim seems highly improbable, inasmuch as Krishnamurti had ceased to advocate celibacy in the 1920's, well before the commencement of the affair.

In any case, Bohm had to be hospitalized for several weeks as a result of his depression. It seems reasonable to surmise that so radical a step may have been required because he had become somewhat suicidal. He may have felt that his life was a failure, both professionally as well as from the psychological perspective entailed by his involvement in Krishnamurti's work. But the hospitalization and whatever medications he was given were apparently to no avail, perhaps in part because his heart condition limited his physicians' choices of medications to prescribe. In any event, Bohm's depression continued for weeks without relief, even after he had been admitted to the hospital.

Finally the attending physicians determined that the only reasonable course of action was electroshock therapy. In the early 1990's, this was not as drastic a remedy as it had been when first introduced; the art of administering electroshock had been refined considerably and the side effects were much diminished. Nevertheless, resorting to this form of therapy was symptomatic of the severity of his depression.

The last time I saw Bohm was in April 1992. He had been released from the hospital and was visiting Ojai in order to conduct another of his annual seminars. I took a leave of absence from my research position in San Francisco and came to visit with him for a week before the seminar. In our daily walks, it was clear to me that he felt diminished intellectually. He felt that his memory was somewhat impaired and that he lacked his former clarity. He was apprehensive about his ability to carry out the seminar, but I felt his intellect remained fully intact and I said as much. In any case, he conducted the seminar with at least eighty percent of his normal energy and lucidity.

After the seminar was over, Bohm asked me to stay on in Ojai for another week. I felt obliged to get back to my job in San Francisco and I was eager to return to my wife, who was at that time not entirely well. Nevertheless, I had reason subsequently to regret my decision not to stay, for I never saw Bohm again. He died of cardiac arrest in a taxicab, on the way home from work, the following December (1992).

Chapter Nineteen

THE SOURCE OF REVELATION

In Buddhist literature, a *bodhisattva* is an individual, real or mythical, who is dedicated to realizing the truth of Buddhism and, in effect, becoming a Buddha as well. Among the most revered of bodhisattvas is one named Maitreya, destined to realize full enlightenment and to transmit Buddhist teachings to the world. Early Theosophical literature borrowed from various religious canons and included Maitreya among the "masters of wisdom," individuals who had transcended the earthly plane but took an active interest in events on Earth. Maitreya was held to occupy the office of World Teacher, specifically responsible for the spiritual education of mankind.

When Annie Besant, assisted by Charles Leadbeater, assumed responsibility for the articulation of Theosophical doctrine, she held that it was the role of the Theosophical Society to find and cultivate an individual who would become the World Teacher. She maintained that Maitreya could manifest himself only in a suitable "vehicle," a body uncorrupted, by virtue of multiple incarnations untouched by alcohol, meat, and other sources of impurity. The selection of Krishnamurti explicitly entailed this process of manifestation, and as late as the mid-1920s, fifteen or more years after his selection for this role, it was widely believed in Theosophical circles that the manifestation was going as planned.

As a result, Krishnamurti's dissolution of the Order of the Star in 1929 and his break with theosophical doctrine were generally interpreted as a failure of the grand prediction that had been made. Krishnamurti wrote to a friend in 1930 that Leadbeater himself was now "against me and what I am saying." Nevertheless, for the rest of his life, Krishnamurti continued to insist that no individual could lay claim to authority in psychological or spiritual matters, and that no religious organization has any kind of monopoly on truth.

And yet by the end of his lifetime, Krishnamurti's actual relationship to the role of World Teacher was no longer quite so definitive or clear-cut. Several factors contributed to some blurring of this issue. Foremost among these was the indisputable fact that his life and career indeed bore an uncanny resemblance to the general form of Annie Besant's prophecy for him. He devoted his entire life to travelling around the world, speaking to audiences on matters pertaining to fundamental issues of daily life and consciousness. He referred to his philosophy as "the teachings," although he regarded them not as the teachings of Krish-namurti, but rather as the teachings of life. When asked in a legal depo-sition in the 1970s whether he was the World Teacher, he answered that he was not in the Theosophical sense, but that he was a world teacher in that he travelled the globe for the purpose of expressing his philosophy. Even on his deathbed, he declared rather pointedly, in order to address some unresolved matters among the Foundations, "I am still the teacher."

The issue was made more complicated by his answers to a series of questions posed by his biographer, Mary Lutyens. In 1979, as she was preparing the second volume of his life, she met with him to inquire into the source of his teaching. Her chapter on this subject is titled, "Who or What Is Krishnamurti?" and she began by asking him, "The teachings are not simple. How did they come out of that vacant boy?" She knew that somewhat similar questions had been addressed to him previously by others, and that he had attempted at some length to answer them. But none of what he said before had seemed satisfactory; he acknowledged there was a mystery involved, but said he was unable to answer it. When she approached him about it now, he put the question back upon her: what did she feel was the answer? She replied that the simplest expla-nation was precisely what Besant and Leadbeater had proposed decades earlier: that Maitreya had selected a young individual, one with a pure body and a rather vacant mind, as the vehicle through which to manifest.

Krishnamurti acknowledged that this was a possible theory, although he did reject it. At first he agreed it was the simplest solution, but he went on to say that the simplest is often suspect. Later he amended his reply to say that Maitreya was "too concrete"—not subtle enough, too "worked-out." In short, he seemed to be acknowledging that some kind of agency or energy was functioning in him or through him that was outside the bounds of ordinary experience. Indeed, at one point he said that he was admitting the operation of something mystical.

One of the reasons this conversation was necessary (apart from the magnitude, depth, and originality of his philosophy) was that Krishnamurti did not come upon his observations regarding life and consciousness through any ordinary process of study or analysis. As he pointed out, other individuals who had articulated penetrating philosophical insights—he mentioned Schopenhauer, Lenin, and Bertrand Russell—were well-read and knowledgeable about what others had said previously. He did not come to his philosophy in that manner. He said if he sat down to write it out, he was not sure he could do it. He did not even prepare for his public talks, and often asked (rhetorically, no doubt) those who were with him, as he was being driven to the venue where he would speak, what he should speak about. He said his spoken observations came to him as a form of "revelation."

In the course of this conversation, Krishnamurti emphasized a few factors that he felt were fundamental to understand the source of his teachings. One was what he called "the vacant mind." He maintained that his mind had been empty from an early age, in the sense that he was not occupied with problems, people, or events, but rather he was quiet, engaged simply in the act of observation, awareness. Not only that, but he evidently felt that his mind had been kept vacant, perhaps by some agency or energy outside the normal parameters of events. A closely related factor was what he described as a kind of protection that looked out for his physical well-being. He said that whenever he flew on an airplane, for example, he knew that nothing bad would happen because of this protection. He felt his body existed in order to speak, and so long as he was able to do so, his mind would remain vacant—except when thought was necessary to communicate, or for practical purposes—and his body would remain protected. These, evidently, were the conditions that enabled the process of revelation to unfold.

It should also be noted that Krishnamurti insisted, not only in this conversation but throughout his lifetime, that he as an individual was of no significance, and all that mattered were the teachings themselves. From this perspective, it is a little less surprising that he seemed unable to answer Mary Lutyens's question; and she, reflecting on it later, wondered whether her inquiry should ever have been initiated. Perhaps a better, more focused question would have been, what was the source of his revelations?

However the question was posed, in the end Krishnamurti declared not only that he did not know the answer, but in addition he could not find the answer. In view of the steady determination with which he examined all other questions, this was a surprising outcome, but he expressed it rather memorably by saying, "Water can never find out what water is." He went on, however, to turn the question around in a tantalizing manner. He averred that someone else, including Mary Lutyens or Mary Zimbalist (who was present and taking notes) could discover the answer if they pursued the question diligently, and that he could then confirm or disconfirm whatever they discovered. He added, however, that in order to find the answer, one would need a quiet mind, an empty mind; and Mary Lutyens was never able to pursue the inquiry beyond this point.

Several other sources of information bear upon this issue. In 1975, the first volume of Mary Lutyens's biography of Krishnamurti appeared at around the time that he and Bohm were engaged in the series of dialogues that were not published in their entirety. In one of these dialogues (June 25, 1975), Bohm inquired at length about Krishnamurti's "process," as it is described in that volume (as well as here in chapter 6.) Once again, Krishnamurti was at a loss to offer any definitive account of this phenomenon, other than to speculate that it might be similar in some respects to what others have referred to as kundalini. He does not endorse this view, but rather merely entertains it as a possibility.

Bohm also remarked that in his reading of Lutyens's biography, he was unable to discern any particular moment or episode that would correspond to any form of enlightenment, transcendence, or definitive or ultimate insight. (Rather remarkably, Bohm does not mention the 1922 events under the pepper tree that Lutyens described in great detail.)

Krishnamurti agreed that there was no particular moment or event. He suggested that his understanding was always present to some degree, but that the language with which to articulate it emerged only gradually, over the course of many years.

Krishnamurti's Notebook, described here in chapter 6, refers repeatedly to a quality or essence that appeared to him at odd moments on almost a daily basis, which he referred to most often as "the other," though at times it was called a benediction or the immensity. A few of Krishnamurti's close associates claimed they too felt the presence of such a force while they were with him. It was something not evident to the senses but experienced nevertheless as palpable and real, indeed, at times, overwhelmingly powerful. It sometimes came precisely when Krishnamurti was discussing issues pertaining to himself or his teaching, and Lutyens records its presence while she was conducting this conversation with him. It came again on a subsequent occasion when she asked him whether it was right or appropriate to include mention of such events in her biography. "There is your answer," he replied, as if the presence of the other was so conspicuous at that moment that it was not even necessary to ask whether she felt it too.

The other also appears in an extraordinary document Krishnamurti dictated to Mary Zimbalist while he was in the hospital for surgery on his prostate in 1977. He had elected to receive a spinal rather than a general anesthetic, evidently on grounds that his body was so sensitive that he might "slip away." Even so, after the operation was over, he experienced or witnessed a dialogue involving his body debating with "the personification of death." Death was insistent, demanding, but the other entered into the conversation and intervened. The opposition of forces took the form of a dialogue stripped of all fear, illusion, or sentimentality. Indeed, Krishnamurti said, "The quality of conversation was urbane," but ultimately the other proved to be stronger than death, and it yielded for the time being.

In the final year or two of his life, Krishnamurti had premonitions of his impending end. He referred repeatedly in his conversations with Mary Zimbalist to the presence or participation of some force or entity that was watching over him and controlling events. She records remarks such as "My life is planned"; "There are things you don't know, enormous things. I am not allowed to talk about them"; and "It is all being decided by someone else. The body exists only to talk. When it can no longer go on talking, then it will end."

On his deathbed, Krishnamurti was asked by one of the trustees of the English foundation what would become or remain of him, of his focus of energy or intelligence, after he was gone. Krishnamurti was emphatic that nothing would remain. In the course of his answer, however, he provided some further clues regarding himself and the manner in which his teachings had been received by the world. This statement, recorded ten days before he died, when he was still lucid but very weak, warrants quotation in its entirety:

> I was telling them this morning—for seventy years that super energy—no—that immense energy, immense intelligence, has been using this body. I don't think people realize what tremendous energy and intelligence went through this body—there's [a] twelve-cylinder engine. And for seventy years—was a pretty long time—and now the body can't stand any more.
>
> Nobody, unless the body has been prepared, very carefully, protected and so on—nobody can understand what went through this body. Nobody. Don't anybody pretend. Nobody. I repeat this: nobody amongst us or the public, know what went on. I know they don't. And now after seventy years it has come to an end. Not that that intelligence and energy—it's somewhat here, every day, and especially at night. And after seventy years the body can't stand it—can't stand any more. It can't. The Indians have a lot of damned superstitions about this—that you will and the body goes—and all that kind of nonsense.
>
> You won't find another body like this, or that supreme intelligence operating in a body for many hundred years. You won't see it again. When he goes, it goes. There is no consciousness left behind of that consciousness, of that state. They'll all pretend or try to imagine they can get into touch with that. Perhaps they will somewhat if they live the teachings. But nobody has done it. Nobody. And so that's that.

In December 1987, almost two years after Krishnamurti's death, I recorded a conversation with Bohm to see if he could shed any further light on the question Mary Lutyens had raised. Bohm did not use the word "mystery," but he stated that in the end some things simply were not clear. He felt that Krishnamurti had endorsed a kind of modified version of the theosophical view, with something more "abstract" than Maitreya operating through him. I also asked him how he would characterize Krishnamurti's overall contribution, including whether, or to what degree, his teaching was original. Bohm replied that nothing is ever entirely original, but that Krishnamurti had put things into his own language and expressed them with particular clarity and force. Nevertheless, he maintained, something seemed to be missing in the teachings or not entirely properly expressed, since evidently no one had ever understood them fully or undergone the kind of radical transformation that Krishnamurti had called for. I asked whether what was missing was a kind of "fine focus," describing the landscape of consciousness with somewhat greater precision and detail than Krishnamurti had done, even though he may have had the whole picture accurately in view. Bohm agreed this was probably correct. The transcript of this conversation appears as appendix 1 of the present volume.

The catalogue of unusual or unique characteristics associated with Krishnamurti may provide further clues to the questions raised here, although they may simply deepen the mystery. Several distinguishing factors have already been noted: the teachings themselves; the vacant mind and the sense of protection; and the fact that his observations occurred to him as a form of revelation, rather than the product of systematic study or analysis. Additional unusual characteristics include Krishnamurti's emphasis on a unique form of meditation, one that was entirely without volition, method, or any purpose external to itself. It came to him unexpectedly, even while driving a car or in his sleep. The meditative mind, for him, was a source of endless beauty, always fresh and new, and it brought a kind of benediction. The meditative mind seemed to be coupled in some manner with the process, the intermittent pain in his head and neck. Krishnamurti had little or no memory of his early life, but he was acutely sensitive to nature, and he had an extraordinary ability, recorded in his diaries and elsewhere, to recall scenes from nature. Any one of these characteristics would have marked him as unusual, but in the aggregate they represent an entirely singular individual and seem to point to something outside the contours of normal existence. At times Krishnamurti wondered aloud whether he might be a kind of "freak," in the neutral, non-pejorative sense of a biological mutation. Perhaps, for all practical purposes, that is the best explanation.

Before leaving this subject, one additional interpretation of the unique suite of characteristics associated with Krishnamurti warrants consideration. He said in his final recorded statement that perhaps one could begin to understand the intelligence and energy that flowed through him if one "lived the teachings." To live the teachings would be to live a life without psychological division, without conflict, and therefore a life of order. He maintained that if consciousness is undivided and in order, it releases a great quantity of energy that is otherwise wasted in conflict. So it seems plausible to consider that many of his unusual qualities—his intense appreciation of nature, the unusual process he underwent, his perception of the presence of the other, and his ability to articulate the teachings as a form of revelation—were byproducts of the direct perceptions expressed in the teachings themselves. In some ways, this is the most satisfying and unifying explanation for who or what was Krishnamurti: he was the living embodiment of the sum and substance of his stated philosophy. The observer was the observed.

In the end it is the diaries that seem to be the surest means of entering into and capturing a glimpse of Krishnamurti's consciousness. Rather than attempt any further characterization of the man and the source of his revelation, it seems appropriate to end instead with a passage, drawn almost at random, from his *Notebook*:

> It was a beautiful drive, in a car that seemed to enjoy what it was built for; it took every curve, however sharp, easily and willingly, and up the long incline it went, never grumbling, and there was plenty of power to go up wherever the road went. It was like an animal that knew its own strength.
>
> The road curved in and out, through a dark sunlit wood, and every patch of light was alive, dancing with the leaves; every curve of the road showed more light, more dances, more delight. Every tree, every

leaf stood alone, intense and silent. You saw, through a small opening of the trees, a patch of startling green of a meadow that was open to the sun. It was so startling that one forgot that one was on a dangerous mountain road. But the road became gentle and lazily wound around to a different valley. The clouds were gathering in now and it was pleasant not to have a strong sun.

The road became almost flat, if a mountain road can be flat; it went on past a dark pine-covered hill, and there in front were the enormous, overpowering mountains, rocks and snow, green fields and waterfalls, small wooden huts and the sweeping, curving lines of the mountain. One could hardly believe what the eyes saw, the overpowering dignity of those shaped rocks, the treeless mountain covered with snow, and crag after crag of endless rock; and right up to them were the green meadows, all held together in a vast embrace of a mountain.

It was really quite incredible; there was beauty, love, destruction and the immensity of creation; not those rocks, not those fields, not those tiny huts; it wasn't in them or part of them. It was far beyond and above them. It was there with the majesty, with a roar that no eyes or ears could see or hear; it was there with such totality and stillness that the brain with its thoughts became as nothing as those dead leaves in the woods. It was there with such abundance, such strength that the world, the trees and the earth came to an end. It was love, creation and destruction. And there was nothing else.

Chapter Twenty

IMPLICATIONS AND REFLECTIONS

Krishnamurti's philosophy is so comprehensive and complex that it does not admit any easy summary or assessment. The areas of his concern embrace conflict, relationship, fear, desire, love, death, conditioning, freedom, beauty, attachment, the nature of knowledge, the illusion of psychological time, the essence of the individual, and the urgency of change. Bohm's most signal contribution to this oeuvre was his focus on psychological proprioception, an issue that was implicit in much of Krishnamurti's work, but was brought out center stage, as it were, by Bohm. One way of evaluating their work together is to assess it in the context of somewhat comparable efforts by others to address the totality of human existence. A second approach is to examine previous revolutions in understanding and to contrast those transformations with Krishnamurti's work. These will be among the objectives of the present chapter.

Throughout history, the list of individuals who have addressed the human condition as a whole, in a comprehensive fashion, is not long. If we confine our reflections to the last two centuries, Charles Darwin, William James, and Sigmund Freud stand out as members of this list, and we may include some of the work of Jared Diamond and E. O. Wilson as well. Considered in this context, Krishnamurti's work appears with greater clarity; against this background, we may perhaps appreciate more fully the meaning and import of his contribution.

In his two major books, *On the Origin of Species* (1859) and *The Descent of Man* (1871), Darwin articulates a perspective on humanity that effectively embraces the whole history of life. Evolution by natural selection lays claim to man as a creature of biology, rather than something divinely ordained or made in the image of God. The implications of this point of view continue to reverberate, and even today have not been fully accommodated, as the controversies surrounding sociobiology make clear. Darwin's view had to be supplemented by Mendelian genetics, and was subject to further modification in terms of group selection theory, "the selfish gene" of Richard Dawkins, and other innovations. And yet in its broad outline, Darwinian theory supplied the basic modern blueprint for examining human nature and society. No contemporary point of view will gain much currency if it stands in fundamental opposition to Darwin.

From this perspective, it is somewhat reassuring that, no matter how radical Krishnamurti's philosophy may be, he accepts Darwinian evolution without hesitation. This point comes up more than once with Bohm, in the *Ending of Time* dialogues and elsewhere, and there is no equivocation about it. What Darwin does not supply, however, is much in the way of detail regarding the nature of individual consciousness, especially in its interaction with society. And so when Krishnamurti and Bohm inquire whether humanity has taken "a wrong turn," their conversation is consistent with evolution, but prepared to contemplate the possibility that something false or self-destructive may have entered into human consciousness, which is, after all, still very young on an evolutionary time-scale.

William James was thoroughly familiar with Darwin; indeed, as a young man, he served as an apprentice to Louis Agassiz, the most famous scientist of his day, and a dedicated opponent of Darwinian theory. In spite of this association, James accepted Darwin and considered his own views compatible with evolutionary theory. James is regarded as the founder of the field of psychology as a subject of study distinct from either philosophy or physiology. His *Principles of Psychology* (1891) is a twelve-hundred page tour de force, a comprehensive examination of every facet of consciousness, with chapters on will, desire, emotion, motivation, and perception, among many other topics. James's methodology is unabashedly introspective, for although he embraced the tenets of science, he wrote in a day before introspection had fallen into scientific disfavor.

Rather surprisingly, Krishnamurti rejected introspection as a means of self-discovery or understanding. In his view, introspection was an analytical process, conducted with preconceived objectives and techniques. What he called choiceless awareness, by contrast, represented a form of inward observation uncorrupted by any form of motive or method. This distinction, however, is by no means immune to challenge or questioning. At the very least, it must be admitted that, among the spectrum of methodologies available to psychology, from neurophysiology to behavioristic experiments to clinical and anecdotal impressions, introspection lies nearest to the approach Krishnamurti recommended. Moreover, it is not clear that choiceless awareness, as a form of inward observation, is in fact so different in practice from introspection.

In both content and method there would appear to exist a broad compatibility between Krishnamurti's work and that of James. In fact, James was an early member of the Theosophical Society, and among his insights was the observation that "the thinker is the thought." Although he did not elaborate upon or emphasize this point to the extent that Krishnamurti did, it nevertheless represents a remarkable adumbration of Krishnamurti's work. In addition, James's *Varieties of Religious Experience* (1909) similarly anticipates Krishnamurti's views by rejecting organized religion and locating authentic religious experience in a more direct and immediate apprehension of another dimension of awareness. All things considered, James represents perhaps the nearest to Krishnamurti not only in scope and method, but also in the substance of his work.

Freud was also comfortable with a biological foundation for his point of view. His perspective was limited in many respects, but what is noteworthy for present purposes is simply the large structure of his outlook, in which man's instinctive nature is at odds with the requirements of society. In *Civilization and its Discontents* (1930), Freud makes clear his view that the benefits of social organization outweigh the alternative, but there is a substantial price to be paid in sacrifice of freedom and the repression of instinctual energy. However limited other elements of his theories may be, this much seems relatively uncontroversial.

To some extent, Krishnamurti's views are compatible with Freud's. He too regarded society as a repressive force, although his language was his own, and his sense of the limitations imposed by society was broader than Freud's. Krishnamurti spoke in terms of conditioning as it is imposed by family, friends, and education, as well as by the culture at large. Freedom from conditioning was fundamental to his prescription for individual clarity and a new society without endemic conflict. It seems not unlikely that Freud would have acknowledged a broad resemblance to his own outlook; indeed, had they had the opportunity, the two men might have become friends, much as Krishnamurti did with Aldous Huxley.

A more recent entry into the field of efforts to understand humanity as a whole is provided by Pulitzer Prize-winning scientist Jared Diamond, especially in his book, *The World Until Yesterday* (2009). Diamond's work belongs to the field of cultural anthropology; he steps outside the confines of the viewpoint of modern civilization and examines from a broader perspective issues facing all cultures, such as warfare, the raising of young, care for the elderly, and so on. He characterizes much contemporary research as based on a highly selective empirical model, "WEIRD," an acronym for Western, educated, industrialized, rich democracies. His aim is to examine human nature rather from the perspective of more than 100 "traditional" societies, each one relatively untouched by modernity.

Diamond's work represents a point of contrast with Krishnamurti's, but it is instructive for that reason. Diamond is engaged in cataloguing similarities and differences across all cultures, both traditional and modern. Krishnamurti is not; his focus is more on the psychology of the individual, and his concern is with features of consciousness that are shared in common by everyone. He would not deny the differences that Diamond describes; rather, he would say they are secondary or even irrelevant compared to the features that are common to all mankind. As he often pointed out, every human being suffers; everyone experiences desire, loneliness, and conflict; everyone is afraid of death. Thus, in a fundamental sense, no individual is deeply different from the rest of mankind; or, in the aphoristic phrase he often employed, you are the world, and the world is you.

Finally, we may consider the work of E. O. Wilson, perhaps the most outstanding living biologist today. Wilson is the world's foremost authority on ants, which may seem far afield from the study of human nature until one considers that ants have developed an intricate and highly evolved form of social organization. No doubt this background prepared Wilson to become one of the founders of sociobiology, which seeks to locate the sources of human nature and behavior within a biological context. In *The Meaning of Human Existence* (2013), Wilson articulates views somewhat compatible with Krishnamurti's. He castigates the divisive effects of tribal and religious ideology in a manner wholly consistent with Krishnamurti's views. He identifies the sense of self as a central feature of psychology and behavior, and he calls into question our ordinary assumptions about the nature of the self. He does not embrace or foresee the possibility of another form or structure of consciousness, but to the extent that he broaches these issues at all, Wilson's outlook and Krishnamurti's are broadly compatible.

Another approach to gaining some purchase upon the place of Krishnamurti's teachings is with reference to other major transformations of awareness through the course of history. He maintains that consciousness is infected with illusory elements that are the source of conflict and confusion, inwardly as well as outwardly in society. To evaluate this claim, or even to locate it within the scope of human inquiry, it is instructive to consider other radically new proposals that have been put forth with revolutionary effects.

Perhaps the paradigmatic case of this kind is that of Copernicus, whose vision of a sun-centered solar system overthrew centuries of a more comfortable arrangement of the universe. Copernicus had to overcome not only the received and sanctioned conventional wisdom of the Ptolemaic cycles and epicycles of the heavenly bodies; he also had to overturn the evidence of the senses of every man or woman who perceives the sun to be apparently rotating around the earth on a daily basis. At first it must have been a deep puzzle how to reconcile the heliocentric concept with the sight of the sun rising and setting every day. To abandon the view that the sun rotates around Earth required a reconstruction of consciousness among not only the intelligentsia, but also the common man.

Bohm was fond of drawing attention to the Newtonian discovery of universal gravitation, which also represented the transformation of an earlier misconception. Prior to Newton, it was believed that celestial objects were held in the sky by virtue of consisting of another kind of substance than the matter with which we are familiar on Earth. It was right and appropriate that celestial objects should remain where they were, in the heavens, because they were constituted of celestial material. So ingrained was this concept that it required a genius of the magnitude of Newton to question it. Newton observed the moon and put to himself the question, why is the moon not falling to the earth? The very question was revolutionary, inasmuch as conventional wisdom held that the moon, made of celestial matter, was not subject to gravity. But if it were subject to earth's gravitational field, what prevented it from falling?

Newton's insight was to realize that in fact the moon *is* falling, but its downward tendency is balanced by its momentum in a straight line forward, and the two forms of motion combine to produce the circular effect of the moon's actual orbit. From there it was a short conceptual leap to the conclusion that the motion of all the planets is governed in a comparable manner; and so the gravitational force exists universally, and is not confined to Earth.

Somewhat similarly, as late as the nineteenth century, it was widely believed, even in the medical community, that the living material of plants and animals was qualitatively different in kind from non-living material. Living matter was invested with a vital essence, which distinguished it and made it subject to different chemical and other properties than ordinary matter. The language of organic chemistry still maintains some traces of that formerly sacrosanct distinction. The breakthrough came when it was discovered that the chemical compound urea, the principal element of urine, could be constructed in the laboratory by ordinary methods. In short, organic chemicals were different to some extent in degree, but not in kind, from other more familiar forms of chemical substances.

Yet another conceptual transition of a comparable nature occurred when Einstein overthrew the comfortable notion that space and time are independent and absolute. Relativity theory showed that space and time are interwoven with one another, and that time is not an invariant feature of the universe, but rather expands or contracts according to the velocity of the observer. These findings have little effect on practical affairs, but they are sufficient to establish the limited nature of our most cherished and unquestioned assumptions about the nature of reality

Against this background, Krishnamurti's radical pronouncements assume a somewhat different aspect. His observations about psychological time, conflict, freedom, and identity represent reconceptualizations on a par with those of Copernicus, Newton, Darwin, or Einstein. In the effort to convey his views, however, he faced formidable obstacles. His field is fundamentally psychological, a realm notorious for idle theories and doctrines without demonstrable empirical support. He had an Indian name and a suspect metaphysical, even occult, background. No matter that he repudiated that background—to anyone not familiar with his work, the early years remain to color present perceptions.

Perhaps Krishnamurti's affiliation with Bohm served in some measure as an antidote to preconceived obstacles to the reception of his message. Not only did Bohm help clarify his language, but the endorsement of a scientist of Bohm's caliber may have helped facilitate recognition of his work. David Peat's biography of Bohm was a missed opportunity to help bring this about. Peat's unfavorable attitude toward Krishnamurti was apparent; he was not able to see that this involvement represented the summit of Bohm's achievement, not a departure from it.

From a critical standpoint, Krishnamurti's work appears unfinished in two respects. As already noted, he had a tendency at times to paint with a somewhat broad brush, one that gives a compelling view but may not offer sufficient detail to allow the listener or reader to see exactly what he means. For example, he often emphasized the necessity to end attachment, since attachment leads to fear of loss, which leads in turn to jealousy and hatred. To end attachment now, he said, entails a kind of death, the ending of all the bonds that one has cultivated. Be with death every day, he said, every second of the day, so that living and dying are always together. In this way, he said, there is not only no attachment, but great beauty, freedom, and love.

Statements of this kind are compelling, but what exactly does it mean to "live with death"? For the ordinary man, this would seem to mean something like, live with the awareness of your inevitable death. That leads directly into a calculation of the probable number of years one has left to live, which surely is not what Krishnamurti had in mind. Perhaps he meant something more immediate and metaphorical. Perhaps there is a way of looking at each moment of the day as a simultaneous process of living and dying, in the sense that one "dies" to each moment as it occurs, only to awaken to the next moment. "Experiment with it," he says. But is this the experiment he has in mind? And if this were the case, would it end all attachment?

These questions exemplify why I suggested to Bohm that Krishnamurti's statements sometimes seem to need fine-tuning. Krishnamurti himself remarked on one occasion to Mary Zimbalist, after one of his talks was finished: "Something new came out. 'Thinking *about* something is different than thinking.'" He evidently pondered this statement for some time until its meaning became clear to him. If he himself had trouble deciphering some of his revelations, it seems little wonder that the rest of us sometimes have a comparable difficulty.

Looking from a broad perspective over all the issues Krishnamurti and Bohm discussed together, one stands out as unresolved like a signal flare. Krishnamurti was adamant about the urgency of change. Neither individuals nor society, he said, could possibly continue on their present self-destructive course. Only a radical revolution of consciousness can save human beings from inexorable deterioration and destruction. This was not a change that could be postponed—it could not happen in time—it is a crisis. The change can only happen now, and it must happen now.

Against this categorical imperative stood another statement, equally adamant, that might be construed as entirely contrary to the former dictum. This was the danger or falseness of any movement of "becoming," the psychological desire to improve oneself or become more or better than what one already is. Krishnamurti identified the process of becoming as at or near the crux of where man in his evolution took a wrong turn. Surely there is a tension between the urgency to change and the urgency not to engage in any form of psychological becoming—a tension that represents a paradox within the whole framework of Krishnamurti's work. Probably this paradox can be resolved only with reference to psychological time: the change Krishnamurti is calling for is not one projected by thought as a goal to be achieved in the future, but rather an imperative requiring the immediate action of insight.

Krishnamurti often cautioned that after he was gone no one was authorized to speak for him as his representative, interpreter, or successor in any sense. His teachings stood on their own and were available as such to anyone. And yet surely he did not intend "no interpreters" to mean that no one else should take up and explore the issues he had raised. He often referred to the Indian aphorism that "nothing grows under the banyan tree." Indeed, where there is a tree so vast as a banyan, the available light and nourishment for other plants to grow beneath it evidently is blocked. Bohm's seminar *Thought as a System* perhaps serves as a model for what may reasonably be accomplished in this regard. No one mistook him for a surrogate Krishnamurti, nor did he himself make any pretense of that kind. Rather, he was a man with a certain level of understanding, informed by Krishnamurti but not copying him, and presenting a set of views that were fundamentally his own. In a sense, we may say that Bohm has shown us one manner in which the work of Krishnamurti may be carried on by others, even though they may lack his deep and comprehensive insight.

Depending upon one's point of view, the collaboration between Krishnamurti and Bohm might be interpreted as either a triumph or a tragedy. It was a triumph of improbability, given their disparate backgrounds and the duration of their work together. It was a triumph of insight and cooperative endeavor, a monumental feat of mutual productivity. The tragic aspect is in a sense a by-product of the very success of their collaboration. So much was accomplished, and yet in the end Bohm was evidently left somewhat bereft, unable either to witness for himself the state of mind he was so adept at describing, or to forge a connection with Krishnamurti that superseded their dialogues. Bohm's depression at the end of his life may have been merely biochemical, organic in origin; but as a form of metaphor, it left little room for doubt or interpretation. The triumph and the tragedy were therefore indissolubly mixed, twin patterns in the complex choreography of life.

The magnitude of what the two men accomplished together has not yet been fully assessed, and may never be, just as a sculpture or painting may not be fully appreciated until centuries after it is created. Their work together is a mountain range, with multiple valleys, difficult passages, and magnificent vistas. But however vast the territory they explored together, the process of exploration is far from finished. For those who have the spirit and the attitude of inward discovery, the opportunities remain unlimited.

Appendix 1

MOODY AND BOHM IN DIALOGUE ABOUT KRISHNAMURTI AND HIS WORK

December 8, 1987

David Moody: I wanted to raise again the question that Mary Lutyens raised in her biography of Krishnamurti. In the second volume, toward the end, she asks, "Who or what is Krishnamurti?" She puts that question to him. He says he cannot really answer. He says, "Water can never find out what water is." However, he adds that she could find out; if she wanted to, she could, and he could verify whether or not it was accurate. And I just wondered what are your impressions of this.

David Bohm: Well, I don't know. I think, finally, some points have been left unclear.

DM: Yes. Like what, his references to "the other"?

DB: Yes, about "the other," and about "the process"—which he said was not necessary for other people to engage in.

DM: Also, in one of the last tapes he made, he says something to the effect that another body of this kind won't come along for "hundreds of years." That's part of the same puzzle, isn't it?

DB: Yes, well, it's clear from these biographies that he feels that there were some special forces at work giving shape to his brain. These forces were not the Masters, but they might in some way be more abstract versions of the Masters, or more implicate versions.

And he's gone through certain things in his life—he was out of the body, essentially lost consciousness, and all sorts of things happened. And what he says is that his brain is being changed. Then he also says other people don't have to go through all that. It's like saying, Columbus discovered America, and other people don't have to discover America again.

You could try to look at it this way: if his brain went through all this, then something in the consciousness of humanity had changed, right? So then other brains could also, deep in the implicate order, move in a different way.

DM: Yes.

DB: He also said that people didn't take advantage of that sufficiently while he was alive; in the last tape, that's what was implied, right?

DM: Yes. But the whole sequence of events seems to make him a bit of a freak.

DB: Yes. But these freaks come along from time to time; and they may open other people up to respond properly; they may open up a movement in the consciousness of humanity. But then, of course, that doesn't close off the possibility that it could happen in some other way.

DM: Yes. It all sounds a bit occult.

DB: Yes. You could say that it contains a somewhat modified form of the Theosophical teachings.

DM: Do you think Krishnamurti was the "World Teacher"?

DB: Well, he evidently said he was, right? That's what he said at the very end, that he was the teacher, you see.

DM: Oh, you mean in another one of the final tapes.

DB: Yes.

DM: So he's not an "ordinary human being."

DB: That's what he seemed to be saying.

DM: But at times he said he *was* an ordinary human being.

DB: Yes, well, so that's one of the things that are not clear, you see.

DM: Yes. So there's some mystery here. It implies it's not possible to answer who or what is Krishnamurti.

DB: Well, we can't see how to answer it.

DM: Hmm. I wonder, then, why he says one could.

DB: Well, he said that if you were to ask him in the right way, at that time, then you could find out.

DM: Oh, I thought he meant that if you wanted to study the question and figure it out, if someone who was serious wanted to really examine the question, they could figure it out; but he couldn't tell them.

DB: No, he used to say in other places, you've got to dig; you see, it's like a gold mine. I think he meant that people hadn't asked him the right questions, or probed in the right way.

DM: So then that implies we'll never know.

DB: Not on that basis, unless, when the next one comes, we can try again. [Laughs.] On the other hand, maybe you could figure it out, you know, by going deeply enough into yourself—because he also told Doris Pratt, "Be me," you see.

DM: Did he?

DB: Well, she came and said, "How can I ever transform, I've been at it all my life." And finally he said, "You've got to be me." And then she said, "I can't, how can I, I'm me." And he said, "Well, you've got to, in the imagination." Well, that's confused all the more, because he was so against the imagination. So I told her that he probably meant the creative imagination.

DM: Yes. Well, let me put the question a little bit differently. Instead of focusing so much on the man, how would you characterize his most essential contribution?

DB: Well, I think it was the question of the nature of thought, as well as the observer and the observed. We can really put it in many ways. It's hard to focus on it; but there is this notion that the operation of intelligence is the absence of the movement of thought.

DM: Has what he said been said before?

DB: Well, I think that some of it has been said before, quite a bit of it. It's a question of whether it's been carried further, more deeply.

DM: Has anyone, before Krishnamurti, said, quite so forcefully, the observer is the observed?

DB: Well, he put it very succinctly and forcefully, but it's kind of implicit in Oriental philosophy.

DM: What about the question of time?

DB: Well, again, the Orient has always emphasized the timeless. However, he put it his own way.

DM: All right. Then what about his insistence that one must understand the whole nature and structure of thought?

DB: Well, I think he put it very strongly and forcefully. I think the Buddhists say you've got to observe your thoughts, one by one. They don't bring it out, really, that you have to see the whole nature of thought, and that it's the cessation of thought, or at least the cessation of its movement in the wrong area, that is the revolution, that is the possibility for the other to operate.

DM: So, this implies that his contribution was not so much in any particular original statement as in the elucidation—

DB: Yes, and in the extreme intensity with which it was carried forward.

DM: And comprehensiveness.

DB: Yes.

DM: Was there some aspect which was, in fact, simply original?

DB: Well, maybe, but I don't think anybody ever produces anything entirely original.

DM: So there's a sense of, not only an enigma, but—I don't want to use the word "failure," but—

DB: Well, it does appear that it hasn't quite worked, you see. I feel that it was not communicated; there may have also been some feature which was not quite right. But it didn't communicate, or at least it was put in a way which gave a wrong impression to the people who heard it.

DM: Yes; for example, he would say, "At the end of this, when you walk out of this hall, you should never taste fear again."

DB: Yes; but then perhaps he did taste fear, you see. Alain Naude said, it's a trivial example, but he said that when they were walking and a dog fiercely came at them, he jumped. You see, somehow he was not putting exactly what was happening, what he really meant. He really meant that deep down, you are now not tasting it so that you can go and look at it; there is something in you which is not overwhelmed by fear, right? and can look. [Laughter.]

DM: Mm-hm. Ah-ha.

DB: There may be adrenaline going and all that, you see.

DM: But the flame of attention remains unaffected.

DB: Yes. And it may take a day, or two days, for something to happen. You see, once somebody came up to him who said, "You are a very nice old man but you are in a rut." He said he looked at it for a few days, but what he didn't make clear is that that's the sort of thing he was constantly doing.

DM: And, in fact, did he not denigrate the idea of someone going off into his room by himself in order to observe himself?

DB: He may have, I don't know; at times he said it's OK, and at times he seemed to denigrate it—he wasn't too clear. You see, he used to say things too strongly. There was the difficulty in his use of the word "all," which he used for the sake of arousing passion, which it does. But it also has a wrong meaning.

DM: I remember one year when he insisted, over and over, "All thought leads to sorrow."

DB: Yes. Well, we can say, technical thought needn't lead to sorrow; but maybe it does because it's connected with the personal thought, right?

DM: Yes. I remember this very well. It was in Pine Cottage, and Mary Zimbalist took strong exception to the statement. She said, you know, what about technical thought, or, two plus two equals four.

DB: And what did he say?

DM: And his response was, "But see the truth in what I am saying. See the truth in it."

It sounded to me as though he was saying, "This statement, 'all thought leads to sorrow,' captures a truth. It may not cover every situation, but it captures a truth, and see that."

DB: Well, but it's not clear how it does capture such a truth. The word "all" may have the meaning of deep intention, passion, right? But it also means, "all, everything." And therefore it implies something which leaves no room for any exceptions; it creates confusion. Now, I wonder if he couldn't have found a better way to put it.

DM: Such as, "thought as a whole leads to sorrow"?

DB: Well, I don't know, perhaps "thought in its essence." But he later said there's another kind of thought which doesn't lead to sorrow. You see, with that way of putting it, you never really seem to quite catch up with it. For the sake of the deep passion, the intention, the feeling, you use a word which also has a meaning. You have to constantly say, it doesn't mean exactly what it says, right? [Laughter.]

So you could say, all thought as it is now leads to sorrow, let's put it that way. And that would be true. Thought as we know it, all thought as we know it, leads to sorrow. I think that would be true, because he has already said, there is a kind of thought which is different, but we don't know it, right? It may at the moment appear that thought isn't leading to sorrow, but it's still connected with the rest, and all these entrained, entangled mistakes are in one web.

So, if you were to put it that way, there is one whole web of mistakes which will lead to sorrow. It may appear that it's only connected with a few strands, but—[Laughter.]

DM: All thought is caught in that web?

DB: All thought is caught in that web—all thought as we know it. Now, if he had put it "as we know it" and explained that a bit, then we could have removed that problem. Saying, there is a kind of thought we don't know, which is not in that web, but, you know, that would be an illusion for us to even consider it seriously until we look at this first; until we get to the bottom of this. We are in the web; thought is in the web, and with that, all thought as we know it leads to sorrow.

I think it was a matter of putting some creative attention into the language. See, that would not confuse anybody—saying, I can see that even technical thought is going to lead to sorrow, because it's in the web. I mean, the highest technical achievements are used for war. It may appear locally as if it's free of it, you see.

DM: Yes. So it leads to a rather unsatisfactory state of affairs, because it implies several things. We're saying, K is in some sense the World Teacher, and we're also saying there is something mysterious about him and how he got to be what he is. There were mysterious, shaping influences, so he is not a transformed ordinary human but another kind of creature—

DB: That's what he implied, right?

DM: Implied; and yet at the same time there is something flawed in his presentation. It's not a personal flaw—

DB: Well, that's the same as the Kabbalah, you know, saying that there was a mistake in the creation; it's up to human beings to help rectify it. [Laughter.]

DM: Hm. He's like the fire-giver, sort of; but it's a fire that has to be shaped, or molded, or something.

DB: Yes. Well, I think it requires some creative action on our part to go on, you know, to go on from here.

DM: To let that be a catalyst, but not to expect it to have all the answers.

DB: Yes. As he said, we don't have to rediscover America. Somebody might say, it was a great and wonderful thing for Columbus to discover America; I want to go through that, too. [Laughter.]

DM: Does it imply, though, does it imply that from K's perspective, he had to regard his whole life as unsatisfactory in some way?

DB: Well, I don't know how he regarded it. I mean, he must have felt that since the communication of this thing was the main point, and it hadn't been communicated, he must have felt that somehow it didn't work. On the other hand, maybe something was started which will work.

DM: Of course. So there's an open-ended quality there.

DB: Yes.

DM: Would you agree, then, that part of the meaning of Krishnamurti's work is yet to emerge?

DB: Yes. I mean, if we take literally what he says, whatever happened to him became a change in the consciousness of humanity, right? Now, he may not have perceived fully what that change was. It may be very, if I may use my language also, in the depths of the implicate order; it is not very clear. Something is moving there.

DM: Something is moving. A process of unfoldment.

DB: Yes.

DM: Which may take centuries fully to unfold.

DB: It may; it may take a long time; you see, at this level, time is not very relevant. The only point being, we're a little worried about whether there's going to be that much time.

DM: Yes. So, I like this open-ended aspect, because it brings back the unlimited, and creativity. It seems to be almost a matter of, he didn't have the fine focus; he had the whole—but he didn't have the whole thing in fine focus.

DB: Yes, his attention was not directed toward the detail, the fine focus. That's why I was saying the wholeness of the whole and the parts. Whereas the other principle is the partiality of the parts and the whole, which is fragmentation—saying that the whole is merely another part, and therefore not really whole at all.

DM: Is there a connection between attention and—

DB: Yes, you can't have attention the other way around. The other way around you will give your attention to the parts, because they're the highest value, right?

DM: Implicit in the very word "attention" is, open to the unlimited, open to—

DB: Yes, there must be a kind of wholeness. It's not broken up but it's a whole and unlimited.

DM: So it seems like perhaps *that's* what Krishnamurti had, in abundance—

DB: Yes.

DM: Whereas, putting it forth in language left something to be desired.

DB: Yes; but, you see, the higher attention might be to attend to the wholeness of the whole and the parts. Which means that attention is simultaneously in the whole and the parts. So we need to have the right focus, the right—what did you call it?

DM: Fine focus.

DB: We need the right fine focus for the expression and for whatever is done. But I think that this fine focus is necessary if the thing is going to work.

DM: So that's the part that remains for us.

DB: Yes.

DM: Shall we leave it at that?

DB: Right.

Appendix 2

MOODY AND BOHM EXCHANGE BY AUDIOTAPE REGARDING TIME

DECEMBER 31, 1989

David Moody:

Good morning, David. This is Sunday morning, December thirty-first, 1989—the last day of the decade. And in this morning's *L.A. Times*, the last page of the book review section has a collection of thoughts about time, some of which I thought might amuse you. I'll read a few of them.

"In order to be utterly happy, the only thing necessary is to refrain from comparing this moment with other moments in the past, which I often did not fully enjoy, because I was comparing them with other moments of the future." Andre Gide.

"The present moment is a powerful goddess." Goethe.

"We cannot put off living until we are ready. The most salient characteristic of life is its coerciveness. It is always urgent, here and now, without any possible postponement. Life is fired at us point blank." Jose Ortega y Gasset.

"No mind is much employed upon the present. Recollection and anticipation fill up almost all our moments." Samuel Johnson.

"The word 'now' is like a bomb through the window, and it ticks." Arthur Miller.

"Take therefore no thought for the morrow, for the morrow shall take thought for the things of itself. Sufficient unto the day is the evil thereof." Matthew 6:34.

"What, then, is time? If no one asks me, I know what it is. If I wish to explain it to him who asks, I do not know." St. Augustine.

"Time is but the stream I go a-fishing in." Thoreau.

"I have realized that the past and the future are real illusions, that they exist only in the present, which is what there is, and all there is." Alan Watts.

"To realize the unimportance of time is the gate of wisdom." Bertrand Russell.

And, finally, "We can never finally know; I simply believe that some part of the human self or soul is not subject to the laws of space and time." Carl Jung.

Now, I have also been thinking about time. In a tape I was listening to yesterday, Krishnamurti says, "Time is the enemy of man." He was searching for a statement about which one either might have immediate insight, or that would require endless explanation, and he chose that. And he went on to explore its meaning somewhat—which came out to be that there is no such thing as psychological evolution. That turned out to be the essence of the meaning of, "Time is the enemy of man."

I'm wondering if we don't need to look with a little bit more precision at time, to get clearer about it, as we have done for proprioception and for the observer and the observed. What is Krishnamurti saying about time? What is the problem with time?

What *is* time? Why is there a distinction between physical and psychological time? Krishnamurti says we can take physical time more or less for granted. He says, of course there is time by the clock—chronological time, physical time, the time it takes to get from here to there. Now, is that correct? Is that point of view true?—say, with respect to the views of modern physics?

In any case, what is time? I remember another meeting with Krishnamurti, in 1976. We were discussing time when suddenly he asked, "Is time, to you, a continuous movement?" And, immediately, I said, "Yes." He said, "I question it," or words to that effect—there may be another way of looking at it.

What is time? What do we take it for? What is the ordinary man's implicit thought about time, or perception, or awareness of time? And what is wrong with that perspective? What is the actual nature of the case?

Also, what is the relationship of time to proprioception? We have found an unexpected connection between proprioception and "the observer is the observed." We came close to saying that the precondition for psychological proprioception may be the perception that the observer is the observed. It may be that this perception is what permits attention to flow in the way that it must in order for psychological proprioception to exist.

Now, let's bring in this third element of time. Is there not also a perception which must occur with regard to time, one which then triggers psychological proprioception?

FEBRUARY 27, 1990

David Bohm:

I'd say Krishnamurti was right: you can more or less take physical time for granted. Relativity changes the concept of time and makes it relative, but it doesn't really change it all that much. For example, it still deals with the time to go from here to there, only this is now relative to the velocity.

We can regard the physical theories of time as maps, as it were; I would say they are maps of the order of process, the action of events which succeed each other. For example, if you have a good watch, it stays in correspondence with the general order of succession. So two people in different places with good watches can agree to meet; and, being guided by their watches, they do actually meet.

Now, we can time journeys; we can time growth; we can time development, evolution; all of this can be described in the order of time. Relativistic theory says this order itself is, in a certain sense, absolute; but that the measure is not absolute. That is, the amount of time may vary according to the speed of the instrument that measures it, or according to the speed of the person who experiences it.

I don't think relativity goes very deeply into the real nature of time. Like other physical theories, it makes a map of the whole of time, and in doing this, it treats all of time as if it were like space: one big block of time. And that leaves out our whole experience of time, you see. To treat time as a kind of space is an abstraction from process and movement. Just as you can make a map and consider a whole country, you could consider on this map of process and movement all that has happened or all you expect to happen. But relativity treats this map rather as if it were the immediate, actual reality; and, in that sense, it isn't very clear.

I believe that a great deal of change is needed in the concept of time in physics. Relativity at root does not agree well with quantum mechanics; and the fact that these two equally fundamental theories don't agree suggests that some new theory is needed, one that goes beyond both. Relativity and quantum mechanics will then both appear as approximations, or limiting cases of a deeper theory.

Now, one thing relativity can't do—indeed, that no physical concept of time can do—is to deal with the actual immediacy of the present. What we do is to draw a line, and we represent different moments as points on that line. So we can say, this moment *now* is to be represented by a certain point. But this point is an abstraction, just as a small dot on the map representing a city is an abstraction. It is in no sense the thing itself.

We should therefore regard physics as dealing with an extreme abstraction of the actual flow, the movement of process, the succession of things that happen. It doesn't give the sense of the immediacy of *now*. There is no place in physics for *now*; and yet *now* is the most immediate meaning of life.

So, in some sense, there is an extreme discrepancy between the way physics deals with it and the way we feel it should be and experience it. Some physicists, including Einstein, say that our experience of immediacy and flow is an illusion, and physics tells us the true reality; that time is an infinite block, like the block of space, and that the succession of things is an illusion.

Now, this view cannot be maintained very consistently, because it doesn't explain our experience of succession. If time is like a block of space, you could imagine a railroad train moving through this block, going through from the past to the future. But then a second kind of time is brought in to describe the movement of the railroad train. So you have merely pushed the problem off.

So the ideas of physics simply do not do justice to the way we experience movement and process and the present. In my view, the best thing is to regard these ideas as extreme abstractions. Just as a map is extremely different from the country, so what physics says about time is different from the concrete actuality of process, movement, and succession.

Now, another view, which is in principle in the implicate order, is that moments unfold one after another. But each moment unfolds from an implicate, enfolded order; and the moments do not then need to be continuous. You may have them fairly close to each other, or extremely close; they may look continuous because you're not resolving the moments— you're getting many of them all at once into your perception, and so on. But, in that view, you could say that we have a creative movement, that everything is created at one moment, again and again; it is recreated similar but different. Thought and memory take hold of this similarity and we see it as continuity, while we see the differences as changes in the continuity.

Now, this is all tied together with the question of the observer and the observed, and proprioception, and literal, figurative, and participatory thought. Because literal thought says that thought is telling us the way things are. Now, if we take the view which I have just been describing, we could say everything *is* now, including memory. Memory is constantly recreated now; it carries some abstraction of the past with it; but memory is never the past, it's always an abstraction actually taking place in the present. We experience it now, and also the anticipation of the future is experienced now.

So memory with its past and future is a small part of the actual now. But it tends to fill our consciousness and becomes the main part. In other words, as Gide said, we mostly fill our consciousness with the memory of the past and the anticipation of the future, which helps to create the illusion of continuity.

Literal thought implicitly denies that it participates. That makes it impossible to see that the observer is the observed. Instead it says the observed is just what it seems to be, and that the observer is simply looking at it without affecting it. So, the trap of taking literal thought too literally is the first point needing attention. We have to notice that literal thought is not actually literal; in fact, literal thought is basically figurative.

For example, when we see a rainbow we see a figure. There is no rainbow there; the light is refracted in a complicated way, but our mind projects a figure of a rainbow, which moves as we walk or go in a car. Everybody projects a similar figure, which might make us think that there is objectively a rainbow; but in fact there is nothing but rain falling and light being refracted from the droplets; there is no bow.

Similarly, we see figurative thought when we project shapes and forms into shadows and clouds and so on. In fact, ultimately all the shapes and forms we see are figurative thought, which are abstractions having a certain correspondence to reality. So we could say with regard to literal thought that its meaning is ultimately figurative.

So the first thing that thought has to realize is that it has figurative and literal aspects, and that it's overdoing the literal aspect, especially when you think about yourself. When you think about yourself, you form inside what you may call a figure of the self. This is not only your self-image, but also a feeling that somewhere inside of you is a center and a periphery. The center may move from the chest, into the solar plexus, into the head; the periphery may be the skin or something else; it's very moveable. But this figure is created by thought. It is taken literally, as saying, it's there, it's real, and it's me.

However, since the figure is incomplete and imperfect, it becomes a problem. There is an urge to make it better. Thought cannot possibly project a complete figure, and if the figure is taken as real, it must be sensed as incomplete, requiring change and so on. It may also be sensed as ephemeral, so that it must be made more permanent.

And therefore, you always have a problem. On the one hand, you may feel, something is wrong with me. Sooner or later, one encounters something wrong with this figure, or one senses that it is inadequate. For example, one may say, this figure contains anger, and I know that this is wrong. It makes trouble for me, so I don't want to be angry; and this implies incoherence.

The awareness of the incoherence should lead you to find the true cause of the trouble, but it does not. For you then inwardly take the same approach you take outwardly, and say: I am distinct from that figure, and I've got to see what it is, and think about it, and do something about it. But this doesn't make sense, because I *am* that figure. I have produced it, and it produces me. That figure affects, profoundly affects the way I think. It produces very powerful compulsions and so on.

And so if you say, I am not the figure, in that very act you are the figure. But when you say, I *am* the figure, then you open the way to ceasing to be it. That is, if you say, "I am momentarily dominated by this figure," you can then see that you are creating this problem. If you are hurt, you are actually experiencing the hurt by assuming that you are there being hurt. That very thought creates the hurt, you see; it attributes the hurt to something real and makes it important.

You then have to see that there is a deeper level of thought—what we have called tacit or implicit thought—which is behind all this. And you can't actually deal with the figure being taken as real at this abstract level, or the level of words.

So there is something deeper. The tacit movement, such as the bicycle-riding movement, is what produces all of the explicit content; and, somehow we have to come into contact with that. A number of years ago I gave the example of attaching a thin wire to a nerve in the hand, a single nerve in the finger attached to a loudspeaker. And every time the nerve works, the loudspeaker clicks. Eventually you are then able to make it click, or even to play a tune on it, in a way you can't describe—which involves some sort of tacit knowledge of the kind that occurs in bicycle-riding. So as long as it's displayed in consciousness (or, it's being displayed by the loudspeaker here), then the tacit movement can be guided by this awareness, which can reach to this implicit source, the enfolded source of the display, and change it in whatever way would be appropriate.

Now, in consciousness we have to display this thought process. If it is displayed wrongly, as something which is not acknowledged to be thought, then the tacit movement can never be guided properly. I take it that when Krishnamurti says, "You *are* the anger, you *are* the fear," this helps to establish a correct display so that you no longer fight against it, but you say, "It is what it is, I can't change it."

But still the tacit movement will work. There is a tacit movement which is really the observer, you see. If thought claims to detach itself from the object (which in this case is the self) when it's not really de-tached, then thought isn't working properly. Thought is then tacitly taking to itself the role of an impartial observer who is not affected by what it observes, when in fact that is not correct. It might be correct if you looked at some object outside that didn't mean much to you, but it isn't true here.

So the first thing is to be free of this false display. This is what Krishnamurti is saying: "You are the world; you are the anger; you are the fear; you are the envy, the sorrow, and so on." It is then being displayed correctly.

Now, this allows for proprioception. The previous split between observer and observed overlaid consciousness with a figure which denied the possibility of proprioception, by implying that was all going on independently of the observer, and that the observer was merely looking at it. It's as if you tried to see something, but overlaid it with a powerful projection of an image, with the aid of very bright lights. You would see something else that was illusory.

All aspects of this whole process have to appear all at once, you see, without time. If you think of Krishnamurti saying that time is not a continuity, that it's just one moment after another, then each moment, we just feel, "There it is!" Once the movement that creates the illusion of separation of observer and observed in a time process is seen to be what it actually is, then its triviality becomes evident. And anything which is seen to be incoherent and unimportant loses force. All the power that generates it is gone, you see, and it must fade away.

So the point, then, is that experiencing in terms of the observer and the observed inevitably introduces time; they are one and the same process. You cannot make a division into parts without introducing time, because if you divide into parts then the connection to the next part must take time to establish. Therefore, in a correct mode of perception, there is no psychological time in the sense of a continuity of existence of a psychological being.

Yes, well, I hope that begins to answer what you had in mind.

Appendix 3

INWARD OBSERVATION

David Moody

Prologue

In reviewing the vast array of problems human beings confront on a daily basis, one is led to reflect upon the nature of the psychological field. Whether on a public scale or in our private lives, it is apparent that various kinds of illusion, self-deception, and other distorted ideas often play a crucial role in establishing the direction of events. Socrates declared that the unexamined life is not worth living; we may add that the unexamined mind is not worth having. And yet in the urgency of daily events we tend to take ourselves for granted, to accept a network of easy assumptions about who we are and what we are doing.

This essay is addressed to those who have begun to examine themselves with greater care, in a spirit of objectivity and critical detachment. Such an examination is not judgmental: on the contrary, to judge what one observes is the denial of objectivity. What matters, therefore, is the quality of inward observation itself. The present essay is designed to sketch the parameters of that process, and to highlight some of the central difficulties associated with it.

I. Ways of Knowing

In order to acquire a sense of what is involved in the peculiar territory of inward observation, it is helpful to begin by considering the process of observation in general. In considering the totality of ways that we have of knowing anything whatsoever—about ourselves, about one another, about the world at large—we may begin by examining the several senses: seeing, hearing, smelling, tasting, and the sense of touch. If we like, we can arrange these in a sequence, moving from outermost to innermost. The sense which gives us access to information at the outermost remove from ourselves is vision: with the naked eye, one can see not only to the edge of the earth, the line where sea and sky coincide, but beyond the earth, all the way to the Milky Way and beyond. Vision gives access to the universe as a whole.

Vision is the only one of our senses that is attuned to discriminate differences in electromagnetic radiation. In nature, there is no sharp distinction between gamma rays, x-rays, radio waves, and the waves we know as visible light: all are varieties of oscillation in the electromagnetic field, where everything moves at the universal speed limit of 186,000 miles per second. Visible light represents only a narrow band within the vast spectrum of electromagnetic radiation, but at least vision does tap into that medium. Hearing, by contrast, relies on a cruder, more palpable medium, that is, the percussive impact of molecules of air. Since molecules of air are all but ubiquitous on the surface of the earth, hearing provides an excellent source of information about events at an intermediate range of distance.

Whereas vision discriminates differences in waves of electromagnetism, hearing discriminates differences in waves that move through matter. Sound consists of a complex mixture of such waves. Waves of motion through matter may vary in both amplitude and frequency: changes in amplitude determine the volume of the sound; changes in frequency determine pitch. The manner in which these changes overlap and coincide is responsible for everything we know with our ears, from the cry of a baby to Beethoven's Ninth Symphony.

The sense of smell, like that of hearing, relies upon air as the medium of transmission; but whereas sound consists of changes in the motion of air molecules, the sense of smell detects changes in the chemical composition of air. Our sense of smell is so constructed that the primary ingredients in the atmosphere—oxygen, nitrogen, and carbon dioxide—have no odor for us. The nose is 'blind', as it were, to these gases; they are undetectable. If it were otherwise, our sense of smell would constantly be assaulted by these odors, just as the ear would be drowning in sound if the mere presence of air could be heard. What the sense of smell can detect are any molecules held in suspension over and above the ordinary gases of the atmosphere. In this regard, the sense of smell can be extremely sensitive. In man the detection of foreign chemicals in the air is somewhat attenuated, but in dogs and other species, as little as a few molecules per million can be readily perceived. Nevertheless, with rare exceptions, the sense of smell gives information about the world only at a near remove from the perceiving organism; thus the dog holds his nose very close to the ground.

With the sense of taste, we move yet another step further in the direction of inward observation. Taste is a close cousin to the sense of smell in that both are instruments designed for chemical analysis. Whereas smell detects the chemical composition of molecules suspended in air, taste detects the chemical composition of molecules dissolved in liquid or detachable from the surface of solids. In order to achieve this form of observation, the perceiving organism must come into direct contact with the object perceived; thus, in the order of nearness, we have come with taste to the physical boundary of the individual.

The sense of touch shares with the sense of taste the observation of events at the boundary of the organism; but touch is a complex set of senses which extends yet further inward from the skin. Even at the surface of the body, touch is multi-dimensional: the skin is equipped with specialized cells designed for the independent discrimination of pressure and heat, as well as for such refinements as the sensations of tickle, moisture, and itch, not to mention the erotic. The proliferation of kinds of information available at the boundary of the organism pays tribute to the bedrock necessity to distinguish self from non-self: the sense of touch defines the global horizon of the physical entity.

The kinds of cells with which we discriminate the pressure of physical contact are not confined to the surface of the skin. Cells of a similar structure and function are liberally distributed at varying depths beneath the surface, as well as throughout the entire musculature. In this connection we come to a qualitatively new kind of information from any we have encountered thus far in our journey from outer to inner. All the previous forms of observation that we have considered represent channels of information about the external world. The sense of touch, however, encompasses information not only about the external world, but also about the perceiving organism: the nerve cells in the muscles tell us how we ourselves are moving or situated. A special word is required to describe this form of observation: it is called *proprioception*, that is, the perception of oneself.

With proprioception we have moved as far inward as it is possible to go in our progressive examination of the physical senses. We have available to us, however, channels of information other than those provided by the senses. Among the most important of these are the emotions. Some would say that the emotions represent the most fundamental of all forms of understanding; others would say that most emotions are distracting and misleading. In any case, however, there can be no denying that the emotions represent an extremely powerful current in our lives.

In the order of progression from outer to inner, the emotions represent a further step inward from physical proprioception. The emotions represent a kind of bridge across the deep divide that separates the physical from the psychological. We generally consider emotions to belong fundamentally to the realm of the mental; yet feelings themselves clearly reside in localized parts of the physical organism. Thus the emotions represent a kind of transitional form of observation, suspended somehow midway between the physical data of the senses, and the psychological space associated with thought.

On closer observation, in fact, it becomes apparent that the emotions are nothing more nor less than the channel of information that tells us about the current state of the vital organs. It is no accident that the heart is considered the seat of emotion, or that many feelings are localized in the stomach. Elation or inspiration literally expand the lungs; remorse releases pancreatic bile. Sorrow and laughter both cause spasms of the diaphragm, as well as the release of cleansing fluids in the eyes. Embarrassment triggers changes in the skin. The kidneys or renal tissues are ordinarily quiet in this dance; but the *ad*renal glands contribute chemicals to the bloodstream that heighten the readiness and awareness of the organism as a whole. Every emotion is associated with a change in the state of the internal organs; and a little reflection suffices to show that the emotions represent little more than the medium of information about those states. Thus the emotions may be considered to represent the proprioceptive capacity of the vital tissues.

The raw fact that emotions convey a form of information about the state of the physical organism does not in any way diminish their meaning or significance. We tend to think of emotions as sublime, subtle, or evanescent—not qualities we ordinarily associate with the state of the physical tissues. But there is no reason why we ought not to consider the state of our internal organs in such terms; indeed, our well-being depends on it, since the state of our organs is ultimately a matter of life and death. The principle is well-established in medicine that the health of the heart, the stomach, and other tissues is intimately linked with the kind of emotional currents that tend to reside there.

We have yet to consider the relationship of emotion to the other side of the bridge. On the physical side, emotion represents the state of the internal organs; on the psychological side, emotion reflects the relationship between perceived values and facts. Where values and facts are perceived to stand in a favorable relationship—I value money and win the lottery—emotion reflects that relationship. Where values and facts are at odds—the stock market crashes—that disharmony is reflected as emotional distress. Emotion is the form of information that reflects the meaning of perceived values and facts for the physical organism. In a phrase, we may say that emotion is the embodiment of meaning.

The bridge of emotion therefore leads us to the psychological realm, the land of knowledge, of concepts and abstractions, of past and future, of memory, goals, and intentions. In essence this is the land of thought, broadly construed. In this territory, observation undergoes a kind of warp; nothing is as simple as it was in the case of the senses. To understand the nature and resolution of this difficulty is the central task involved in the art of inward observation.

The first thing to notice about the kind of observation associated with the land of thought is that it is private: nothing here is accessible to others. From this fact arise the notorious difficulties associated with the effort to treat psychology as a science. Because independent observation is a cornerstone of scientific method, the primary data of psychology are intrinsically off-limits to science.

But there is another equally fundamental discontinuity between the data given by the senses and those given by thought. In the case of the senses, it is possible to direct the attention at will: if you ask me to look at a rainbow or listen to the whippoorwill I can do so without hesitation or difficulty. But if I seek to direct my attention to thought, I find that the object of my investigation is elusive. To be sure, if you ask me to say in general what I have been thinking about, I can tell you easily enough; but if you ask me to observe the process of my thinking as it is in the act of unfolding, something very curious occurs. I cannot simultaneously think something and be aware I am thinking it. If I am listening to the radio, the listening and the awareness that I am listening are, or can be, simultaneous. But in the case of thought, that simultaneity is impossible. I can think something, and I can be aware that I have thought it; but the awareness cannot occur in the very moment when thought does arise.

From this fact there follows a nest of difficulties. Perhaps the most salient of these from the standpoint of daily life has to do with the manner in which we understand and deal with emotion. The bodily sensations which are the substance of emotion are akin to the senses in that we can direct our attention to them at will. But emotions are a bridge between the physical and the psychological. On the physical side, we can watch the emotions as they unfold in the present; but on the psychological side, we cannot. As a result, we lose track of the fact that emotions have their origin in thought. We tend to attribute our emotions to facts and circumstances in the external world; we lose sight of the fact that emotion is the embodiment of meaning, and that meaning resides in our minds.

Our failure to understand the source of emotional states leads to the contradiction that we then try to control them. To say that we must not be afraid is contradictory because fear has its source in the very cognitive apparatus that says to have no fear. Thus the admonition not to be afraid (or angry or envious or depressed) is not only ineffective; it is also a source of conflict in the organism as a whole. The admonition sets up a predisposition in the nervous system that cannot be fulfilled, and the energy so directed becomes blocked. Tension is the condition that results when such energy cannot find a natural outlet or form of expression.

A similar contradiction occurs in connection with the effort to control thought itself. One becomes aware that one has been having certain thoughts, but these thoughts are not observed as such in the moment when they arise. Rather, we see them only in retrospect, when they are a little removed in time from where we are now. That distance, that degree of separation, introduces the implicit notion that we who are observing the thought are separate from the thought we are observing. That notion in turn sets up the implicit expectation that we can somehow influence or control the thought in question. But since the thought was the product of the same apparatus with which it is now perceived, the impulse to control is circular and self-defeating.

As serious as the foregoing contradictions may be in daily life, they take a back seat to the most fundamental discontinuity introduced by our inability to observe thought directly, in the process of its unfolding. Unable to see thought at its source, we invent a source for it. If we were to watch it as it first arose, like a worm emerging from the soil, we would see that it arises of its own accord, as it were. But since we only observe thoughts as finished products, delivered to the plate of our attention a moment or a month after they are first formed, we implicitly infer the presence of a thought-maker, a psychological entity at the source. Since thought is crucial for our daily functioning, the entity at the source of thought occupies the hub if not the circumference of our lives.

But the thought-maker is only inferred; we don't notice that the thought-maker itself is the product of thought. We infer the characteristics of the thought-maker according to the kinds of thoughts it produces; but those characteristics are attached to an entity which is itself only inferred. We never stop to examine whether the thought-maker does or does not exist in actuality.

One of the tasks of inward observation, accordingly, is to inquire into the source of thought. Is it possible to put aside all inferences and observe the matter directly? If the thought-maker exists in actuality, is it accessible to observation? And what is the thought-maker's role in asking these questions?

Before we proceed too far down that path, however, it may be worthwhile to recall what got us to this point: the inaccessibility of thought to immediate perception. That inaccessibility, as we have seen, is responsible for a kind of warp in the entire field of inward observation. Whatever inquiry we may undertake with respect to the thought-maker will in all probability intersect with the inaccessibility of thought in general. In short, we may need to expose the entire continent of thought before we can go in search of its capital.

In reflecting, therefore, on the range of ways we have of knowing anything at all, we see that another kind or set of rules appears to apply in the observation of inner events. The difficulty already begins to emerge in connection with the emotions, where it is not at all apparent what the observed sensations indicate or represent—notwithstanding that they largely rule our daily life. And by the time we come to the more strictly psychological realm, observation per se evidently comes to a halt. The art of inward observation thus appears to be a rather subtle and mysterious one. In any case, it would seem we are well advised to proceed with caution, mindful of the possibility of the unexpected, but also with a certain urgency, born of the realization that the entire structure of our understanding is at stake.

II. Thought and the Thought-Maker

We have seen in connection with our review of the range of ways we have of knowing anything at all that something peculiar obtains with regard to the observation of inner events. Part of this peculiarity has to do with the nature of the inferred entity at the source of thought. We realize that the question of the actuality of the thought-maker in all probability cannot be resolved independently of the larger issue of the general inaccessibility of thought to immediate observation. Nevertheless, with an urgency born of necessity, we plunge into the core of the thicket. It may be necessary to expose a continent in order to discover the capital, but if so we shall do so in the effort to make that discovery.

What is the origin of thought? Where and how does it arise? Is there a thought-maker, a thinker, an entity who speaks in a silent soliloquy? When the question is framed in this blunt manner, we find that the simple answer is to say, we don't know. We hardly even know where to turn to look for an answer. The mind somehow forms the intention to look in a place where it imagines a thinker might reside, but is that looking actual or imagined? Boundaries blur.

How, then, shall we proceed? If we cannot observe the source of thought as readily as we can perceive that the radio is the source of a sound, what approach is possible? Is there a mirror that will enable thought to see, as it were, its own face? Or are we simply faced with an impenetrable puzzle, a black hole at the center of consciousness? If thought itself is inaccessible to direct observation, how much more so must be the source of thought?

Who is the thinker? Does the thinker exist? If not, where do thoughts come from? In asking these questions persistently, repeatedly, with pauses or interludes of rest, something fundamental begins to occur. One must try this to observe its effects for oneself. It introduces a kind of stillness into the mental realm, a watchfulness, one in which thoughts do not cease but perhaps come with somewhat reduced frequency. One approach to the issue of the actuality of the thought-maker, accordingly, is simply not to be deterred by any initial absence of success. Let the question stand. Let it work on its own.

Another approach that presents itself for consideration is to ask, what would the thinker look like if it existed? That is, what assumptions do I currently hold about the thinker? What do I think it is like, whether I have examined the matter closely or not? What would come as no surprise if I were suddenly able to observe the thinker directly for myself?

The thinker is great. The thinker is noble. The thinker is honest and true. The thinker is kind and wishes well of others (with a few rare exceptions, perhaps). The thinker may be weak, confused, or erratic on occasion, but that is only because it is faced with extraordinary challenges. In general, the thinker seems to be the very core of goodness, its observations and intentions worthy of trust absolutely. These, in any case, seem to be our implicit assumptions most of the time. To be sure, there are occasions when the thinker is afflicted with a paralyzing sense of its own inadequacy; but on the whole, the thinker seems to think well of itself.

Does this constellation of values give insight into where and how to observe or comprehend the source of thought? Perhaps not at once; but again, it may serve as a point of reference as we proceed. The source of thought, we seem to assume, is not merely a mechanical device, but the source of truth, goodness, and beauty as well.

In the somewhat meditative frame of mind induced by an inquiry of this kind, another layer of assumption about the thinker comes into view: the element of time. The thinker is the historian; it is the repository of information about that which has occurred. In fact, the thinker is imbued with the record of its past thoughts and experiences; in some sense it is that record. I am that which has happened to me. I am what I remember about myself.

We have discovered that, whatever may prove to be the actual attributes (or actuality) of the thought-maker, we hold a vast array of intensely meaningful assumptions regarding it: the barnacles on this hull have more mass than the hull itself. Whether this brings us nearer to an understanding of the actual thinker remains to be seen; for the time being we are content merely to note all potentially relevant data.

Yet another approach to the thinker is to try, insofar as is possible, to put aside all assumptions whatsoever. To do so would be to consider what is the source of thought without regard to any kind of expectations, preconceptions, or implicit ideas. What is the source of thought? Where does it come from? As simple as that: no assumptions.

When the issue is considered in this manner, it is not at all apparent why there should be any requirement for a thought-maker at all. Thoughts evidently simply arise; they seem to be the by-product of the entire disposition of the nervous system. Thoughts are the expression in words or images of something that is already felt or seen in the nervous system at a non-verbal level. It is the natural product, it appears, of that layer of the brain whose stock in trade consists of words and images. There is no need to invoke any psychological entity; the physical organism, with its brain and senses, is source enough.

What, then, we are entitled to ask, of the thinker as the repository of the past, as the sum of its experiences? Even if my present thought does not require a thought-maker, who is the historian? And whose story is it? Is there not an entity who is the sum of all my experience? Is not that the one who thinks?

We seem to be approaching the thinker simultaneously from two directions. On the one hand we have a large set of operating assumptions about it; on the other hand, we have the cold reality that we cannot put our hands on any thinker, or observe it directly; nor can we see any reason to infer that it exists. To be sure, thought appears to reside in some kind of psychological space; but that seems no reason to presuppose or conclude that the source of thought is similarly non-physical. The material substance of the brain appears by both observation and reason to serve as a sufficient substrate for thought. Evidently, only long and deeply held habits of mind mitigate against the direct realization of this fact.

In reflecting upon this overall state of affairs, we are drawn to consider further the nature of the psychological space which both thought and the thinker appear to occupy. At the same time, it seems reasonable to inquire into the nature of psychological time. Is there a kind of time with which we measure events in the psychological realm? Does the thinker occupy the same sort of past, present, and future as does the physical organism? Or does psychological space entail a corresponding kind of time?

To begin with, does psychological space exist? If it does not, where does thought reside? Are we content to say merely that it resides in the brain, in the neurons and the synapses? Or is it necessary to invoke an alternative kind of medium, one not subject to the laws of Newton?

Suppose that we concede that thought is weightless, odorless, undetectable by the senses: does it therefore follow that it is ethereal, non-material? What if thought were the by-product of electrical impulses in the brain (as in fact it very largely does appear to be)? Would it not then appear exactly as it does?—that is, as a swift current of energy and information. Therefore, why do we need to invoke psychological space? Whatever my assumptions may be, thought need occupy no space more mysterious than the circuitry of the cerebral cortex. Psychological space, like the thinker, is then just a fiction I have invoked with which to explain something I have never closely examined.

By the same token, psychological time is only the interval in which the psychological entity seeks to become that which it is not. The thinker is well aware of its limitations; these are brought home every day. But the thinker is also aware of its own inherent fund of goodness: whatever it may not be now, it could become in the future. Improvement is always possible. We don't notice that the time in which that improvement is expected to occur is not really ordinary time, as measured by clocks and calendars, but a time appropriate to events in psychological space. I will become better tomorrow. But tomorrow is never any specific date; in psychological time, tomorrow is always the same. That is the tip-off to the fact that it too is fictitious.

The crucial point to recognize regarding psychological time is that we do not ordinarily see or sense a distinction between it and chronological time. We have already suggested one basis for such a distinction: the interchangeability of all psychological tomorrows. In addition, psychological time is typically imbued with a particular content, an expectation of what will take place. Psychological time, therefore, is a projection of psychological events, whereas time by the clock is the projection of nothing but itself.

To be sure, within the projection of chronological time it is possible to anticipate, with varying degrees of certainty, the occurrence of events in the physical world. Next week I will fly to New York for an anticipated series of events: these can imbue the chronological future with specific content, just as psychological time is prone to do. What can be accurately scheduled, however, is of the order of planes, taxis, and human bodies; what cannot be scheduled are states of mind. What distinguishes psychological time is that there we attempt to project the qualities and characteristics of the thinker. To do so is to project a future that corresponds to a fiction; that future itself, accordingly, is fictitious too.

At the end of it all, therefore, what remains? Not the thinker, nor the space in which the thinker resides, nor the time in which it improves. What remains is only thought, the simple fact of thought, and its consequences. And it is that to which we may now, therefore, turn our complete attention.

III. The Proprioceptive Mind

We return to our point of departure: the inaccessibility of thought to direct inspection as it is in the process of unfolding. We have seen several difficulties this blind spot generates, and we have examined one or two of these in some detail. We have yet to understand, however, why the blind spot exists, much less what can be done to resolve or shed light on it. Until we come to terms completely with this fundamental issue, we cannot expect to master the art of inward observation.

Let us begin by recalling what the condition of psychological proprioception would be like, or what it appears to us (who do not have it) that it would be like. We are looking for a state of mind in which thought appears to us as such, qua thought, in the very moment of its occurrence. We may think of this state as akin to what presently occurs when we listen to the radio, or to someone else who is speaking: our awareness of what is being said and of who is saying it is simultaneous. In the case of thought, by contrast, there appear to be two separate moments: the one in which thought occurs, and the subsequent moment in which I am aware of what I have thought.

This apparently innocuous gap, as we have seen, represents the gateway to a world of psychological difficulties. In the interest of closing or resolving this gap, we may consider the following hypotheses designed to account for its existence:

Twenty-one Hypotheses

The following hypotheses are offered in an effort to account for the essential inaudibility of ongoing cognitive processes.

1. Simple inattention.

2. Thought moves too fast. You can see it/hear it as it occurs, if you want to, but only if you slow it down.

3. As with any perceptual object that is difficult to pick up, the problem may lie in the lack of appropriate or sufficient contrast with a background. Perhaps if other ongoing, *non*-cognitive processes (e.g., sensory awareness, outwardly or inwardly), were brought to attention, then the ongoing cognitive processes would show up against that background.

4. Or perhaps the background of the thinker needs to be brought into attention in order to illuminate the foreground of thought.

5. (a) Perhaps it is the temporal aspect that is elusive. Maybe it is necessary to get on the wavelength, as it were, of the present, since observation is always and only of the present. Outward awareness may then serve as a kind of tempo-setter, or wavelength adjustor, for one dimension of ongoing cognitive processes.

   (b) Perhaps the next step is to locate thought in space: outward sensory awareness; inward sensory awareness (feelings, emotions, intentions, etc.); then ongoing cognitive processes.

6. Maybe what blocks the awareness of thought is the presence of the observer. According to Bohm, proprioception is the awareness of the connection between the intention to act, and the result. Perhaps only when the observer is seen to be the observed, when the thinker is collapsed back into the thought, can the true, actual intention to think be observed. That is, the idea of the thinker serves as a kind of screen or block against awareness of the actual origin of thought.

7. Maybe the problem lies in motive, in the process of seeking. So long as awareness is with an end in view, it is not choiceless and therefore not fully aware. The only ongoing cognitive process to be aware of in that case is the motive.

8. Perhaps the problem lies in the distinction between implicit and explicit thought. There is thought in the foreground, the ongoing interior monologue; and thought in the background, the implicit realm of assumptions, presuppositions, and other elements of the known in varying degrees and stages of unconsciousness. Maybe it is necessary to pick up the implicit as a background against which to tune into the ongoing explicit soliloquy.

9. Thought is too quiet. The silent soliloquy is not really totally silent, just very, very low volume. After all, if we say thought is a material process, perhaps it follows that it has a certain volume. But it is a very light material process, and has correspondingly low volume. You can only pick it up if all other sound ceases totally; otherwise it gets drowned out.

10. There are too many distractions. You could listen to thought as it occurs if you gave it your total attention.

11. When you are looking for thought, it isn't there. But it's almost always there when you relax and are not looking for it. One needs to adopt an attitude in between, letting it come, but also on the lookout at the same time.

12. Maybe it doesn't matter. Maybe one doesn't need to observe thought exactly as it arises. It's good enough just to weave back and forth: letting it come for a bit, then looking back on it, then letting it come some more, etc. That may be close enough to get the gist of what's going on; and perhaps, with successive approximations, it may then become possible to bring the two modes into one.

13. It really can't be done. What you are trying to achieve is a sense of separation between you, the observer, the listener, and the (sought-after) object of your attention, the interior monologue. But the whole point of what K is pointing out is that that sense of separation is an artificial one introduced precisely by the presence of the observer, the thinker, which in turn is the result of the presence of thought. In other words, the achievement of the sense of separation is contingent upon the movement of thought as separate from the thing observed. Ergo, the movement of thought can never have that sense of separation from itself. This is somewhat akin to the fact that the physical eye can never see itself.

14. It could be we are looking for the wrong kind of thing. Maybe we should be looking for an ongoing process of meaning, rather than of sound, something heard in the mind's inner ear.

15. Thought is the past. To observe thought in the moment is to distinguish it from non-thought. The distinguishing factor is time: thought is the past.

16. It can only be done if it is done with the right intention, the right approach. If it is done with a motive, with an end in view, as a means to some reward, it cannot be done; whereas if it is done out of the fullness of immediate awareness, out of the motiveless impulse of intelligence to observe, then there is no problem.

17. There is a "blind spot"—precisely analogous to the optic nerve in the retina. Unfortunately, psychologically as well as with vision, perception is designed to "paper over" the blind spot—we do not see what we do not see. It requires special experimental arrangements even to discern that the blind spot exists.

18. We have thought mis-categorized when we go to look for it as "thought." Already, one is looking for something outside of oneself. Rather, we should look for "me," the voice of the me. That is how we experience thought, and that is where we shall find it if we set out to look for it.

19. Either you have the intention to observe thought or you do not. If you do not have the intention, you do not do it. If you have the intention, you have nothing to observe: in the place where thought was before you tried to observe it, now there is nothing but that intention. You could say, "Well, then, observe that intention," and that might be correct—in fact, it might be a big step. Nevertheless, this is not an entirely satisfactory result, for several reasons. First of all, the intention to observe thought is a rather static affair in itself. That is, if such an intention is in fact a thought (as it almost undoubtedly is), it is just a big, unitary, monolithic thought—kind of a big, gray fog—without much there to observe. In any case, it is not at all like the lively, bouncing, fantasy-filled, emotionally reactive thought that seems to take place very often when we don't have the intention to observe it.

    In addition, now the field of action seems to have changed a little. We started out with the intention to observe thought; now we have the intention to observe an intention. Is it the same thing, or isn't it?

    On top of that, it's not so easy to observe a big, stationary, monolithic thing like the intention to observe thought. What exactly is one observing here? And is there a division between the observer and the observed?

20. You've got to shut your eyes in order to do it. Just as you can hear music better with your eyes closed, so you can hear the subtle

"sounds" of thought better without the distraction introduced by the visual field. This is even physiological: when the eyes are closed, an inhibitory nerve that dampens the auditory apparatus switches off.

21. Let's say listening to thought is like tuning into a certain TV channel. Let's say one day our TV set starts being able to tune into that channel, and we start watching it—and it turns out after all this, there is nothing on it worth watching! Let's say the programming is really boring, trivial, mundane, disconnected. We would say, "What's the point of watching this channel?" We wouldn't watch it for ten minutes before we shut it off.

The point of this little parable is this: Why do we want to watch that channel in the first place? What do we expect to get out of it? Maybe we've been stuck on this point for so long that we've forgotten the reason for it—that is, if we ever had it clearly in mind in the first place. Maybe we just picked this up as an inference from K, and have been pursuing it rather blindly ever since.

The deeper point is this: Maybe the whole difficulty in observing thought springs from the lack of clarity in the intention. Maybe if the foundation of the intention were clear, the whole thing would occur quite spontaneously. Maybe that is the only way it can ever happen.

So why do we want to observe thought? Can we get clear on the intention? The actual intention, as well as the "right" intention?

Let's begin with the actual. This we can only find out through observation. And in observing this, we are in fact, at some level, beginning to observe thought—no?

As indicated in hypothesis number 6, our inquiry with David Bohm into the nature and dynamic structure of consciousness finally brought us to a certain point: a focus on the issue of psychological proprioception, and a proposal for a resolution of this issue. What, I asked David, is the basis of proprioception generally? What is the essential nature of that process, as it occurs physically and as we would like it to occur psychologically? He answered that the basic nature of that process consists in an awareness of the relationship between the intention to act, and the action. Proprioception, he said, is to be aware that *this* intention produces *that* effect, that action. To see or sense the dynamic unity of the impulse to act and the action, he said, is the quality of proprioception itself.

I asked him, is there in fact an intention to think? Does thought require, or is it preceded by, any kind of intention at all? I am not sure David was clear on this point; he may have suggested that there is such an intention, but that it is only implicit, or that it occurs only at a subtle level. In any event, I followed this point up with a proposal: that there may be an intimate connection, indeed a virtual identity, between psychological proprioception and the insight that the observer is the observed. My reasoning was that if we assume the presence of an observer, a thinker at the source of thought, that image will serve effectively to block attention to the actual source, the actual intention to think. That is, only with the dissolution of the illusion of the thinker does it become possible to give attention to the actual source of thought, i.e., to the intention to think as it arises from the subtle and implicit ground of consciousness.

With this proposal, we come to the end of our present inquiry. What we have done is to sketch the contours of the territory of inward observation, and to point out the major issues that require resolution. No one, however, can undertake the process of observation for another; what remains is for whoever is interested to participate on their own. At that point one is likely to find that the action or movement or intention to listen to thought at its source engenders a kind of stillness in the mind, just as any listening typically does. In that stillness, thought has subsided; indeed, that stillness is the stillness of thought. Thus, the very act of listening suspends or holds in abeyance that which one is intending to listen to.

Inward observation, accordingly, is an extremely subtle art, one for which there are no simple formulas or recipes. In the stillness that listening engenders, thought cannot be held in abeyance forever; sooner or later, another thought occurs. Perhaps, one may say, that is the very moment of inattention, the moment of the failure of listening; or perhaps, when thought occurs in a moment of stillness, another kind of attention is in fact possible. Only an active, experimental approach will resolve these issues; and again, no one can resolve them for another. In the land of inward observation, a map can take us only so far; what follows is all frontier.

Appendix 4

PHYSICS AND THE LAWS OF NATURE

Edited Transcription

David Bohm in conversation with David Moody and Saral Bohm. Circa 1989.

David Moody (DM): What would you say is the subject matter of physics?

David Bohm (DB): Oh, it's the general laws of nature, I suppose —the study of matter.

DM: The study of matter. Is that the answer from the perspective of the common man? That's my position—right, Saral?

Saral Bohm (SB): What do you mean?

DM: Everything has got to be expressed in the simplest terms—the terms of ordinary language, the terms that the ordinary man—

SB: Well, not necessarily; I mean, some things can't be expressed that way. And, you might devalue—

DM: Then you translate; you translate.

SB: No, some things just can't be. I mean, if you put everything into the lowest common denominator—

DM: OK; but that is going to be our goal. We may not succeed in every case, and where we cannot succeed we say so.

SB: All right.

DM: We push in that direction.

SB, DB: All right.

DM: See, every man knows matter, has an immediate experience of matter.

DB: Yes.

DM: But don't we also need to bring in light?

DB: But that's also considered part of matter now; you see, they have extended it. That's why I say, the laws of nature in general. Matter may be extended to include light.

You could also say that fields are another form of matter, a more subtle aspect of matter. The idea is that they all have energy and momentum and so on, and so they all interact with particles, in the form of combined systems.

So this whole system is an extension of the notion of a material system. Therefore we could include space and everything in such a system. The idea of what is physics is constantly extending and changing.

DM: Okay. Now I'd like to bring in this book by Einstein and Infeld called *The Evolution of Physics*. When do you suppose they say physics began?

DB: When?

DM: With Galileo. They say, physics began when Galileo said—how did he put it?—the velocity of an object is due to the change of force, rather than to the force.

DB: The change of speed is due to the force—rather than saying the speed is due to the force, right?

DM: Okay. Right.

DB: Well, I don't know if you'd say that's when physics began. I mean, people were doing it before, but it developed at that point into a direction—

SB: Maybe what they meant was that modern physics began—

DB: Well, maybe modern physics began then. But even during the late Middle Ages people were building up a lot of information which laid the foundation for that.

DM: What would you say? When did physics begin?

DB: Well I don't know when it began. Aristotle used the word *physics*. I mean, *physics* means nature, the nature of things, right?

DM: Newton thought of his own investigations as natural philosophy.

DB: Natural philosophy. Many people did.

DM: He didn't even have the concept of physics—it didn't exist for him, did it?

DB: Well, I don't know if it existed; they used the word, but it wasn't given the emphasis that we give it today. But Aristotle used the word, which was known long before, in Greek times.

DM: A word meaning *nature*.

DB: Yes, but Aristotle used it in much the same sense, to study motion; and he had a different idea. He considered the same problem as Galileo, but he studied it under simpler conditions. Under ordinary conditions on the surface of the earth, an object moves only with the force on it, because of friction. So Aristotle took the view that that was general, that an object would only move if there were a force on it. And that was true in the area which he knew, right? He took that as a general law.

DM: What about when Thales said, "everything is water"?

DB: That was physics too; he was discussing the nature of reality.

DM: So physics is just the study of nature.

DB: Well, it's the systematic study of nature.

DM: Look what a different feeling that gives to the common man.

DB: What do you mean?

DM: If you say to the common man, "Okay, today I'm going to tell you about physics"—you've already lost him! It's already abstruse, right? But suppose you say, "Today let's talk about the laws of nature." He thinks, "All right, maybe there's something in that."

DB: Yes, well, one view was to say that nature is explainable; you could say that was the beginning of physics, with people like Thales.

SB: With who?

DB: Thales, of Miletus.

DM: He's the one who said everything is water.

DB: Some other people said everything is fire, like Heraclitus. Somebody else said everything is air, in different degrees of condensation. So they had the idea of explaining nature, rather than just accepting and saying, this is what it is.

DM: We should also include what Democritus said, that everything is made of atoms. That was an inspired intuition, wasn't it?

DB: Well, it arose from a philosophical question. You see, there had been Zeno and the Eleatic School, which said that all is being—that non-being is not—that motion is illusory in some sense. Zeno developed a number of paradoxes on that basis, saying that motion cannot be rationally understood. If something is moving it occupies a series of positions, but its motion can only be understood as a relation between its present position and the previous one, right? But the previous position does not exist at present, so you cannot have such a relationship.

There are many such paradoxes: he showed that the notion of a vacuum or a void was impossible, and so on. So there were various purely philosophical paradoxes concerning the nature of motion, the nature of substance, and so on.

On the other hand, Heraclitus said there is nothing *but* movement; he said, everything is flux, all is flux, you see.

DM: This was a period of pure logic, of reason. Thought was developing its basic categories.

DB: Yes, pure logic. Thought was putting forth its categories. Heraclitus said all is flux, all is fire, and so on; opposites are one.

DM: And Pythagoras said, all is number.

DB: Yes, he said all is number. He gave a mystical sense to number, you see.

SB: It seems that everyone was emphasizing the *all*.

DB: Well, they were explaining all; that was the beginning of it. The attempt was to explain everything, the whole of nature, the whole of existence, by assumptions. They didn't regard them as assumptions—

DM: By reason.

DB: By reason, but they had to have some principle behind it, which they had to put forth as their reason.

Now Democritus came about because he answered Zeno's paradox. See, Zeno said motion is impossible, and all sorts of things that we take for granted are impossible. So Democritus made the assumption that all is atoms. Atoms were beings, the same as the Eleatics said; but he made being multiple, and the Eleatics had not allowed for multiplicity. All was one for them.

Democritus also said there is an empty space; he admitted the existence of the void, in which the atoms could move. You see, if there was no void you would say there is no movement, right? And previously they had said a void is impossible. So Democritus said there is a void, and that atoms move in the void. In that way, ordinary large-scale properties could be understood by the atoms changing their arrangements in space. At the same time the atoms were still eternal beings. The word *atom* meant it couldn't be divided.

DM: Literally, it means "not cut."

DB: Yes. So that's how Democritus came to suggest the atoms. That idea remained largely dormant for a long time because there was no way to test it. The atoms were much too small for them to have done anything with them at that time.

DM: So the Greeks were tremendous physicists. They're not usually thought of as physicists.

SB: They were thought of as philosophers, weren't they? And philosophy and physics were not separate.

DB: At that time they were the same, yes.

SB: Even today you would say they're not really separate.

DB: You see, they believed in reason as a basic way of proceeding. Aristotle also believed in reason. But he also believed in observation, which he could apply in areas like botany. They couldn't observe atoms, obviously, so he couldn't get anywhere with that.

DM: So all of this is—

DB: This was speculative reason, which was regarded as a positive activity in those days—a way to understanding and knowledge.

DM: And it was accessible to everyone who wanted to stand and listen to the argument of the other fellow.

DB: Yes; well, if they were somewhat educated, they could understand it. I don't know if the ordinary man could have got very far with it at that time; you know, he was occupied with whatever menial work he did, right?

DM: But it didn't take twenty years in the University to learn what was being discussed.

DB: There wasn't as much to learn, but even what Aristotle said occupied any number of books, and it would have taken some time to learn that. And his language, at least what has survived, is often obscure.

SB: Their language was probably as remote from the common man of the time as the physicists' language today.

DB: Well, not as much, but still—I've seen translations of some of

Aristotle's arguments and they're not at all easy to follow; not merely because they're subtle, but because they're not put in a very precise way.

DM: I am assuming someone who is able to read.

SB: Ah. Well, the educated class.

DB: It would have taken a sharp person to follow what Aristotle said, some of it, or even Zeno's paradox.

DM: I'm assuming someone who can read, and who's motivated to find out.

DB, SB: Yes, yes.

DM: But not someone with layers of specialized knowledge.

SB: Yes.

DM: That's what I feel is unfair. Got to stand up for the rights of— [Laughter.]

DB: So I think physics was there in ancient times. Insofar as you were interested in the general laws of nature, the general explanation of nature by reason, that was physics. The idea that it could be tested wasn't foreign to the Greeks, but they didn't give it a high value, although Aristotle gave a lot of importance to observation. Later on in Europe there was added the notion that the thing has to be tested by observation and experiment, you see.

DM: Galileo.

DB: Even before Galileo, many people were doing it. It started with people observing carefully, like Copernicus, and so on. People were doing measurements and experiments. It hadn't developed to the extent of Galileo, but they were doing something, right? Galileo represented a sort of a milestone, a qualitative leap of some sort.

DM: Did anything of significance develop between Aristotle and Copernicus?

DB: Well, the Romans didn't do a lot of physics. There was a fellow called Lucretius who developed the idea of atoms further.

DM: He was aware of Democritus?

DB: Oh yes, the Romans studied the Greeks; they had a very high regard for their philosophy. And of course when the Middle Ages were finished people began to get interested in worldly things. They began to pay attention to the writings of the Romans and Greeks; this was a very big factor in the European Renaissance.

Also, the Arabs brought that knowledge to Europe. They kept it going, you see, while Europe had largely forgotten about it. A little bit was kept going by the Church, but they weren't very interested in that sort of thing.

DM: "Kept going" just means, they remembered—they preserved the documents.

DB: They preserved them, but they didn't talk a lot about them. But by the time of St. Thomas Aquinas, some of the philosophical questions were discussed as they affected theology, you see. Aristotle was very important to him.

DM: This was in the twelfth, thirteenth century.

DB: Thirteenth century, I think.

SB: He was sort of the Aristotelian.

DB: Yes, but there was already a revival of interest in that direction.

SB: There was also an interest among the Arabs, and in Spain.

DB: Yes, the Arabs kept it going during that period. They had a strong interest; they discussed it quite a bit, and they wrote books about it and so on.

DM: What did they say?

DB: Well, I don't know, precisely, but even Maimonides wrote about Aristotle. But there were others who were much more involved, who were very active in reading and writing their own views.

DM: What about in the East? Was any physics developed there?

DB: You mean in India, or in China? The Chinese made some discoveries, the magnet and quite a few others, but they didn't do any very systematic physics. And some of the Indians had a bit of interest in physics. There was a materialist school in India which was interested in algebra. In fact, the zero was apparently invented by the Indians, by Hindus.

SB: I thought that was done by the Arabs.

DB: No, the Arabs took it over. The Indians were the right people to invent zero, you see. As K pointed out, nothing is complete security. [Laughter.] The idea was, they put a symbol for nothing; that was a tremendous step, right? [Laughter.]

SB: What about infinity?

DB: I don't know who invented that, but it may well have been the Indians too. I think they invented both zero and infinity—that is, they invented the symbols. They were the right ones to do it; their philosophy led them to do that, quite naturally. They were doing some algebra before the Arabs. The Arabs took it up, and developed it, you see.

DM: But this isn't really physics, is it? This is not—

DB: Well, it's a speculation with ideas, you see, with thought. Algebra is still part of thought.

DM: But this is not about the laws of nature. If we want to understand the laws of nature, we may use zero and infinity, but they're not quite the same thing. What did these people think of nature? What did they think of matter?

DB: There was a materialist school among the Indians, in which there was interest in these things. But most of the philosophy of the Indians was directed toward the transcendental, toward yoga, or toward liberation. There was a group who were interested in materialist philosophy as well, but I don't know how far they got; the interest was obviously a lot less.

DM: Okay, let's go back to the basic meaning of physics. It would seem you can't just equate it with laws of nature, because physics is not chemistry, physics is not astronomy, physics is not—

DB: No, but it is concerned with the most general laws, you see. In chemistry you begin to specialize in some particular area.

DM: Would you say astronomy is just another specialization?

DB: Yes, in a sense it is. Nowadays most of the work in astronomy is really astrophysics—a great deal of it, anyway.

DM: Would you say biology is another specialization?

DB: That would be one way of looking at it, unless you wanted to say life was something different, you see. One view is to make physics specialize in inanimate nature—

DM: All right.

DB: And then biology is different. But the original view would probably not have separated them.

DM: But now, the modern understanding of physics observes that distinction of inanimate nature at its most general level.

DB: Yes. Which means that it claims ultimately to be able to explain things like chemistry, and astronomy, and so on, as subdivisions of its basic laws.

DM: So every society must have some understanding, some conception of inanimate nature.

DB: Well, early man may not have had any such conception at all. There's no evidence that people had. They may have felt that all the trees and animals were on the same level as people. They felt the whole universe was alive, the rocks and so on. I don't know when the idea of inanimate developed; but the original philosophy of the human race was animism.

DM: Let me put it differently. Every society must have some understanding of that portion of reality that *we* call inanimate nature.

DB: But they may not divide it off—they may regard it as all one.

DM: Nevertheless they must account for it. They must say—

DB: Well they may account for it as animate, you see. You could say, starting with animism, they might gradually slough off a part of it and call it inanimate. If they start with animism as a whole, then at some stage a society begins to recognize some things as inanimate, right?

DM: Yes.

DB: And then that area spreads and spreads until in modern times scientists want to make the inanimate include even life, and mind. Something which was originally sloughed off as a part gradually expanded and began to take over the whole, right?

DM: Yes.

DB: You see, the notion of inanimate must have developed gradually, as a relative category; some things were less alive, or less obviously alive. Then at some stage people may have recognized that certain things were not alive at all.

DM: When did that occur?

DB: Nobody knows for sure; probably at the beginning of civilization. You see, people were experimenting with flint tools, and so on; we don't know how animate they considered it, or when they began to think of it as inanimate. It could have been well before agriculture. But at some stage people began to treat things in a more manipulative way—they were tacitly treating them as inanimate, and gradually more so, right?

You know, when these people want to cut down a tree, they talk to the tree, surround it and say "don't worry" and so on; they are not only regarding the tree as animate, but as having a certain kind of consciousness, a spirit. And to a certain extent they were regarding rocks and so on that way too, as well as areas, regions, especially those that were sacred. Even now, people may get angry at something like an object or a tool; they get angry at it as if it were animate, right? There's a survival of treating these objects as animate, and conscious.

DM: All right. Now, could we explore a little further what we mean by the study of the inanimate? Einstein and Infeld imply different things at different times. Sometimes they imply that physics is the study of matter, and sometimes that physics is the study of changes in matter, which is a little different. Then in another place they say, for a long time physics was the study of matter and forces; and then there was a transition, after which physics became the study of matter and fields.

DB: Well, that came about gradually.

DM: But what is the case? We've said, physics is the study of inanimate matter, but within that, what are the basic, simplest categories? Is there matter proper, and then quasi-matter, or—

DB: I think the first definition of inanimate matter was that it was to be distinguished from animate matter. The idea arose gradually, and the qualities of inanimate matter were said to be mechanical. Once the idea came that everything was a machine, then it became clear; what they said was, it's all a machine.

At first the idea of a machine was just a qualitative idea; it wasn't well defined. People made machines; even the ancient Greeks made some machines. This idea of something mechanical was there for a very long time. But with the growth of physics what was meant by mechanical became more defined. There was the idea of a clockwork, a very precise machine, which gave rise to the clockwork analogy to the universe.

The idea reaches fruition at the time of Descartes—that everything was a machine, including animals and plants—everything except the human soul, which was immortal. So by that time some of the leading people were saying it was all inanimate, including the animate.

DM: But I want to come back: within the category of the inanimate, don't we recognize certain distinctions, such as between matter and forces?

DB: Well, forces are inseparable from matter, you see. By the time of Kant that was already becoming clear. Maybe originally they thought of force as some sort of spirit, but later it was clear that force was considered to be a property of matter.

DM: Would you say, physics wants inherently to reduce everything to one substance?

DB: That's one of its approaches, yes; it's trying to find a single explanation.

SB: That's like saying, all is water, all is—

DB: All is fire, and so on.

SB: Why should physicists want to reduce it all to one thing?

DB: Well, that would help make it possible to put it all together into one law.

SB: But why do you need that? Why shouldn't you have multiplicity?

DB: Fundamental multiplicity would be very hard to understand. We would have to say there is a great deal of arbitrariness in nature, or perhaps that it was the will of God.

You see, in science we are trying to get a rational comprehension of the whole thing, as far as possible. It therefore aims toward unity, right? All the ideas of unity may prove to be limited, and then it has to introduce some diversity; but then it aims for a higher unity.

I mean, if you just said there are all sorts of different things, then you would have several different areas that were unrelated, and that seems strange. Or if they are related, then you would say there are three things, *a* and *b*, and also their relationship *c*; and you would say, why are all these things separate?

DM: Yes, but wait. Physics recognizes a category of phenomena called matter, right?

DB: Well, it's not phenomena—they're assuming that matter exists.

DM: Yes, put it that way. Physics also assumes that there exists something called fields.

DB: But then it has said they are basically the same, you see. That is, it has put them together.

DM: So physics has not only put together matter and energy, and matter and forces, but also matter and fields?

DB: Yes, because particles are considered to be aspects of fields, you see, starting with Einstein. Even during the nineteenth century, particles were considered to be vortices and structures in the ether.

There are different principles of explanation which have been adopted by physics, but one of its basic approaches has been to try to find one principle, whatever it may be, which would encompass everything else. So sometimes you turn things upside down. Whereas you might have said matter was your fundamental idea and fields secondary, you can now turn that upside down and say field is your fundamental idea and matter is part of it. And maybe someone will get another idea.

But the general approach now is not to worry about that too much anyway because the principle is the equations themselves, primarily. The approach is to say that, independently of what we think these things mean, the equations just work, right?

DM: So, in terms of everything we've been discussing, this is the abandonment of nature for mathematics.

DB: Yes, that essentially is it, to say mathematics is the essence of nature, you see.

SB: Doesn't mathematics just express the relationships?

DB: Well, that's a different view. Sir James Jeans said, early in this century, being inspired by relativity theory, that God must be a mathematician. In other words, the plan of the universe was basically mathematical. You see, imagine God trying to be the architect of the universe; he would do it through equations. [Laughs.]

SB: You can't say mathematics *is* the matter of the universe.

DB: But mathematics expresses its basic nature—

SB: *Expresses* it.

DB: Yes, but so do words, so does thought, so does anything.

SB: But surely they only point to what something—

DB: But there's nothing to point to, you see. Anything beyond that is unknown, you could look at it that way. Either you're going to point to something that could be expressed in words, or to some sense impressions you could get from very abstract bits of apparatus; and if you look at the way the apparatus functions, you will get very little enlightenment.

So you can't point to your sense experiences, right? In fact, they are comprehended as, their meaning is in the mathematics. By themselves they are such trivial experiences that nobody would even bother with them.

So now, where will you point? You can either point to sense experiences or to some picture given by ordinary thought, or say it's totally unknown. Anything further would be totally unknown, so we would be stuck with this, right?

SB: But it's still pointing to that which is unknown.

DB: But it doesn't point, you see; I mean, your equations don't point to the unknown. You can study the equations as long as you like and you'll be no closer to the unknown than you were. They are merely somehow expressing some regularity in the unknown, but that's about all you could say. They are expressing some regularity in the way that the unknown manifests to us.

SB: But they're not in themselves—

DB: No, nobody is claiming that the world is made of equations.

SB: Well, this is what it sounded like.

DB: No, but you have to get it clear: the essential principle of the world is contained in equations rather than in verbal concepts. You can't say the world is made of verbal concepts either.

SB: No, I wasn't assuming you could say that. But the way you put it—

DB: I'm trying to put it that you replace verbal concepts and pictures by equations.

SB: Yes, but that's only another language, a symbolic language.

DB: But it doesn't symbolize anything except itself, you see. Previous to this, in the beginning, mathematics expressed in another language, perhaps more precise in some ways, things that you could already express verbally and by ordinary concepts and thoughts.

DM: But now you said that now it symbolizes nothing but itself?

DB: Or also, it symbolizes the unknown, if you wish, the way in which the unknown will manifest to us when we make experiments.

DM: That seems different than to say it only symbolizes itself.

DB: Well, it is in the first instance a structure of thought which symbolizes within itself. It is later interpreted as also symbolizing how the experiments are going to go. And you can test that interpretation. See, as a piece of mathematics, it symbolizes nothing but mathematical thought.

DM: Is that the same as to say it symbolizes itself?

DB: Yes, well, it symbolizes more of the same sort of thing; one mathematical thought symbolizes another and another, but it's all one structure which is sort of reflecting on itself. It's a bit like the observer: you can observe your thoughts, but it's one part observing another; it's all reflecting on itself.

SB: You mean it's not pointing to anything—

DB: Well, pure mathematics is not supposed to point to anything, right?

SB: But at least it points to the relationships between the parts.

DB: But there are no parts; there are only concepts which are mathematical concepts and that's all. I'm talking about pure mathematics.

SB: Supposing you use a and b—

DB: But a and b don't stand for anything except for what you can do with them. You see, you haven't understood the attitude to pure mathematics. It began by saying a and b symbolize something else, right? Then it gradually got to the point of saying a and b are unknown; it is only implicit what they symbolize. You can't say.

SB: Yes, but the relationship is not implicit, it's explicit.

DB: But the relationship is another thing of the same kind. It is a relationship between a and b and nothing more.

SB: Then how can you use it for physics?

DB: Well, people like Wigner are writing articles saying he's very puzzled by the unreasonable effectiveness of mathematics in physics, you see. [Laughs.] It hasn't been explained, right? If you would take that attitude, it hasn't been explained.

But let's try to look at it the way people look at it. We have the idea of pure mathematics, which I've explained, right?

SB: Yes.

DB: Now we discover, interestingly enough, that a certain part of pure mathematics—a rather small part, maybe less than one percent, or a tenth of one percent—happens to work in physics. That is, it works if we add to it rules of interpreting these symbols in physics. Now, in the past the rules of interpreting were very simple, in that these symbols stood for things that could be ordinarily seen or thought about, right?

SB: Right.

DB: Now, they don't any more.

DM: But then they must stand for something which arises in the experimental situation.

DB: Well, some part of them stands for something which arises within the whole structure. You can't say every part stands for something, but within that whole structure there are parts which stand for what could be seen in the experiment and you could test those parts.

DM: That's enough, isn't it?

DB: It's enough to test that it works, right?

DM: But not enough to know what it's talking about?

DB: Well no, you don't know what it's talking about except that it's a set of mathematical rules. But then if you're religious you can take the attitude that that's the sort of rules that God used in creating the universe, you see. So you could say by knowing those rules you will know the universe as well as you could ever hope to know it.

DM: So Pythagoras was right. The universe is made of mathematics.

DB: Well, the essence of the universe is mathematical. It's not that it's constituted of mathematics, but its essence is mathematical relationship.

DM: And you, do you agree with this?

DB: Well no, I don't think it's necessarily so; I think that physicists have focused on that aspect and given it undue importance. They have sort of worked on each other and convinced each other and created a professional structure in which people who think that way are rewarded and so on. Students are told that from very early and they believe it and it builds up.

It's sort of a self-fulfilling prophecy once it gets set up, right? Once it gets set up, that's the way they go, and nobody looks at it any other way. And they're bound to have a certain amount of success with it, and they regard that as proof that that's the way the world is, right? That it can't be any other way.

SB: You mean, if a physicist looks at that sunset, he sees it as just a piece of mathematics?

DB: Well, no: most physicists don't worry about all this. They generally say it's all been settled by some people, we're not interested, we're in a profession and we've got a job with certain things we've got to do.

Of course a few physicists do worry about it; they have different opinions about it, right? But the most common opinion is the one which I just expressed. Most physicists have sort of absorbed it by osmosis, tacitly. For the ordinary physicist, this is a jumble in his mind; he doesn't think it's very important anyway. But among the people who do think of these things, there is a vast difference of opinion, of confusion and whatnot, right?

SB: That's why you have conferences.

[Break. Conversation continues after participants come back from a walk.]

DM: We were talking about the paradox of Zeno, and his denial of the possibility of motion. And I think we traced that to the fact that motion is tied to time; it seems to be time which is the weak link. And apparently this paradox has never really been fully resolved.

DB: No.

DM: Newton, with the calculus, adopted an approach which seems to gloss over the problem.

DB: Yes. The calculus provides rules for dealing with continuous movement. But these rules break down if the movement is not continuous. Quantum mechanics brings that point out.

DM: Yes, and this was a very interesting point, because quantum mechanics is in part based upon the very calculus which is violated —

DB: Yes; by quantum properties themselves. Relativity also is based on the idea of perfect continuity; and yet the attempt to bring in quantum mechanics will lead it to violate that continuity. And once again, rules have been found which gloss it over, which use Feynman diagrams and so on.

DM: We were also discussing the relationship between relativity and quantum theory and the difference of their domains. You were saying that relativity deals with what is the character of space and time at velocities approaching the speed of light; whereas quantum theory addresses the fine structure of matter.

DB: Yes; relativity could also address the fine structure of matter; it doesn't deny it, you see.

DM: And similarly, quantum theory could address what happens to space/time at velocities approaching light?

DB: Yes, it does try to do that, through making what is called the quantized theory of gravity.

DM: So you might say that each of these has its own area of strength, and yet each has been extended to reach that area of strength of the other?

DB: Yes.

DM: So that there are both incompatibilities and compatibilities between these two.

DB: Yes.

DM: And so they are different paradigms, but not entirely incompatible paradigms; therefore the differences between them can be glossed over by most physicists.

DB: Mm-hm.

DM: And also, you pointed out that Feynman diagrams help make these two paradigms somewhat more compatible.

DB: Yes.

DM: And therefore I was asking whether the modern experimental approach—even though it is at the service of theories whose meaning is not entirely clear—nevertheless does this experimental approach produce results which are interesting in themselves? And you said, not really so very interesting, not all that creative—

DB: Well, the experiments are done primarily to answer questions raised in the theories, you see, and therefore without the theories they would never have been done. People would never engage in such expensive, complicated experiments, requiring teamwork over years, and the total commitment of a large organization.

DM: And this led us to an interesting point: the curious fact of the high degree of confidence that people who work in the field have about what they can say regarding the Big Bang, and a millionth of a second after the Big Bang, and so on. Evidently the experimental results you get with these linear accelerators and so on do corroborate—

DB: Well, not the Big Bang, but they check some of the features of the theory of elementary particles, you see.

DM: They continue to give confidence in mathematics as a guide to physical reality.

DB: Yes, they continue to give confidence in mathematics, although I think that people are inclined to overestimate the impressiveness of the results; but still they are getting results which encourage them in their assumptions, and which lead them to believe that they're on the right lines. In fact some physicists feel they're not too far from getting the whole thing, you see.

DM: But then there remain anomalies in the field of cosmology—

DB: Yes.

DM:—just as there are incompatibilities between relativity and quantum theory. In the field of cosmology, for example, there is the possibility that the red shift is the result not of galaxies receding, but of a thinly dispersed plasma in interstellar space.

DB: Yes. That's one, but there are others; a fellow wrote a book on such anomalies, and just recently we had the discovery of this bubble structure and some kind of vast wall of galaxies, which will require some explanation. Of course, physicists would not merely say, "Well, we don't understand it," but rather, "We're going to explain it, give us time"—that's their attitude. So we have to say, wait and see, right?

It looks as if the explanation will declare almost a kind of design, you see, which goes against the spirit of the whole enterprise. To have that much design in the very early universe would be rather odd, unless you could show that there was some process going on which would tend to bring about this result.

You see, they can always have some hope that maybe they will find some explanation. These things are matters of degrees of confidence, and hopes; maybe it will work, maybe it won't.

DM: Now, let me shift the focus again a little bit. As you look back over the whole history of physics, is it accurate to characterize that history as periods of stasis, followed by moments of revolution?

DB: Well, I think that's been somewhat exaggerated. There has been relative stasis and relative revolution, but I think that there were slow changes going on during the periods of stasis which people tended to ignore. It was always changing; there was never a paradigm that was absolutely fixed. And if there had been less pressure toward a common paradigm, you would probably have had a lot more diversity of points of view, even in the stasis periods.

DM: Yes. But would you agree that there were moments when that relative stasis was punctuated by—

DB: —by rapid change, yes.

DM: Rapid change. And would you be willing to say, from Aristotle to the present, what is the one greatest or two or three greatest changes?

DB: Well, the first big change was Newtonian mechanics, you know.

DM: That was the triumph of the machine model of the universe.

DB: That's right, and that was followed by a period of extension and consolidation of that. But during the nineteenth century there appeared fields, Maxwell's field theories, and the difficulty with the ether and so on was building up. And then at the end of the nineteenth and early twentieth centuries we had this big change, bringing in relativity, and the beginnings of quantum theory. And then the full quantum theory came out in the nineteen-twenties and early thirties.

DM: And has everything since then been mere minor modifications compared to those?

DB: Well, there has been nothing comparable. I mean, there have been further discoveries; there was a slow, steady period of discovery of new particles, you see. People thought that the electron and the proton would be the fundamental particles; and then came the neutron; then came the meson, and then other kinds of mesons in the fifties. There's been a slow, constant increase in the number of particles that people are dealing with, and the attempt to put them into a new system, which is called the standard model. The standard model has had some success in systematizing all the particles and in dealing with certain properties like collisions.

There has been a series of achievements and some predictions, but nothing at all comparable to quantum mechanics and relativity. The more recent discoveries are much more limited and tentative and much less elegant; and, see, a bit of brute force has gone in to hammer it out, you know.

DM: Part of the reason I ask is this: Einstein and Infeld wrote their book in 1938. And then in 1960, Infeld wrote a new preface in which he said, look, there really hasn't been that much happening since then.

DB: Well, by '60 there hadn't been much happening; a bit more has happened since then, but it's still not anything very fundamental. A lot of new things have been discovered, but the sort of thing that's been found is an extension of the sort of thing that was there before. There have been some surprises and some differences, but—I think they're waiting to get the grand, the great unification, you see. However, string theories have sort of settled down; they're not likely to be able to do much with them, to detect them, and I think many people are losing confidence in them. It has become a kind of bandwagon; but the fashions change in these things, you see.

DM: But you think that the progress from 1960 to 1980 is greater than from 1940 to 1960?

DB: Probably; that's my momentary judgment, you know. There's certainly a lot more work on this from '60 to '80 than from '40 to '60. That was the period of the war, partly, or the immediate post-war. The number of physicists exploded by about '60, you see.

DM: So they've discovered a great deal more detail.

DB: Yes, and systematized it and extended it, with some new ideas as to how to do it, but not radically new ideas. They have different kinds of particles, like quarks, and sub-quarks, and gluons, and this and that. In other words, they've gone on that line and multiplied the number of particles and put them into systems, and they've got some evidence for some of these systems. But the amount of actual evidence is not all that great, you see, and probably some very different theories could equally well fit it.

DM: Now, looking back over that whole period, how would you say, in one sentence, or very briefly, what was the contribution of Newton? Was it that he made the thing into a machine?

DB: Well, it was done by the whole system, but he made a very big step to turn it into a whole that would stand up as a totality, you see, with one universal law expressed mathematically.

DM: And, what did Einstein change in that?

DB: Well, he kept that scheme, except he extended it to fields, and he changed the notion of space and time within that area.

DM: And then what did quantum theory add to that?

DB: Well, quantum theory denied a lot of that, because it said the Newtonian concepts of determinism and continuity had broken down.

DM: So it looks to me like quantum theory is the greatest single revolutionary break with the past.

DB: Yes, quantum theory is far more revolutionary than relativity.

DM: This is not commonly understood.

DB: It hasn't really been assimilated in the same way. Relativity can be understood to some extent; physically and mathematically it's fairly clear what it means by now, and how it works, although it was very mysterious at the beginning. But quantum theory has not really been assimilated—in fact it has gone into greater and greater confusion as to what its meaning and its interpretation is.

All the factors I mentioned earlier contribute to this, with every new generation of physicists. The tendency is to say the interpretation doesn't matter. Textbooks are written with a few words of interpretation, then they start laying down the formulae, from on high, right?

DM: Yes.

DB: Physicists are therefore tacitly encouraged to think that that's the way knowledge comes about. It comes from various authorities, and they hope that eventually they'll be one of the authorities that lays it down.

DM: So let me try to say something, and tell me if it's wrong. Newton made nature into a complete machine. And part of what it took in order to do that was absolute space and absolute time. That is, space and time existed totally independently—independent of one another, or of anything else.

DB: Yes. Newton also assumed absolute determinism.

DM: And absolute determinism. Now, Einstein brought down some of that—

DB: Some of that; his space and time were still absolute, although in a more subtle way. The ordinary measurements of space and time became relative, but the basic structure of space/time was a different kind of absolute; it was still deterministic.

DM: Still deterministic, and yet there was some monkeying with the fundamental structure.

DB: Yes.

DM: Even though it was not overturned, or radically broken, it began to get loosened in its moorings.

DB: Yes.

DM: And then came the much more radical break of quantum theory, which arose from investigating the fine structure of matter. When you look at the fine structure, then these fundamental, guiding assumptions—absolute space, absolute time, absolute determinism—they go out the window.

DB: Well, yes, at least as far as we know it now. It doesn't mean they're out forever, but it means at least at this stage, they're out.

DM: Okay. So that gives an overview kind of map. But I raise all that with another objective in mind, which is: I notice in reading Einstein and Infeld that they discuss pre-Einsteinian physics in ways which are familiar. But once they begin discussing Einstein and beyond, relativity and beyond, their discussion is saturated with mention of the observer.

DB: That's part of it, yes. They have brought in the observer; the first step of Einstein's theory, which made relativity, was to express all the measurements as a relationship to an observer. That's the special theory; but in the general theory it works the other way. Einstein went back to an absolute point of view of a more subtle nature, you see. The way he put it is, he used relativism for a while, as a heuristic tool, to sort of break the old mold.

DM: So relativism itself entails the observer.

DB: Yes; but he said he was using that just to break the old mold, by bringing in the observer to analyze the situation in a new way.

Then when he went on to general relativity with fields and so on, he came back to something absolute, but which would contain the observer within it. He never really got very far in doing this, but to complete the theory he should have given an absolute account of the observer, as part of the whole structure.

DM: But then quantum theory came along and really made the observer center-stage, right?

DB: Yes, apparently so, but again it doesn't have to be; it can be looked at in other ways.

DM: Well, but what about the Heisenberg uncertainty principle: you have to bring in the observer in order to say what Heisenberg said, right?

DB: That's right, yes.

DM: And that's fundamental to quantum theory, is it not?

DB: Yes. Except that, once again, you don't have to give the observer so much emphasis. See, in the theory I'm proposing you can say that the whole universe is participating, and the observer is a particular case of that. So you don't have to give special emphasis to an observer. Heisenberg did; but that was his philosophy, you see. A great deal of the interpretation depends on the predilections of the person who is making it. The same situation can be interpreted in a number of different ways.

DM: I just think it's very, very curious that physics got into these various muddles—anomalies, and the abandonment of determinism, and so on—

DB: Yes.

DM: and the observer is right there in the middle—

DB: Yes; in the middle of the muddles.
  [Laughter.]

DM: It's not only interesting in and of itself, but it also makes a fascinating point of comparison between the physical realm and the psychological realm.

DB: Yes. You see, Einstein brought in the observer in the beginning and he tried to get rid of the observer later. The notion that there is a separate observer may be one of the basic faults in the whole structure.

DM: But don't you at least have to account for the observer?

DB: You have to account for the observer once you understand the theory in a more subtle way.

DM: I see. You're talking about relativity.

DB: Yes, relativity or quantum theory.

DM: But at least you have to account for it. You can't just bring it in and make certain statements about it and not finish with it.

DB: Yes. But if you give the observer a fundamental role, you then find it very difficult to see what you would mean by cosmology. When the observer is sort of outside the cosmos, then it's not cosmology, right? That's been one of the criticisms, and several people are now trying to get an observerless quantum theory, in order to be able to construct cosmological quantum theory.

DM: Is that a good idea?

DB: Well, yes, if you can do it. You see, I think that if you give the observer a fundamental role, it's going to be the same problem as with the psychological question. At the very least it makes cosmology impossible; but of course Bohr would not have minded that. He said that cosmology would be intrinsically impossible; you can't get the whole anyway, as far as Bohr was concerned. You see, you could take that attitude.

But bringing the observer in may cause confusion, if you bring him in in a fundamental sense of saying he's an axiomatic element. See, the observer can be seen as arising as part of the whole system. But I think fundamentally we need a law of the system which doesn't bring in an observer, but sort of refers to itself; it would be a self-reflective law.

DM: Are there any examples of such a law?

DB: I don't think we have them yet; but it's similar to the problem of proprioception of thought.

As long as we try to think of the universe as a machine, out there—as long as we use mathematics in the present spirit—we always have a residue of that thought. That is, the mathematics is supposed to describe something out there different from the mathematics, right? So I think our whole approach tacitly brings in the observer in some way, because it says something is out there and something else is describing it.

DM: Is this the Achilles heel of the mathematical approach to physics?

DB: It may be, yes.

DM: You're saying the observer is implicit in the mathematical approach in a way that is not fully understood by the mathematics.

DB: Yes. People are trying to say these equations imply an observer, but in some way there's still a residue of the problem. I mean it may be useful to do that in some ways, but I think there's something in the whole mathematical attitude which excludes, which makes it difficult to bring in the notion of participation. It's a kind of abstraction, which tends to symbolize something other than itself. It is the vehicle of absolute truth symbolizing something else that it's the truth about.

DM: Therefore you end up with the dualism of subject and object.

DB: Yes. And then you would raise the question, how this mathematics could ever have arisen in the universe, or how this universe could ever produce the mathematics by which it knows itself. It's a bit along the line of Godel's theorem and so on.

DM: What does Godel's theorem have to say to physicists?

DB: Well, I think it sort of implies that we're not going to get a final theory. You know, Godel's theorem says that any consistent and coherent system of axioms is incomplete; although it may be true, it depends on something outside the system to be true. And then you can always say, what about that thing outside the system? It may be limited, right? And it may depend on something else in turn. You could extend the system to include that, but then that depends on something again, by Godel's theorem.

Some people have criticized Godel's theorem by saying, in order to prove that theorem you also have to make assumptions which would have to be criticized. In other words, some people are not certain of the logic behind that theorem. You see, one feels there's room for some trouble there. Somewhere he must be making an assumption, using some system of assumptions to prove his theorem; and, according to the theorem, it must depend on things he is unable to state. If he does state them he makes a bigger system and that will depend on something he is unable to state.

So one could feel a little uneasy about the theorem itself. It raises an interesting question, but one might feel a little uneasy as to how much he's proved. But if you take it as so then you could say that it does look questionable whether you could ever have a theory that explains everything.

DM: All right. Now I wonder if we could come back one more time to the question of matter and fields. Does quantum theory give complete authority to fields?

DB: What do you mean?

DM: Does it regard fields as absolutely valid, as the foundation of physical reality?

DB: Well, quantum theory can be applied to any classical theory, you see. It's a set of rules which turns a classical theory into a quantum theory. Now if it's applied to particles, you get a certain theory. You can also apply it to fields, and you get what's called quantized field theory. And in the quantized field theory the field becomes discontinuous, and it has particle-like properties.

See, just as quantum theory applied to particles gives wave-like properties, quantum theory applied to fields gives the fields particle-like properties. It gets to a situation where particles can be treated as particular states of the field. But one has no very clear picture what that means.

DM: How can a field—what is a field?

DB: What is a particle? You see, a particle is defined as a point, and you can't say what that is either. A mathematical point has no extension; and they have not yet been able to make a theory of an extended particle that's compatible with relativity.

You see, I think the way physics is now, it's a bit like mathematics: we make certain assumptions and systems, and we work with them, and on the basis of a few assumptions we comprehend a large number of things. It does not attempt to explain what its ultimate assumptions are. No theory can do that; that would only lead to further assumptions that would have to be explained. You would say, a field is an x, but what is x? Or, a particle is x. If I say a particle is a point, you would say, what is a point, right?

DM: Last night, I believe you said a field is a property of space.

DB: Yes, but so is a particle, in a sense.

DM: But if space is the void then it has no properties.

DB: Well, but physics has already committed to the idea that space has properties.

DM: Well, then it's not space.

DB: We call it space because what we call empty space has properties, that's all.

DM: But why call it space if there's something in it? It's not empty.

DB: We say by space only that area which we experience as empty, but actually may be full, right? Space is, when we look at things and say matter as we know it is not there. But it may still be full of something, which doesn't show directly.

DM: Then, one wants to know what that something is.

DB: Well, we call it field, movement; whatever you say it is, you'd have to explain what that is, you see. You cannot finally say what something is, right? I mean, what's there, we say, is fields.

DM: [Laughs.]. So that's what a field is. It's that which is not understood—which has observable properties.

DB: Well, but the particle is the same, you see. The particle is not understood either—there is no consistent theory of the particle. If you say it's a mathematical point, nobody quite understands what that means, and it leads to infinities, and wrong results; and if you say it's an extended region it also breaks down in relativity; and anyway you have no good theory of why it should be extended and so on, you see. You cannot actually say at present what a particle is, except by what it does.

DM: Is that why they keep trying to smash particles? Is that related?

DB: Well, they're trying to find their structure, you see.

DM: Will that resolve this question of what is a particle?

DB: Well, if you can say that it has a certain structure, then it helps to tell you what it is, right? If you say, what is a house, well, it's made of bricks and it has a certain structure. Then you have to ask what are bricks, and they are made of grains of this and that; and then what are they, they are made of atoms; and eventually you stop at a certain point, and say that we stop here—

DM: Just a minute. If I understand you, you're saying there's a fundamental theoretical difficulty with regard to particles: that is, according to theory, they cannot be either infinitely small, nor can they have extension.

DB: Yes.

DM: Now, isn't experimental physics pursuing the same question in a different manner? That is, it's trying to find the nature of particles.

DB: It's trying to find it, but to do so we must make some assumptions. We have somewhat inconsistent assumptions now; but if we simply assume that the particle has a certain kind of structure, even though that may not be entirely compatible with everything else, then we may get some consequences that are right. You can always get right consequences from a theory which is not entirely right.

DM: It seems that we're getting an accumulation of anomalies. One is that Zeno has never been properly answered. Another is that quantum theory and relativity are not fully compatible.

DB: Yes.

DM: And now we have this one, which is that—

DB:—we don't know what a particle is; we can't even say one way or the other what a particle is or what its structure is.

DM: It can neither have extension, nor be without extension; neither way works.

DB: Nevertheless we can make theories in which particles are, say, without extension; and by means of certain rules we can remove some of the unwanted consequences of that and get some results that are right, you see.

DM: Is this anomaly commonly acknowledged?

DB: In a way it is; I think again people play it down all the time, but it's there. I mean, those who think about it will know it's there. But most physicists probably won't think about it. They're thinking about their own thing first, right?

DM: So it's semi-acknowledged.

DB: Yes.

DM: Now, do the experiments in any way help address this theoretical problem?

DB: Well, they're trying to; for example, we have not yet found any structure to the electron. If there were structure, certain consequences would follow in the scattering of electrons. And they don't follow, so it looks as if the electron has no structure, at least none any bigger than ten to the minus sixteen centimeters. If it were smaller, an experiment might miss it.

Now, other particles, like protons and so on, have been found to have a quark structure, because the scattering shows they have three centers. But then, what are quarks? You only push the question back, right? You could say they're made of sub-quarks, or something else; but then, what are they?

You see, the problem will arise somewhere, but you can say that at a certain level of experiment it may not be important, and you can test some features of structure without ultimately solving the problem. You can see that bricks are making the house without knowing what the structure of bricks is. And we can do something like that in physics. We know now that the protons have a quark structure, but we couldn't say what the quark structure is.

DM: But does all of this experimental work address in any way the theoretical contradiction between a particle that has extension versus—

DB: No, not finally. Ultimately it doesn't, because all it could do is to say the particle which has extension is made of smaller ones, but the smaller ones will still have the same problem.

DM: So it will never answer the theoretical problem.

DB: Not unless some new idea comes from the theory. The experiment can't answer the problem.

DM: Does this anomaly about extension/no extension arise primarily in relativity, or does it also come up in quantum theory?

DB: It comes up in relativity; and it also comes up in a stronger form in quantum theory.

DM: A stronger form.

DB: In relativistic quantum theory. In ordinary quantum theory, it would be possible to deal with that, but the attempt to make quantum theory compatible with relativity gives the same anomaly only stronger. The quantum theory makes it impossible to localize things; it makes them jump around a lot more, so that the attempt to hold a structure is much harder than it is in simple relativity.

See, the basic point is, how will you account for the stability of a structure if there is one? Relativity would say there must be forces between all parts of the structure; and you can make what is called a non-linear field theory that would stabilize structures in simple relativity. They are somewhat arbitrary now, somewhat contrived, but you could make a kind of theory that would explain a particle as a stable pulse of the field.

Now, if you try to do that quantum mechanically, it breaks down because there are further quantum movements. You can't control the movement so you can't explain how the structure holds together.

DM: So you begin by investigating matter—and you end up with total mystery.

DB: Well you can achieve a lot of correct results, but the foundation of the theory is set in doubt, right?

DM: Set in doubt? It seems like a huge cloak of doubt.

DB: Yes. The most reasonable assumption is that the theory is an approximation of some kind that breaks down at a certain point.

DM: And yet, this is at the very moment when the leading figures think they've got the whole thing under control, and it's just a few more decimal points before they understand the whole thing.

DB: The point about all these troubles with the quantum theory is that there are what are called renormalization techniques using Feynman diagrams. You start with a certain theory, then you apply these techniques which really change the theory in some unknowable way, and you come out with finite results for many things. And they're hoping that eventually it will work all the way down, so that when you combine the theory with these techniques the problem will not bother you, you see.

DM: That's quite a leap of faith, isn't it?

DB: There's a great element of faith in it, but there are always elements of faith in people pursuing physical theories. I mean, that's the way it works: people believe in them, and they get comfort in believing that they're really going to work; otherwise it would be hard even to proceed with them, right?

DM: Are you saying that the renormalization techniques are the band-aids which hold the whole structure together?

DB: In a way, yes. They do enable you to calculate a lot of results very precisely, when you remove these infinities in a certain way. There's a hope that someday maybe somebody can make a new theory that will get rid of the infinities, and then the renormalization approach will be an approximation to that. But there's really no sign that any of this is going to happen.

You see, there's a great element of faith and hope as far as the fundamentals are concerned.

DM: What could happen to make people take these difficulties more seriously?

DB: Well, I don't know, it's been known for so long, I don't think people want to pay too much attention to it. They feel that along these lines they're going to make steady progress, in the sense of predicting more and more experiments, and eventually they will be able to predict everything—they will have the theory of everything. You will have a set of rules that enable you to predict the outcome of every experiment.

DM: And then their work will be done?

DB: Well, I suppose if you take the attitude which Hawking suggests, then we may be replaced by computers. See, he could only say that on the assumption that the purpose of the whole thing is to get a set of rules that will enable you to compute everything; otherwise, why would he say that the computers can then take over?

DM: But you're implying that, although we might come to the point where everything could be predicted, that wouldn't necessarily entail that very much had been understood.

DB: Yes. But they could hope that everything that was really important could be predicted, or that everything predictable could be predicted, let's put it that way.

DM: But given the rather striking anomalies at the foundation of these paradigms, doesn't it seem that at some point the anomalies will produce some step which defies prediction, or in which the results are very different from—

DB: Yes, I think so, but that may be far off, you see. What seems most likely is that, if the theory is going to break down, it will break down at a place called the Planck length of ten to the minus thirty-three centimeters. At that point essentially all the approximations break down. That length involves the constants from the three theories—relativity, gravitational theory, and quantum theory. Where these three theories come together, at that length of ten to the minus thirty-three centimeters, perhaps they all break down.

Now, that's very short, you see. We saw that the structure of the electron was investigated only to ten to the minus sixteen so far, so that's a very long way to go.

These high energies are one of their hopes of getting there. I think even then it won't break down in any clearly obvious way, because it's a very complicated mess. When you bombard something with such a high energy particle and it collides, it gives off a vast mess of other particles, and who knows what you can say about it? So there's no obvious connection between that and the breakdown of theory.

DM: What does Planck's length arise from?

DB: Well it arises from the attempt to make a quantum theory of gravity, a relativistic quantum theory of gravity. When you do this, you find that the quantum theory implies fluctuations of the gravitational field. The fluctuations get bigger as you consider shorter distances; and at ten to the minus thirty-three, the fluctuations become so big that they make the whole notion of space and time indeterminate. Because the gravitational field is supposed to affect the meaning of what is meant by length, and time, and so on, you see. That's basic to the Einstein theory of gravity.

DM: Up to this point we've been discussing relativity and quantum theory; but now, is gravitational theory another, separate theory, or—

DB: Well, it's general relativity rather than special, you see. Einstein began with special relativity, where gravitation could be neglected.

DM: When I said—what is relativity?, and you said, it's what happens to space/time at velocities approaching light—

DB: That's the one I was talking about.

DM: Special.

DB: Yes. But general relativity goes further and says space/time are affected by gravitational fields.

DM: So does this produce what is in essence yet another paradigm?

DB: Well, Einstein regarded it as a generalization of the other one; he didn't feel it was a radically different paradigm. It brings in quite a different attitude, not only gravitation, but the idea of space/time being connected to gravitation, which was a new idea. Also it gave the field much greater importance, and it moved away from emphasis on the observer. So in general relativity the observer is not nearly that significant; although, you know, you can always go back to special relativity and put him in.

DM: When was Planck's length discovered?

DB: It was never discovered—it was noticed that this was a basic constant in physical theory. You find these three theories coming together at that point, and causing a breakdown.

DM: That's a very interesting construct, Planck's length. Just the fact that such a point of contact between the three theories exists—it's a constant in all of them.

DB: Yes. Yes, it's a place where at least one or two of them must break down, or perhaps all three.

ACKNOWLEDGMENTS

This book is the product of an uncommon collaboration in its own right. My sister Leanne Grove and her husband Barry assisted me financially and otherwise when it was needed most. This book would never have seen the light of day without their support.

My good friend Friedrich Grohe and his associates also provided much needed assistance. Claudia Herr is an angel of intelligence and good will.

Adelle Chabelski supplied the initial encouragement and the vision to say that this task must be done. Adelle is a formidable force in the universe, a kindred spirit of Helena Blavatsky and Annie Besant.

Several friends provided valuable commentary on an early draft of the manuscript. Lee Nichol, my comrade at Oak Grove School, commended me for undertaking this effort, which was very encouraging. He also made specific recommendations on an early draft of the manuscript, all of which I appreciated.

Kent Richland provided line-item editorial guidance as well as comments on the substance and themes of an early draft. Perhaps without intending to, he showed me that my draft was not yet ready for prime time. Our mutual friend Alan Newman also helped me understand the audience I was trying to reach.

Javier Gomez clarified the relationship between Bohm's contribution and Krishnamurti's and enabled me to describe this issue more accurately.

Michele Sender was diligent and thorough in her review of the manuscript. She helped iron out many inartful or inaccurate words, phrases, and sentences.

Many others were helpful and supportive in more indirect ways. Professor Krishna has a comprehensive and subtle understanding of Krishnamurti's teachings. I might never have become involved in this work were it not for Mark Lee. Ulrich Brugger, Rowan Lommel, Jaap Sluijter, Michael Krohnen, Suza Francina, Theodore Kneupper, and David Skitt are among those who have formed the background and context that made this volume possible.

Marilyn Mosley Gordanier was a motivating presence, playful counterpoint, and spiritual companion throughout the composition of this book.

BIBLIOGRAPHIC ESSAY

This essay describes the essential publications pertaining to the lives and work of David Bohm and J. Krishnamurti. References to specific chapters indicate chapters in the present volume. Complete bibliographic information is given following the essay.

Many of the recorded dialogues of Bohm and Krishnamurti have appeared in print. The first of these was a single conversation that took place in 1972 and was included with other Krishnamurti talks and dialogues in *The Awakening of Intelligence.* That conversation is the subject of chapter 9.

The question of whether to publish the twelve dialogues that occurred in 1975 was a matter of disagreement and controversy, as explained in chapter 11. Selected portions of three of those dialogues appeared with other material in *Truth and Actuality*, and portions of several more were published two decades later in *The Limits of Thought.* Although the transcripts of all twelve dialogues are now available online, approximately half of this material remains to this day unavailable in printed form. My efforts to persuade the Krishnamurti publications committee to publish the full set of dialogues in a single volume were unsuccessful. The dialogues could not be published in that form, I was told by the committee, in part because they presented intractable editorial difficulties. My efforts to determine the specific nature of those difficulties were also unsuccessful.

In 1976, Bohm and Krishnamurti met with American psychiatrist David Shainberg for a series of dialogues that were recorded by video as well as audio and are available in print under the title *The Wholeness of Life*. The video recordings, called "The Transformation of Man," are available through the Krishnamurti Foundation of America, at kfa.org. This series represents a comprehensive introduction to the work of Krishnamurti accessible to any interested reader or listener.

The fifteen dialogues conducted in 1980 were published as *The Ending of Time* and are the subject of chapters 12-15. *The Ending of Time* was re-published in a slightly revised and expanded version (now with the rather misleading subtitle *Where Philosophy and Physics Meet*) in 2014. The new version also includes the last two recorded conversations between Bohm and Krishnamurti, conducted in 1983 and previously published as *The Future of Humanity*.

The sole existing biography of Bohm is *Infinite Potential: The Life and Times of David Bohm*, composed by his friend and science writer F. David Peat. This work provides a competent description of Bohm's scientific career, but fails to convey the meaning and significance for Bohm of his relationship with Krishnamurti. There exists a compelling need for a more comprehensive and definitive biography of Bohm. Such a book would encompass not only his work in theoretical physics and with Krishnamurti, but also a multitude of related fields to which he made important contributions, including dialogue, creativity, and the philosophy of science. The challenge will be for someone sufficiently well versed in all of those fields to bring them together into a coherent whole.

Bohm's first book, *Quantum Theory*, presented an unusually lucid account of the standard, Copenhagen interpretation of the strange world of events inside the structure of the atom. His mastery of this field no doubt enabled him to provide his path-breaking alternative to that interpretation, published as "A Suggested Interpretation of Quantum Theory in Terms of Hidden Variables, I and II." *Quantum Theory* remains in print well over half a century after its initial publication.

Causality and Chance in Modern Physics describes the interlocking principles of causation and probability throughout the fields of science. In language accessible to the layman, this book places the controversial nature of quantum theory in a larger context, one in which it is possible to see the prevailing interpretation of subatomic events as a philosophical predisposition rather than one grounded in empirical evidence. The exposition is fascinating in its own right, as well as for its refutation of the resistance to Bohm's alternative interpretation of quantum mechanics.

In *Wholeness and the Implicate Order*, Bohm describes the inherent contradictions between the two major paradigms of modern physics, quantum theory and the theory of relativity. He proposes a radical and profound resolution of these contradictions with the introduction of the "implicate order," a deeper way of describing physical reality than is possible with the familiar, linear, Cartesian order on the surface of events. In the implicate order, wholeness prevails, rather than fragmentation into ever more minute parts, and matter and consciousness are brought into a coherent relationship with one another.

The definitive, textbook account of Bohm's understanding of theoretical physics is *The Undivided Universe: An Ontological Interpretation of Quantum Theory*. A festschrift celebrating Bohm's contributions in many fields, with articles by Richard Feynman, Roger Penrose, J.S. Bell, Maurice Wilkins, Karl Pribram, and others, is *Quantum Implications: Essays in Honour of David Bohm*.

Bohm's psychological observations, as informed by his work with Krishnamurti, appear in *Thought as a System*, the subject of chapter 17. This book represents the transcript of one of several seminars conducted by Bohm at Oak Grove School in Ojai, California. The transcripts of all the seminars he conducted there are available through University Dissertation Services. Other elements of Bohm's contributions outside the field of science, including on creativity and dialogue, were published in volumes edited by Lee Nichol.

Well over 30 books exist of Krishnamurti's work, and these represent only a fraction of his recorded talks and dialogues. Much of this material, including audiotapes and videotapes, is accessible online at jkrishnamurti.org and is available for purchase through kfa.org. Works discussed in chapter 5 include *The First and Last Freedom* and *Last Talks in Saanen 1985*.

Chapter 6 is largely devoted to the three diaries Krishnamurti composed later in life. These were published as *Krishnamurti's Notebook*, *Krishnamurti's Journal*, and *Krishnamurti to Himself*. The diaries feature exceptionally vivid scenes from nature interspersed with penetrating commentary regarding consciousness and the human condition. Of the three, *Krishnamurti's Notebook* is the longest as well as the most revealing of the extraordinary quality of his inner life and experiences.

As discussed in chapter 7, Krishnamurti's authorized biography appears in three volumes composed by Mary Lutyens: *Years of Awakening*, *Years of Fulfillment*, and *The Open Door*. *Years of Fulfillment* is especially noteworthy for its chapter (discussed here in chapter 19) entitled, "Who or What Is Krishnamurti?" A fourth, summary volume composed by Lutyens is *Krishnamurti: His Life and Death*. Another biography, by Pupul Jayakar, includes a great deal of material that supplements the work of Lutyens, and is also discussed in chapter 7.

Krishnamurti experienced a rich and unusual inner life, as is reviewed in chapters 6 and 19. The meaning of these experiences is open to interpretation, and the available evidence suggests that Krishnamurti himself did not subscribe to any particular point of view, but rather acknowledged an element of mystery: "Water can never find out what water is." Nevertheless, in *The Inner Life of Krishnamurti*, Aryel Sanat construes the available evidence according to a basically Theosophical point of view. His analysis is rather one-sided, in my view: he interprets ambiguous events and statements as if their meaning is clear, and he disregards evidence to the contrary of his chosen perspective.

Krishnamurti's Insight is a scholarly summary and assessment of the scope of Krishnamurti's philosophy, replete with diagrams representing relationships among key terms in the teachings. The author is Hillary Rodrigues, Associate Professor and Chair of the Department of Anthropology at the University of Lethbridge, Canada. The author italicizes and hyphenates Krishnamurti's frequent use of "what is," with the unfortunate effect of turning ordinary language into something mysterious. Otherwise, the treatment of the material is fair and objective, without any discernible biases for or against Krishnamurti or any particular point of view.

Numerous memoirs of Krishnamurti have been composed, and new ones continue to appear. Several of these are discussed in chapter 7. All but one of the existing memoirs portray Krishnamurti in a positive light; the exception is *Lives in the Shadow with J. Krishnamurti,* by Radha

Rajagopal Sloss. The numerous distortions and inaccuracies contained in her account are described and refuted in meticulous detail, including source material not previously published, in *Krishnamurti and the Rajagopals,* by Mary Lutyens.

Not reviewed in any detail in chapter 7 are two more recent recollections of Krishnamurti and his work. *A Jewel on a Silver Platter*, by Professor P. Krishna, examines the man and his teachings from a variety of perspectives. Krishna's own observations are supplemented by his interviews with several others who knew Krishnamurti well. His book also includes an elucidation of several important points in the teachings, as well as a glossary of key terms. The net effect is somewhat kaleidoscopic, and a rich addition to the literature. *Knocking at the Open Door*, by Mark Lee, is a rather personal account of the author's interactions with Krishnamurti over a period of more than 20 years. Lee's observations are colored accordingly, and so are the source of interesting insights as well as a few distortions.

The most detailed and comprehensive description of Krishnamurti's daily life has appeared only recently in the form of a series published online called "In the Presence of Krishnamurti" (inthepresenceofk.org). These are the recollections, recorded in her daily records, of Mary Zimbalist's life with Krishnamurti during his final decades. A summary of this material, *In the Presence of Krishnamurti: The Unfinished Memoirs of Mary Zimbalist*, is available as an e-book through the same website.

BIBLIOGRAPHY

Albert, David Z. "Bohm's Alternative to Quantum Mechanics." *Scientific American* 270 (5) (1994): 58-67.

Bohm, David. *Causality and Chance in Modern Physics.* Pennsylvania: University of Pennsylvania Press; Reissue edition, 1971.

Bohm, David. *Ojai Seminar Series I, 1986-1989.* Ann Arbor, MI: UMI Dissertation Services, 1996. (UMI Number: LD03357)

Bohm, David. *Quantum Theory.* New York: Prentice Hall, 1951.

Bohm, David. *The Special Theory of Relativity* (Routledge Classics). London: Routledge, 2006.

Bohm, David. "A Suggested Interpretation of the Quantum Theory in Terms of Hidden Variables I," *Physical Review* 85 (1952): 166-179.

Bohm, David. "A Suggested Interpretation of the Quantum Theory in Terms of Hidden Variables, II," *Physical Review* 85 (1952): 180-193.

Bohm, David. *Thought as a System.* London and New York: Routledge, 1992.

Bohm, David. *Wholeness and the Implicate Order.* London: Routledge and Kegan Paul, 1980.

Bohm, David, and Charles Biederman. *Bohm-Biederman Correspondence: Creativity and Science.* Edited by Paavo Pylkkanen. London and New York: Routledge, 1999.

Bohm, David, and B.J. Hiley. *The Undivided Universe: An Ontological Interpretation of Quantum Theory.* London and New York: Routledge, 1993.

Bohm, David. *On Creativity.* Edited by Lee Nichol. London and New York: Routledge, 1998.

Bohm, David. *On Dialogue.* Edited by Lee Nichol. London and New York: Routledge, 1996.

Bohm, David. *The Essential David Bohm.* Edited by Lee Nichol. New York: Routledge, 2003.

Field, Sydney. *Krishnamurti: The Reluctant Messiah.* New York, NY: Paragon House, 1989.

Grohe, Friedrich. *The Beauty of the Mountain: Memories of J. Krishnamurti.* Krishnamurti Foundation, 2006.

Hiley, B.J., and F. David Peat. *Quantum Implications: Essays in Honour of David*

Bohm. London and New York: Routledge and Kegan Paul, 1987.

Jayakar, Pupul. *Krishnamurti: A Biography.* San Francisco: Harper & Row, 1986.

Krishna, Padmanabhan. *A Jewel on a Silver Platter: Remembering Jiddu Krishnamurti.* Peepal Leaves Publishing, 2005.

Krishnamurti, J. *The Awakening of Intelligence.* New York, NY: HarperOne, 1973.

Krishnamurti, J. *The First and Last Freedom.* New York: Harper and Brothers, 1954.

Krishnamurti, J. *Krishnamurti's Journal.* London: Victor Gollancz, Ltd., 1982.

Krishnamurti, J. *Krishnamurti's Notebook.* Ojai, CA: Krishnamurti Publications of America, 2003.

Krishnamurti, J. *Krishnamurti to Himself: His Last Journal.* London: Victor Gollancz, Ltd., 1987.

Krishnamurti, J. *Last Talks at Saanen, 1985.* San Francisco: Harper and Row, 1985.

Krishnamurti, J. *Truth and Actuality.* San Francisco: Harper and Row, 1978.

Krishnamurti, J. *The Wholeness of Life.* San Francisco: HarperSanFrancisco, 1979.

Krishnamurti, J., and David Bohm. *The Ending of Time: Where Philosophy and Physics Meet.* New York, NY: HarperOne, 2014.

Krishnamurti, J., and David Bohm. *The Future of Humanity.* San Francisco: Harper and Row, 1986.

Krishnamurti, J., and David Bohm. *The Limits of Thought.* London and New York: Routledge, 1999.

Krohnen, Michael. *The Kitchen Chronicles: 1001 Lunches with J. Krishnamurti.* Ojai, CA: Edwin House Publishing, 1997.

Lee, R.E. Mark. *Knocking at the Open Door: My Years with J. Krishnamurti.* Hay House Publishers India, 2015.

Lutyens, Emily. *Candles in the Sun.* Philadelphia and New York: J.B. Lippincott Company, 1957.

Lutyens, Mary. *Krishnamurti and the Rajagopals.* Ojai, CA: Krishnamurti Foundation of America, 1996.

Lutyens, Mary. *Krishnamurti: His Life and Death.* New York: St. Martin's Press, 1990.

Lutyens, Mary. *Krishnamurti: The Open Door.* New York: Farrar, Straus, Giroux, 1998.

Lutyens, Mary. *Krishnamurti: The Years of Awakening.* New York: Farrar, Straus, Giroux, 1975.

Lutyens, Mary. *Krishnamurti: The Years of Fulfillment.* New York: Farrar, Straus, Giroux, 1983.

Lutyens, Mary. *To Be Young: Some Chapters of Autobiography.* London: Rupert Hart-Davis, 1959.

Moody, David Edmund. *The Unconditioned Mind: J. Krishnamurti and the Oak Grove School.* Wheaton, IL: Quest Books, 2011.

Moody, David E. "Can Intelligence be Increased by Training on a Task of Working

Memory?" *Intelligence* 37 (2009): 327-328.

Moody, David. "The David Bohm Biography." *The Link* 14 (1998): 20—22.

Moody, David E. "Gaia Comes of Age." *Natural History* 119 (3) (2010): 40—42.

Moody, David. "The Insight Curriculum." *Journal of the Krishnamurti Schools* 2 (1998): 13-15.

Moody, David E. "Review of *On Gaia*, by Toby Tyrell." *Progress in Physical Geography* 38 (1) (2014): 138-141.

Moody, David E. "Seven Misconceptions Regarding the Gaia Hypothesis." *Climatic Change* 113 (2012): 277-284.

Patwardhan, Sunanda. *A Vision of the Sacred: My Personal Journey with Krishnamurti.* Ojai, CA: Edwin House Publishing, 1999.

Peat, F. David. *Infinite Potential: The Life and Times of David Bohm.* Reading, MA: Addison-Wesley, 1997.

Rodrigues, Hillary. *Krishnamurti's Insight: An Examination of his Teachings on the Nature of Mind and Religion.* Varanasi, India: Pilgrim's Publishing, 2001.

Sanat, Aryel. *The Inner Life of Krishnamurti: Private Passion and Perennial Wisdom.* Wheaton, IL: Quest Books, 1999.

Sloss, Radha Rajagopal. *Lives in the Shadow with J. Krishnamurti.* London: Bloomsbury, 1991.

Smith, Ingram. *Truth is a Pathless Land: A Journey with Krishnamurti.* Wheaton, IL: Quest Books, 1989.

Zimbalist, Mary. *In the Presence of Krishnamurti: The Unfinished Memoirs of Mary Zimbalist.* inthepresenceofk.org, 2016.

PHOTOS

Thirty-year-old David Bohm entering the hearing room of the House Committee on Un-American Activities, May 25, 1949. Present on the committee to interrogate him was the newly elected Congressman from California, Richard M. Nixon.

Krishnamurti in Pergine, Italy, 1924.

Some sixty years after Krishnamurti arrived in Ojai, the young pepper tree in front of his cottage has fully matured.

(CREDIT: PHOTOGRAPH BY FRIEDRICH GROHE, COPYRIGHT © FRIEDRICH GROHE: FGROHEPHOTOS.COM)

David Bohm at age 70.

(CREDIT: PHOTOGRAPH BY MARK EDWARDS, COPYRIGHT © KRISHNAMURTI FOUNDATION TRUST)

Krishnamurti in London, 1968.

(PHOTOGRAPH BY MARK EDWARDS, COPYRIGHT © KRISHNAMURTI FOUNDATION TRUST)

Krishnamurti addressing an audience from a public platform in Saanen, Switzerland, 1985.

(PHOTOGRAPH BY MARK EDWARDS, COPYRIGHT © KRISHNAMURTI FOUNDATION TRUST)

INDEX

Printed in Great Britain
by Amazon